Posthumous Pieces

"When all relativities are seen as non-existent nought remains to be apperceived."

The Great Pearl (HUI HAI)

So what is this book* about? Just that.

* Like those of Nagarjuna, Arya Deva, and Candrakirti, but inferior in all respects.

Also by Wei Wu Wei

Contents

Author's Note

The people, places and events that take place in England are all figments of my imagination. Many of the towns, landmarks and buildings set in the USA actually exist. Interested readers can find out more by consulting any guidebook about Route 66 or California Highway 1. If it isn't there, it isn't real. This may be because I invented a scenario or expanded on something that happened during my real-life travels. Sometimes, this is to protect the innocent – or the guilty! A case in point are the made-up names of the Golden Sunlight Hotel and Wrendale. The complete story of Wrendale did happen, without any embellishment from me, at a hotel in a town far away from Missouri.

Clint Eastwood is real, obviously. Sadly, the film premiere was not. The other named characters in the USA are fictional, with the exception of Jesse Martinez and his dog Ona. They bravely walked most of Route 66, spending many a night sleeping under the stars. Their commitment and determination filled me with awe.

PART ONE
Lost in England

CHAPTER 1
The Bombshell

'Tom, I'm home.' Carla dumped the heavy bags on the hallway floor and congratulated herself for finishing the grocery shopping in record time. 'Hello? Tom?'

Frowning, she took off her jacket and hung it on the Victorian coat stand, a recent purchase made on impulse in a rare moment of madness. It looked totally out of place in their contemporary home, but she had fallen in love with it. She turned around and collided with her husband.

'Tom! Don't creep up on me like that. You nearly gave me a heart attack.'

He looked uncomfortable, shifty... not at all like Tom. Then she noticed the suitcase in his right hand.

'I'm going,' he mumbled.

Carla stared at him, her face as white as his was red, her mouth opening and closing, giving a passable impression of a goldfish on display at a fairground stall.

What? Why? Who with? Where to? When? Any of those questions would have been a start. Well, maybe not *when*. But she said nothing, nada, nichts – the language didn't matter, for she was quite simply dumbstruck. They stared at each other for seconds... minutes... surely not hours? No, not hours. Then Carla did what she did best when faced with a difficult situation. She pushed past him and rushed upstairs. As she stumbled into the bedroom, she heard the front door close, and he was gone.

* * *

Carla didn't know what happened next. She had no recollection of anything other than being vaguely aware of the sky changing from light to dark on more than one occasion. She lay in bed staring at the ceiling, sleeping intermittently, and crawling to the bathroom for a drink of water to quench her raging thirst. Was it shock, a breakdown? She had no idea. All she knew was that she was staring in the bathroom mirror at a woman she barely recognised. And to make matters worse, she was actually having a conversation with her.

'You look like hell.'

'Thanks a bunch. You look pretty awful yourself,' said the woman with the sunken eyes and greasy hair.

'How did you let yourself get into this state?'

'Well, it's not every day your husband of thirty-two years walks out on you, is it?'

'True. When did it happen?'

'Who knows? You look like you need a bath, so it must have been a while ago. And by the way, you stink.'

Jesus, Carla, get a grip!

The timescale was a complete mystery. She checked the date on the electronic alarm clock on Tom's bedside cabinet and established she'd lost five days.

What the...?

Whatever had happened, life as she knew it was over and she had no clue what to do.

The only way is up, right?

First off, Carla cleaned her teeth and luxuriated in a bubble bath. She got dressed, dried her hair and applied some make-up. After shedding a few pounds in her food-free 'coma', her jeans fitted perfectly. She felt good. Carla had never been one to suffer from false modesty or a lack of confidence in her appearance, and she refused to allow Tom's bombshell to do more than temporarily dent her self-esteem. She looked younger than her fifty-seven years and was fit, too. She realised her spirits had lifted, even though nothing had changed. She would pick herself up and go out and smash it. Smash what and where she wasn't yet sure, but she was determined to do something special with her life. In the meantime, she was ravenous, so scrambled eggs on toast and a pot of steaming hot coffee were in order. She shuddered at the thought of the long-defrosted and not-so-fresh food lying on the hallway floor, where it had remained since Tom's sudden departure. She'd tackle the task of what to do with her life first and deal with the abandoned groceries later. Right now, the lure of coffee was triumphing over everything else.

CHAPTER 2

The Proposal – 1984

What am I doing here?

W   Carla looked about her, depressed by the crush of tourists and the fug of smoke and sweat in the typical West End pub, with its high ceilings, ornately carved mahogany décor, etched mirrors and fancy lights.

Damn.

Now her brand-new Armani power suit would have to be dry-cleaned and her Princess Di hair would need washing. She was drinking champagne with her work colleagues, their voices gratingly loud. Men with Eton accents competing with the Cockney twang of would-be barrow boys made good. They were so busy trying to outdo one another that they hadn't noticed her disquiet.

It's banking, we're not trying to save the universe! she thought to herself.

She could be at home with her feet up now. Instead, she was 'bonding' with her work mates.

Her annual review had been somewhat of a mix. Believing her boss didn't like her, she'd entered his office filled with trepidation. Stifling a yawn, she'd listened to him drone on and on about the usual guff – it was clear he loved the sound of his own voice.

To her surprise, he'd suddenly changed tack then and said, 'Your future in this company was discussed at our board meeting yesterday. We are anxious to do our bit to encourage women in the workplace. It's been eight years since the Sex Discrimination Act came into effect, yet we don't seem to have made much headway with getting our girls into management.'

Girls?

'We think you have a lot to offer the company, so we've decided to put you on a management development programme and fast-track your promotion. How does that sound?'

'That's fantastic, Mr Gant. I won't let you down.'

'There's just one area you need to improve in.'

'Oh, what's that?'

'I'd like you to make more of an effort with your colleagues. Teamwork is important in this business.'

Carla frowned. 'I thought I got on well with everyone here.'

'You do, but how can I put this? You don't mix after work. You need to go down the pub with them, be one of the boys.'

So, here she was being 'one of the boys' and absolutely hating it. The music ramped up, U2's rousing 'Pride (In the Name of Love)' drowning out her colleagues' inane chatter. At least the music was good.

She was wondering how soon she could escape without appearing rude when someone tapped her on the shoulder. She turned around to see an attractive man who didn't seem to fit either the yuppie or tourist mould towering over her. Her evening suddenly seemed more interesting. Bono continued to sing at full volume, rendering normal conversation impossible. The man's delicious lips were moving ineffectually.

Carla leaned in to him and shouted, 'What did you say?'

The man yelled, 'Hello, I'm Tom. Will you marry me?'

As he spoke, the music suddenly stopped, meaning everyone heard the proposal. The deafening silence remained as the drinkers craned their necks, eager to discover who was behind it. Carla stared at him, lost for words. It was only when she heard her colleagues sniggering behind her that she recovered herself.

'Don't you think you are being a bit premature?'

'Sorry, it does rather look like that, doesn't it? I'm just trying to save time on small talk. No point in wasting any more of my life without you, is there? So, will you?'

'Maybe I will,' she grinned.

And just six months later, she did.

* * *

As they strolled hand in hand down a muddy lane at the edge of Staverley, Tom's village, Carla could tell something was up. Tom had a swagger, and he looked exceptionally pleased with himself.

'Shut your eyes, and don't open them until I tell you.'

'What's this all about?'

'Just let me guide you, it's only a few yards away.'

'What is?'

'Our marital home.'

'Wait a minute, don't I get a say in where we live?'

'Trust me, you'll love it. OK, you can open your eyes now.'

'It's only a field,' Carla said, unable to hide her disappointment.

'I know it's only a field, but it's a really nice field, a really huge field, and it goes right down to the river. My mum and dad are giving it to us as a wedding present. I've got an architect coming round next week. We'll plan the house together and then I'll build it. It'll be everything you ever dreamed of. We shall live happily ever after in our own little castle until death do us part.'

'Oh, Tom, that sounds wonderful. I can't wait. I love you so much.'

She flung her arms around him and hugged him tight, enjoying the warmth and comfort of his body. He knew exactly how to make her feel special.

'Hmm, not as much as you love my parents.'

'You're probably right – they really are the best people in the world.'

'Shall we live in a caravan while I build the house, or would you prefer to stay with them?'

'You are not seriously expecting me to answer that question, are you?'

'It's not the idea of living in a caravan that bugs you, is it? You just want their undivided attention. I think you're only marrying me for my parents!'

'Guilty as charged! Let's not forget, though, that you're a product of those wonderful people, and you're not at all bad yourself.'

Barney and Brenda treated Carla like the daughter they'd never had. They adored Tom and had tried for many years to give him a brother or sister. It wasn't meant to be, and Carla was happy to fill that void, lapping up the attention they lavished on her. It was true that she'd fallen in love with the whole package – Tom, his parents, and the warmth of their home. Now that she was part of it, she was feeling the joy of unconditional love for the first time in her life.

CHAPTER 3

The Secret

With her caffeine levels back to normal, Carla dragged her mind back to the moment when her life had been turned upside down.

When Tom uttered those two dreadful words – *'I'm going'* – why had she just stood there gaping at him? Why hadn't she asked him to explain himself? It was all so unexpected. There'd been no hint of trouble. She realised she must have gone into an immediate state of shock. She had turned her back on him, and he had let her. Was he relieved at her lack of fuss, giving him the chance to escape before she could compute what was happening and challenge him? She had so many questions, and she didn't know the answer to any of them. Even so, he couldn't care about her, otherwise he would have phoned to check if she was alright or at least explain why he'd left.

Carla topped up her coffee cup and stood at the kitchen sink. The view through the window was always a joy, and for a few minutes she was distracted by the abundance of small birds hopping around the lawn flitting between the hedges and

11

trees. Before long, her thoughts inevitably swung back to Tom. Could he have another woman? Casting her mind back, she couldn't think of any clues he might be having an affair. As far as she knew, he hadn't bought any new underwear lately, and he showed no signs of taking more care with his appearance. She hadn't caught him furtively checking his phone, nor had there been any unexplained absences. Up until his leaving, he'd been the same old Tom. They hadn't even rowed recently, and he didn't seem distracted by anything, so it didn't make any sense. Perhaps he was having a crisis, a breakdown of his own, and she hadn't noticed the change in him. A new thought struck. What if he hadn't intended to leave? Maybe it was a cry for help, or a test that she had failed. She had turned her back on him and walked away.

Oh my God, where was he?

What if he was in some lonely hotel, desperately hoping for a call? A wave of guilt swept over her, followed by brain-freezing panic.

Of course, that had to be it; he wouldn't have left if he'd been thinking straight.

Carla grabbed her phone. The battery was dead, and the charger was nowhere to be found. She didn't know Tom's mobile number off by heart, so she couldn't call him from the landline, and the last thing she wanted was to ask one of her children for it and trigger some awkward questions.

Oh, what a fool I've been, Carla thought. *I hope he's alright.*

Suddenly feeling the need to keep busy, she decided to clear up the mess in the hallway. After throwing away most of the rotten groceries, she picked up the letters on the doormat and automatically sorted them into three piles – Tom's, hers and junk. She immediately dumped the junk into the recycling bin and found herself drawn to an item in Tom's pile. The red envelope stood out amongst the heap of bills and invoices. She picked it up and stared at the unfamiliar handwriting, noticing the postmark was from ten days ago. She turned it over, but there was no return address. Clearly, the envelope contained a card of some sort. Who could it be from and what was it for? Tom's birthday wasn't even close.

For as long as they'd been married, they'd always opened their own mail and left it on the kitchen worktop for the other to read afterwards. Until now, they hadn't kept any secrets from each other.

Carla put the letter back in Tom's pile and went to make herself another coffee. She'd never felt the need to open his mail before, but he wasn't here now, was he? Should she open it?

No? Yes? No?

Oh, for goodness' sake, Carla told herself, *just open it! The rules don't apply any more.*

Hands trembling, she slit the envelope open with a penknife and removed the card. The picture on the front was innocuous enough: a drawing of two fishing boats in a harbour. She took a deep breath and peered inside.

Dear Tom,
Sorry I didn't get back to you. I was on one of my hush hush jobs and didn't get your message until today. I tried to call you a couple of times, but your phone wasn't available, and I can't call you now I'm back at Rose Cottage. As you know, it's in a twilight zone, so I'm sending you this card instead. I'm so glad you are coming. Can't wait to see you.
Love Jane x

So, he was having an affair after all. Wow, he must be a clever liar; she hadn't seen that one coming. Carla burst out laughing – a genuine belly laugh as opposed to a hysterical howl. She didn't feel jealous, angry or any of the other emotions she might expect to be experiencing. A weird sense of relief washed over her; it was as if a weight had been lifted from her shoulders. She didn't need to worry about Tom's welfare after all. He had slunk off to where the grass was greener, found something she couldn't offer: the excitement of a new relationship. Thirty-two years of marriage offered a lot of things, but the first flush of romance and sexual tension wasn't among them. Well, Jane was welcome to him. She could take care of him in his not-so-distant old age. Carla had had his best years. They had shared so much: love and friendship, dreams and disappointments – and they'd made exciting plans for their fast-approaching third age. She hadn't imagined they wouldn't be together 'until death do us part'. But now he had chosen someone else to share his life with and disappeared without an explanation or even an attempt to sort out whatever was bothering him. Confronting this knowledge offered a welcome release. Carla couldn't compete with the excitement of new love, nor could she fight or change it, so she would just have to embrace her new situation.

Her euphoria lasted all of three minutes, maybe four. Who was she kidding? She thumped the table, grimaced and rubbed her hand. What was that card all about? Jane must have known there was a possibility Carla would see it. Maybe she'd decided it was time to take charge of the situation. Having covered their tracks for so long (how long?) to keep their affair a secret, she must have decided to up the ante, afraid that Tom was getting cold feet. Had Jane gambled on Carla throwing Tom out so he would join her at Rose Cottage?

Carla realised she had been well and truly taken for a fool. She couldn't believe she'd had no inkling of Tom's infidelity. So many questions rattled around in her head. Where did they meet? What did she look like? Although Tom had an eye for a pretty girl, he had never shown any desire to do more than look (as far as she knew – doubts were now creeping in). Had Carla unwittingly met this Jane woman and missed what was going on right under her nose? She couldn't think of an occasion when that could have happened. And most of all, when had Tom found the time to have an affair? Clearly, he was not the workaholic she thought he was. There was no point dwelling on it. She thought of the Shakespeare line, 'O, that way madness lies; let me shun that.'

'The good old bard, he's got an answer for everything,' she said to the empty room.

CHAPTER 4

The Family... And Sally

Carla eventually found her charger under her bed. With her phone working again, she was shocked to find there were no messages or missed calls, and the landline answerphone remained silent. Five days she'd been incommunicado. Five days! And not one person had noticed.

She switched on her laptop and checked her emails. Nothing, apart from the usual spam. Next, she clicked on Facebook. As a prolific poster, she reckoned that surely one of her five hundred and fifty-five friends had noticed her absence and sent her a message? But no. How was it possible that none of her family or friends had realised she was in trouble?

Carla had always been there for them. She constantly put everyone else's needs before her own, and now that she was struggling, they were nowhere to be found. She felt lost in confusion and overwhelmed by her misery. She was losing her grip and slipping back into oblivion. Or she would have been, had she not been disturbed by the distant sound of her mobile. She looked at the screen to see her son's name. James was her eldest. At thirty years old, he was still the apple of her eye.

'Hello, Jimmy, love,' she said with a singsong tone of delight.

'Hi, Mum. Melissa's been called into work unexpectedly and I've got an important meeting ahead, so I'll drop Mariah round in about half an hour if that's OK?'

Carla thought a simple 'How are you?' or a 'What have you been up to this week?' would have been nice. Clearly, she wasn't even considered worthy of a cursory preamble to the topic in hand.

Carla adored Mariah, her beautiful three-year-old granddaughter, and valued the time she spent with her, but just then, something inside her snapped. 'Sorry, James, it's not convenient.'

'Oh... oh! What am I going to do with her, then?'

'You could always ask Andrea,' Carla said mischievously.

'I already did; she's busy today.'

Typical! Melissa's mother always got first dibs on Mariah while Carla got the crumbs, for which she was supposed to be grateful. And she usually was. Whenever called upon, she would cancel her own arrangements, not wanting to miss out on precious time with her gorgeous little girl. She accepted that the downside of having a son meant she had to play second fiddle to Melissa's mum. A wife almost always regards her mother as the most important grandparent in the family. This was so blatant, though, that she couldn't believe the total lack of thought for her feelings.

'I'm sure you'll think of something. I have to go now. Bye, James.'

She clicked off the phone without giving her son a chance to respond.

Shivering, even though it was a warm day, Carla made herself yet another cup of coffee and clasped her hands tightly around it to warm up. She sighed and wondered how her adoring little boy had become so distant and unfeeling in adulthood. He had stopped confiding in her, and she had felt helpless watching him change from a happy, smiley boy to the withdrawn, serious adult he had become since meeting Melissa. It wasn't all down to his partner, though; her overbearing mother was causing most of the problems, and on top of that, his job was stressful too. Carla knew better than to interfere.

* * *

Carla jumped. Away with the fairies, she realised her mobile was ringing again.

Emili!

Carla knew her daughter would be after something. Emili never phoned unless she wanted her help, and she always left it until the last minute to ask. At least she usually spoke sweetly and showered her mum with compliments when Carla complied with her wishes, as she always did. But not this time.

'Hi, Mum, I can't talk. Old McGregor will bollock me if he finds out I'm in the loo making a private call. Kev's landing at Heathrow in about an hour. He's cut short his New Zealand trip because he misses me so much. Can you pick him up and drop him at my flat?'

'No, I'm sorry, I can't.'

'How's he going to get back, then?'

'He'll just have to get the train, won't he.'

Carla's voice was curt and definite – a tone Emili rarely heard from her mother.

'I promised him you would,' she wailed.

'It's not your place to promise things on my behalf.'

Carla clicked off the phone without saying goodbye and

19

then slammed it on the table. How dare her daughter treat her with such disdain?

Emili was used to getting her own way. She'd arrived unexpectedly, ten years after James. Both Carla and Tom were delighted with the arrival of their beautiful bundle of joy, while James, used to being the centre of attention, hadn't been so sure. But he'd adapted quickly. Better, in fact, than Carla and Tom, who soon found that juggling two children was a lot harder than one, especially as their work responsibilities had grown. They also couldn't rely on Tom's beloved parents in the same way they had when James had been little. They'd loved having their grandson while Carla and Tom were at work; unlike Frank and Janet, Carla's parents, who had shown no interest in him at all. James had been surrounded by so much love: from Barney and Beryl on weekdays, Tom in the early evenings and Carla at weekends. He'd grown up feeling safe and secure in this happy family unit. By the time Emili came along, Tom's parents' health was declining, and they couldn't look after her. Tom and Carla had no choice but to send her to a day nursery, for which they were racked with guilt. Even though Tom was always there to pick Emili up, both he and Carla overcompensated for not being around as much for their second child, often giving in to her in return for a quiet life.

Now, at twenty, Emili's sense of entitlement knew no bounds. Outside of her home life, she was delightful and popular, a credit to her parents, but she had little respect for her family. Carla hoped she would grow up soon. As yet, she was showing little sign of it. Right now, though, Carla had more important things to worry about, and her daughter would just have to lump it.

* * *

Ring, ring, ring. This time it was the landline.

No calls for five days and now it's like Piccadilly Circus around here, thought Carla, wryly.

The caller ID said 'Dad'. Carla knew this conversation wouldn't go well; her overbearing father would waste no time tearing strips off her about something or other. Despite everything she did for him and her mother, it was never enough. She was surprised it had taken him five days to find a reason to berate her.

'Hello, Dad.'

'What's got into you, Carla?' His voice boomed down the line, forcing Carla to hold the earpiece at arm's length. 'Your mother waited in all day yesterday for you to come round and cut her toenails like you promised, and where have you been all week anyway? You didn't even phone to say you weren't coming. You are so selfish, always putting yourself first and not thinking of us. After all we've done for you —'

Usually, Carla would revert to child mode and say sorry to her bullying father just to keep the peace. Not this time. She didn't have the energy or will to fight, so she disconnected the call. The phone remained unexpectedly silent. Ordinarily, she would have wondered why her father hadn't called again, then she'd feel guilty and call him back. But not now, not when she was barely able to focus on herself, let alone anyone else.

* * *

Silence filled the air. Carla had now officially fallen out with her husband, both children and her parents. For the first time in a long while she felt completely alone. Needing to talk to someone, she decided to call her friend, Sally, whom she'd met at a fat-burning aerobics class following James's birth. Carla had quickly got back into shape, which is more than could be said for Sally, who enjoyed the taste of pastries and cakes rather too much. They were an unlikely pair, with little in common, yet somehow a friendship had formed.

Sally would understand. Goodness knows, Carla had listened to her tales of woe enough times. She knew all her trials and tribulations, both real and perceived. Carla had given Sally no end of kind words and reassurances over the years, from which Sally always walked away with a spring in her step. If she could unburden herself to Sally, maybe she would feel better and be able to make some sense of the mess she was in. She dialled her number and Sally quickly answered, but before she had the chance to speak, Sally launched into an epic speech.

'Hi, Carla, you must be psychic! I was just about to ring you to tell you the latest. You are never going to believe what Mike's done this time.'

Not waiting for Carla to hazard a guess, Sally ploughed on, barely pausing for breath. 'We were supposed to be going out for a meal last Saturday night, but he didn't turn up. I called him half an hour after he was due to pick me up, but he didn't answer. I kept texting him, but he didn't reply. I was going to call you, but I was too upset – I thought he'd dumped me again. Then he phoned me on Sunday to say sorry. He'd met up with some of his mates at lunchtime and they'd gone to watch the football. He got so drunk he clean forgot he was supposed to be taking me out. He'd also left his phone at home by mistake and didn't get my messages until Sunday morning. He told me he'd ring me in the week, but he didn't call until today because he's been so busy at work.'

A likely story! thought Carla.

'I was so cross, I told him I'd had enough of him messing me about and didn't want to see him anymore. Then I hung up.'

Finally!

'But then, a couple of hours later, the florist turned up with a beautiful bouquet of flowers with a little note attached that said, "I'm sorry, please forgive me." So, of course, I had to, didn't I? I told him I was giving him one last chance.'

Again!

Carla had listened to Sally's sorry stories about Mike's shortcomings countless times, and they were all variations on the same theme. She doubted anything would be different this time, although she had to admit the flowers were an improvement on Mike's usual behaviour.

'Anyway, it's been great talking to you, but I really must dash. Mike is taking me to The Bell to buy me a slap-up meal to say sorry for being an arse.'

And with that, Sally was gone.

CHAPTER 5
The House

Time passed. How much, Carla couldn't say. She had no idea of how long she'd been sat in the kitchen, and she wasn't aware of any conscious thoughts. She couldn't even call it despair; it was just blankness. Her mind had shut down again, and when she came to, the sky had turned pink and the light was diminishing.

Without Tom she was bereft, rudderless.

'What's the matter with you, Carla? It's 2017, for goodness' sake,' she said aloud. 'These days, women are supposed to need a man like a fish needs a bicycle. Well, I reckon whoever came up with that stupid saying has never been in love.'

And now she was talking to herself again.

She sighed. Looking around the kitchen, she noticed how empty it felt – just like her life. She had always loved it here in the hub of the household. Just as he'd promised, Tom had built the house of her dreams. They'd spent hours discussing what it should look like and how to make the best use of the land, and the result was a simply stunning property. From the front, the farmhouse-style building with its Cotswold stone walls and slate roof was complemented by an enchanting cottage garden, so traditional that it satisfied even the most conservative of their neighbours in the village. However, the back of the house could not have been more different. Ultra-modern for its time, oversized windows had been fitted in the kitchen/diner and upstairs bedrooms to maximize the view of the rear garden and surrounding countryside. They'd spared no expense in the kitchen, furnishing it with oak cabinets, a fan oven, a built-in fridge-freezer and all the latest mod cons, including a dishwasher and microwave. Wall-to-wall grey mottled carpets throughout the house provided the final touch of luxury. Carla shuddered now to think how they had also put carpet in the main bathroom, and she was glad her first project post-redundancy had been to drag the smallest room of the house into the twenty-first century.

The house had done more than provide a roof over their heads. For the first time in her life, Carla had felt she belonged somewhere, and building it changed the course of Tom's career. Before, he'd been cruising at his job as a bricklayer with little enthusiasm – he was just working to live. Brenda and Barney were smart cookies, though, and they knew their son better than he knew himself. They persuaded him to leave his job and subsidised him for the year it took to build the house, generously covering all the materials, meaning that Tom and Carla were left with a mortgage-free forever home. When it was complete, Tom felt incredibly proud of his achievement and, brimming with newfound confidence, was inspired to start his own business building bespoke homes for wealthy clients. His bank manager liked his business plan and lent him the start-up money, using the house as collateral. Tom gained immense satisfaction from a job well done and making his customers happy. The company expanded slowly but surely, eventually employing ten people. He thrived on the pressure of it all, up until Carla's unplanned early retirement, which made him reflect and complain that it was getting tougher with age. It was the ideal time for him to retire too, and for them to embark on a new chapter in their lives. But despite a few vague promises, and for reasons best known to himself, Tom had been dragging his heels ever since. And now he'd upped and left her.

Carla's home had been her sanctuary, where she was cocooned from the outside world. All the good things in her life belonged here, and she had never imagined moving anywhere else. Now that illusion had been shattered, and she wondered what the future held for the house that had been built just for her.

Ordinarily, she loved sitting at the kitchen table looking out at the garden, enjoying the spectacle of its flower-filled borders: a riot of colour that contrasted beautifully with the lush green lawn, which was painstakingly cared for by their part-time gardener. Beyond the lawn stood a six-foot hedge, behind which was a series of hidden garden rooms. Outside the garden boundary, there was an uninterrupted view of wheat fields surrounded by bushy hedgerows. These gently sloped towards the tree-lined river that ran through the valley below, behind which were open hills.

Usually that sight, together with a strong cup of coffee, would lift Carla's spirits, but not today. She had to face up to it; her life as she knew it was over – the life she'd enjoyed before The Day That Tom Left. She was truly alone. She groaned as she stood up, stretching her limbs to release the stiffness in her joints after being sedentary for too long. She made herself a cup of camomile tea, dragged herself upstairs, threw her clothes on the floor and climbed into bed. Almost immediately, she fell into a long, dreamless sleep.

CHAPTER 6

The Secret Garden

C arla awoke to sunshine streaming through her bedroom window. She'd been so out of it last night that she hadn't even closed the curtains. She felt refreshed from her deep sleep and jumped out of bed, took a piping hot shower, got dressed and hurried downstairs ready to face the day.

The sinking feeling in the pit of her stomach had disappeared, to be replaced with a hearty breakfast of poached eggs and smoked salmon on crumpets. Realising her caffeine intake was fuelling her anxiety, she switched to mint tea, which she drank while wandering around the garden, enjoying the sound of the chirping robin and the beauty of her flowers. She loved her garden with a passion, even more so than the house. Until now it had always relaxed her.

She remembered the first big row she'd had with Tom. It was after she had bounded into the kitchen and presented him with a grand design for their outside space, her eyes sparkling with excitement.

'Take a look at these plans I've drawn.'

Tom had studied them carefully and then said, 'It's a

beautiful design and it would be amazing, but it will take too much work to landscape it and the upkeep would be time consuming and a real nuisance. I'm sorry, I can't justify the time and effort needed to create it. It will be much easier if we just get the whole garden turfed, plant a few trees and dig out a couple of borders for flowers. Neither of us has the time to commit to maintaining a fancy garden, and it would just end up being a horrible mess.'

Crushed, she'd turned to leave the room but then thought better of it and strode back.

'No, Tom, we are going to have this garden whether you like it or not. We did the house your way and we're going to do the garden my way.'

'That's not true, Carla – we agreed all the house plans together.'

'Yes, but I didn't have any input in their creation. I was happy to go along with your plans and you've built a beautiful house. I *want* a garden to go with it, and I'm going to *have* a garden to go with it. It won't take up any of your time; I'll employ a landscape gardener to create it and then I'll find a regular gardener to look after it. I'll pay for it out of my savings.'

She'd been right, of course. The huge expanse of dirt was transformed, and the mature garden was now every bit as splendid as the one she'd envisaged all those years ago.

Carla walked through the gap in the centre of the hedge and scanned the fruits of her labour. The garden was divided into sections, each one surrounded by neatly trimmed, low-growing box hedging, exactly as she had planned. To her left, she gazed at the first room and smiled wryly at the sign, which read *Tom's Veg Patch*. In a ridiculous show of machismo, he'd insisted the first room should be given over to vegetables, even though he'd previously objected to a labour-intensive garden.

Letting him win that battle, she had allocated that room to him; she'd even asked the landscape gardener to put in good soil for him to plant his seeds. He never did. Carla had left it fallow for two years, not once commenting on the lack of attention, and neither had he. The following year, she had planted the shrubs she'd planned to put there in the first place and the sign remained as a permanent reminder of Tom's stubbornness.

To the right, the sign read *The Bee Garden*. Carla had created a formal lavender parterre, and when the flowers were in full bloom, the bees busily buzzed around the fragrant bushes. She loved the sight and smell of lavender, and the symmetry of the design of the parterre appealed to her tidy nature. The flowers were just starting to bloom. She grasped a handful, let go and sniffed the aroma from her cupped hand. She closed her eyes, inhaled deeply and felt a tiny bit of tension release from her rigid body.

She smiled as she strolled into the Rose Garden. She had dreamt of having a pergola in the shape of a giant birdcage and had hunted high and low for it, adamant it must be Victorian-style wrought iron. All that fuss, and now she could barely see it; the pergola was swamped with spectacularly beautiful, scented blooms, the colour of blazing sunshine. She could just about squeeze inside. Tears pricked her eyes as she recalled taking Tom into the newly installed birdcage.

'Face me and hold my hands,' she'd said. 'Close your eyes and imagine we are inside a giant rosebush. Breathe in deeply and smell the roses.'

'I can't smell anything.'

'Imagine you can. When the bushes climb to the top and the flowers bloom, the aroma will engulf you, and whenever you come in here, you will be reminded of this day. Open your eyes and look at me.'

He did as he was told.

'We're going to have a baby!'

The smell of the roses was overpowering, and it seemed like only yesterday they had stood here, hugging and crying on one of the happiest days of their lives. She wished Tom was with her now.

Recovering herself, her next stop was the Secret Garden. Hidden behind a tall hedge, the children had loved this place. It had a Wendy house, a swing and a slide, and best of all, it was a keeper of secrets, or so they'd thought. They'd spent hours playing with friends in here. They could not be seen and believed they could not be heard. Little had they known that she and Tom had often stood at the other side of the hedge listening to their conversations and trying their hardest not to laugh at their innocent chatter. Recently, their granddaughter had discovered the Wendy house and made it her own, where she 'made tea' for her dolls. Dear, sweet little Mariah.

Damn you, Tom. Did you even once think of the fallout that would come from your flit? Of course you didn't!

Calming herself, she unbolted the wooden gate and entered her favourite spot. The grassy area was home to a couple of apple trees and a small wildflower patch in the corner, which had been planted to attract butterflies and insects. Expensive garden furniture adorned the large patio and barbeque area. This would have been enough for most people, but Carla had gone one better with the addition of a fully equipped summerhouse and landing deck, which overlooked the river and the hills beyond. Here, the family enjoyed the cool shade on hot summer days.

She watched as two graceful mute swans glided by, their beautiful, white-feathered wings raised like sails, their fluffy, grey offspring paddling furiously behind them. She went into the summerhouse, opened the French doors and sat down.

Motionless, she watched for more wildlife to pass by. Sometimes, a heron would settle on the other riverbank and patiently wait for an opportunity to catch a fish. If she was really lucky, a colourful little kingfisher might flit past and, maybe, an otter too. They were so lucky to have all this, and now Tom had thrown it all away.

CHAPTER 7
The Sadness

C arla needed to think about where to go from here. First, she had something more pressing to do. She switched on her laptop and logged on to Facebook. After all, what could be more important at this precise moment? A plan was emerging... she had to declutter her existing life before she could build a new one. Five hundred and fifty-five friends.

How popular am I!

She snorted at that thought. She systematically scrolled through and deleted all the 'friends' she had never actually met. How had she ended up with them in the first place? Now she had two hundred and fifty-one. Then she did the holiday pals whom she'd only met once, promised to keep in touch with and never did. In her defence, these friends were useful for stealing holiday photos from and, in any case, they hadn't bothered to contact her either.

She was now down to two hundred and twenty-five. Next, it was all the people she hadn't seen or heard from in the last two years. That left her with ninety-nine. Who was left? Family members she only saw at weddings or funerals. She culled them, leaving seventy-four names. Then there were the stalkers who looked at her posts and never commented or posted anything on their own timelines – gone. That left seven – Tom, James, Emili, Melissa, Kev, the cat lady next door, and Sally.

'Funny how you think you're popular and have a good social life, yet when the chips are down, it's just you,' she said aloud.

Carla knew she was being disingenuous. She'd never had many proper friends, and that was the way she liked it. She had Tom, and he was her best friend; she hadn't needed anyone else. And with a busy career and children, it was hardly as if she'd had the time for them. No wonder she had gone into shock when Tom walked out. Everything she had believed in had turned to dust. She hovered the cursor over Tom's name to delete it but found she couldn't bring herself to do it. Instead, she logged out of her account and shut the laptop with yet another sigh. She reckoned she'd sighed more in the previous twenty-four hours than in the last twelve months.

Her head was thumping. Well, that was a simple fix. If only a broken heart was as easy to sort as caffeine withdrawal. Two cups of coffee later, her head had cleared. She thought about the conversations she'd had with James, Emili and her parents. Her responses had been so out of character that it was hard to grasp why not one of them had called her back to find out what was going on. Sally's silence was no surprise. She only ever thought about herself, and Carla had already thrown her into her mental trash bin. She would waste no further time thinking or worrying about what had always been a one-sided friendship. If only she'd cut her off earlier.

As for her family, did she really mean so little to them they neither noticed nor cared what she might be feeling or going through? All those years of picking up the pieces of their traumas. She was always ready with a cuddle, a smile or just a cup of tea... and for what? It hurt. Without her family and without her job, she had nothing. Now she understood the anguish suffered by her male colleagues when they were thrown on the scrapheap. Her job had ceased to define her once the children arrived, and when redundancy came, it wasn't something she feared. It was different for men, she realised, and now here she was questioning her professional life and everything she had ever believed in.

Mr Gant's faith in her had not been misplaced, and she had proved her worth in a male-dominated industry. She had never doubted her own abilities, and believed her strength of character and independent spirit was formed at an early age as a direct result of her parents' lack of attention. Also, the teachers at her all-girls' school had fostered independent thought and self-belief in their pupils. As a result, it had never occurred to her that men might be considered superior to her in the workplace, and with her forthright attitude, no one at the bank thought so either. After becoming the youngest person in her branch to pass her exams, she quickly moved through the ranks, transferring to the bank's investment arm, where she settled comfortably into middle management. She knew she could have gone further had she not married and had children, but it was a compromise she was willing to make. Besides which, she'd realised in middle age that there was more to life than breaking the glass ceiling – she was happy to leave that to the talented young women coming up behind her. But her decision to coast had backfired following a perfect storm of technology advancements, her high salary and reaching her mid-fifties (i.e. becoming over the hill). Suddenly, a whole swathe of middle-management positions became surplus to requirements and a posse of grey-haired and not so grey-haired men and women were out on their ear. Some of the men she knew were devastated, but Carla had seen it as an opportunity.

And look how that had turned out.

* * *

She wandered aimlessly from room to room, feeling like a stranger in her own home. She decided there was not much point dwelling on the past; her rose-tinted glasses had been shattered and her memories would never be the same again. She sat behind the large mahogany desk in the study and smiled in spite of herself. It had belonged to Tom's dad – dear, kind Barney. How she had loved him and Tom's mum, Brenda. She missed them now more than ever. They had died five years ago, less than six months apart, and she and Tom had mourned their loss in equal measure. She knew neither of them would ever stop missing Barney and Brenda, and she wished they were here now. They would have comforted her and told her everything would be alright. She doubted Tom would have acted as he had if they were still alive. A thought struck her. *Could it be a delayed reaction to his parents' death that had caused Tom to go off the rails?*

What a ridiculous thought! Carla was clutching at straws, looking for an explanation only Tom could provide. He hadn't made any attempt to contact her and was presumably now holed up in the 'lovely Jane's' country cottage, whispering sweet nothings in her ear. Carla was probably the last person on his mind.

She slumped back in her father-in-law's huge leather office chair. Its aromatic smell filled her nostrils and took her back to happier days. She wallowed in her memories of him and Brenda. Carla had been so lucky to have them in her life. The downside was that until meeting Tom's parents, she'd had no idea her relationship with her own wasn't normal.

She was an only child too. She had spent her whole life seeking her mum and dad's approval, even though they did not deserve her. For the last few years, they had needed her, but not as a daughter or a loved one – they just wanted a skivvy to clear up and run errands for them. Well, no more. If she was to reclaim her life, she had to change it, and the first thing she had to learn was acceptance. Whatever she did or didn't do for them, she would never have the parents she wanted. They would have to learn to manage without her. They could afford to pay for help, so she had no need to feel guilty if she abandoned them. Maybe she should call her father and tell him her thoughts, but she didn't feel strong enough to handle him. There were enough negative emotions floating around already, without him adding to them. He would soon work it out and open his wallet. Her mother would not have to go without. Whatever her father's other faults, he had always treated his wife like a princess. Carla had nothing to worry about on that score. For now, she put that aspect of her life back into its box.

The mental exhaustion of the previous few days overcame her. She dozed off and dreamt happily of Barney and Brenda. An hour or so later, she awoke with a start, feeling disorientated. The landline phone was ringing: the caller ID said it was her father. She stared at the phone, her heart pounding, willing herself to pick up the receiver. She could not face his wrath or, at best, his indifference to her needs, so she ignored the incessant ringing and eventually all was quiet again.

CHAPTER 8

The Friend – 1967

Carla's magnificent dolls' house dominated the corner of her bedroom. Three storeys high, it was similar in design to Queen Mary's dolls' house, which she had fallen in love with on a rare family outing to Windsor Castle. The front of the house opened out to reveal lots of rooms, a fully decorated interior and intricate, hand-built furniture. Carla cherished it with all her heart.

'Do you like my new dolls' house, Judith? Father Christmas left it for me by the Christmas tree.'

Judith nodded.

'You can play with it if you want.'

Judith didn't say much, but Carla didn't mind; she talked enough for the both of them. Judith was Carla's best friend, her only friend outside school. They kept each other entertained for hours on end, and there was never a cross word between them. They were busy reorganising the furniture when Carla caught her finger on a jagged edge. She squealed and snatched her hand from the house. Blood trickled down her finger. She daren't cry.

'My finger hurts, Judy,' she whimpered.

'Shh! Be brave. Your daddy will get cross if you make too much noise.'

Carla sucked her finger. 'Let's go and find Mummy. She'll put a plaster on it.'

The two girls tiptoed down the stairs. Hearing voices in the living room, they crept in and saw Carla's parents huddled together. They were talking in low tones, oblivious to the children's presence.

Her father was saying, '...and if we send her to boarding school, we'll be free to get on with what we want to do, without having to worry about her.'

'It's not her fault we had an accident, and she's no bother, is she?'

Carla screwed up her little face and peered at her friend. Nobody had told her about Mummy and Daddy's accident. Judith shrugged. Mummy looked serious and Daddy looked angry.

She whispered to Judith, 'Come on, let's go. My finger has stopped bleeding.'

They sneaked out without being spotted and crept back upstairs to play.

Mummy and Daddy got better from their accident; Carla never did go to boarding school.

CHAPTER 9
The Decision

As darkness fell, the study turned gloomy. Carla turned on the lights, and the warm glow from the desk lamp immediately made the room feel cosy.

Her gaze shifted to another lamp, positioned at the other end of the room. *That's curious, I've never noticed that before.*

Tom had presented it to her one Christmas; it was a replica of a movie studio light, and it was attached to a tripod. From it, a shaft of light beamed onto a map of the world, which she'd hung on the wall back in the days when she and Tom were dreaming of taking off across America. How she'd been looking forward to her husband's retirement.

'Damn, now it'll never happen,' she muttered out loud.

She picked up a glass paperweight and threw it across the room, narrowly missing a window. It hit a curtain and landed safely on the carpet.

Or will it?

Leaping out of her seat, she yanked open the top drawer of the filing cabinet. It was crammed with all sorts of paperwork, but she knew it was in there somewhere and she rummaged through the drawers until she found the A4 exercise book entitled *Route 66 – Here We Come!*

A couple of years ago, she'd researched Route 66, also known as the Mother Road. She'd planned a six-week trip, starting in Chicago, Illinois and travelling 2,500 miles across the middle of the United States to Santa Monica, California. She'd planned everything to the nth degree, including the hotels, landmarks, car rental companies and restaurants.

Now all that needed to happen was for the bookings to be made, and for the small matter of Tom to retire. Back then, he'd promised he would sell the business so they could get away. Time had ticked by and, tired of asking when they could go, Carla had busied herself with the minutiae of day-to-day life. She had managed to drag Tom to New York for a few days last December, which they'd both enjoyed, but it hadn't whetted his appetite for a bigger trip, and so nothing had changed.

Well, if he wasn't going to do it, she would damn well go on her own. The more she thought about it, the better the idea sounded. Right now, she knew she was in no fit state to decide what to do with her life in the long term. She had a husband who didn't want her, two children who took her for granted, ungrateful parents and a self-centred friend. Far from feeling sorry for herself, though, she suddenly felt an enormous sense of freedom. She was done with putting their needs before her own. She would worry about the rest of her life when she got back.

A few clicks later and it was done: her American Airlines flight from Heathrow to Chicago was booked for 9.15 the following morning. She wondered whether she should call her family, or at least let someone know where she was going. No, bugger them. They probably wouldn't even notice she'd gone. She knew she was being childish, but if she were to do this, it had to be without any recriminations ringing in her ears. She could face the music later. And if any of them dared to criticise her, she'd have something to say about it.

This was going to be the start of a New Carla. Actually, it would be more of a return to the Old Carla, the independent, strong-minded woman she used to be. Meeting Tom and having the children hadn't changed her, but it shocked her to realise that since her enforced early retirement, a wrench that coincided with the deaths of Tom's parents, she had slowly but surely – and without even noticing – lost her sense of purpose and self-worth. She'd become so wrapped up in the lives of everyone around her that she'd gone off track herself. Now it was time to get herself back. With her excellent redundancy package and an inheritance from a distant uncle still largely intact, she could afford to travel in luxury if she chose. But that was not in the plan: she was going to find the real America and meet real Americans along the way.

Feeling excited, and with a renewed sense of purpose, Carla rushed upstairs and packed a few old clothes in a small carry-on suitcase, vowing to buy new outfits as soon as she arrived in Chicago. She plonked it by the front door with her e-ticket, passport and ESTA – the visa waiver she needed to get into the USA. She had gone into a blind panic trying to remember where she'd put it when she and Tom got back from New York, eventually finding it with his documents.

Phew!

She booked a taxi to the airport, luxuriated in a hot bath, climbed into bed and immediately fell asleep.

* * *

When the doorbell rang the next morning, Carla was dressed and ready to go. She hesitated, then took off her wedding ring and placed it with her phone in a kitchen drawer. Where she was going, she wouldn't be needing either. Before she had the chance to change her mind, she locked the front door and climbed into the taxi, glancing over her shoulder only once as it pulled away. No more looking back, it was time to look forward and embrace the adventure to come.

PART TWO

Get Your Kicks On Route 66

CHAPTER 10

Crossing The Atlantic

With time to kill, Carla browsed the magazines in WHSmith. Feeling a tug on her skirt, she looked down and was surprised to see a tiny angel dressed in a white satin dress with wings attached. The little girl, who was of a similar age to her granddaughter, rewarded her with a beautiful smile. Suddenly, a harassed-looking woman appeared and swept the child up in her arms, staring daggers at Carla as if she were some kind of child snatcher before rushing off, presumably for an imminent flight departure.

The child reminded Carla of Mariah, and a wave of sadness and guilt washed over her. She knew she ought to contact James before she got on the plane, but she couldn't face a conversation with him. She needed to hold onto her resolve and make a success of this trip, without being upset by condemnation or complaints from her son.

Catching sight of a rack filled with postcards, she purchased one of Buckingham Palace – it reminded her of a school trip to London with her friend Judith – and quickly wrote:

Hi Jimmy,
Gone away for a while. Don't worry, I'm fine. Give Mariah a hug
for me.
Love Mum x

Scrabbling around in her handbag, she found a book of stamps lurking at the bottom of it and then located a post box. Task completed, she headed to her gate. She was finally on her way to the US of A.

* * *

Gazing out of the cabin window, Carla hoped the seat next to hers would remain empty. No such luck. A young boy climbed into it and repeatedly jumped up and down, practising his trampoline skills.

Great, I've got a bouncing bomb next to me, she sighed to herself.

His mother, a thin, tired-looking woman with scraggy blonde hair and hollowed eyes, appeared not to notice as she struggled to put her bags in the overhead locker. The boy sat down and immediately started to fidget and play with the foldaway table.

At least I'm not sitting in front of him, Carla concluded.

The boy's mother slumped into her seat, not paying her son any attention or seeming to care that he was being a nuisance. Carla immediately regretted being a cheapskate and wished she'd upgraded her seat. After all, it was the real America she was after, not the real England. She'd had a lifetime of being with Brits, and the prospect of spending the next nine hours with a snotty-nosed, hyperactive kid was not a pleasant one.

Carla had always ensured her children behaved in public. She struggled to understand why people had kids if they weren't prepared to look after them properly. She thought of James and Emili and felt a further pang of guilt. She quickly let it go. She'd done more than enough for them over the years, and now it was time they learned to stand on their own two feet. Despite herself, she wasn't entirely convinced by her own sentiment.

She was looking forward to the drinks trolley doing its rounds. A few glasses of wine would surely dull her fraying nerves. Seatbelt on, the boy calmed down at last and peered over to the window, the excitement clear on his face as the plane trundled down the runway and took off. Carla had to admit, he was a cutie.

The entertainment system was switched on and the boy's mother found him a cartoon to watch. Then she put her chair back and immediately fell into a deep sleep.

Charming!

After her first glass of wine, Carla noticed the cartoon had finished and the boy was looking up at her with sorrowful eyes. With his cherubic face and his little body huddled in that big seat, he looked so vulnerable and lost. Carla's heart melted. He looked anxiously across at his sleeping mother, a deep frown on his forehead.

'Are you alright?' Carla asked him.

'My daddy's just run away with an ugly bitch,' the boy said, matter of factly.

'Is that what your mummy said?' Carla asked solemnly, trying not to smile at his words.

'Yes, and now we're going to 'Merica to see my Auntie Joanne.'

'And you've got a horrible feeling in your tummy, haven't you?'

'How do you know that?'

'I've got one too,' Carla admitted.

'Did your daddy run away with an ugly bitch too?'

This time, she did laugh. 'No, but my husband did.'

'It sucks.'

'Yes, it does.'

They sat in silence for a few moments while they mulled over these words of wisdom, then Carla said, 'Let's forget about them, shall we? How about we let your mummy catch up on some sleep and we play some games?'

'Yes, please.' His face beamed brighter than a ray of sunshine.

What a polite young man. Carla realised his mother wasn't neglectful, she was just struggling to cope with the sorry situation she had found herself in. She felt guilty for judging her so harshly. She of all people should understand that you can never know what's going on in someone else's life.

'What's your name?'

'Stevie, what's yours?'

'Carla. Pleased to meet you.'

Trying his hardest to look grown up, Stevie held out his little hand and Carla gently shook it while smiling reassuringly at him.

'How old are you, Stevie?'

'I'm six.'

'Gosh, you are a big boy. Right, let's get started.'

They played noughts and crosses, crayoned in the colouring book that the flight attendant had given to Stevie, and drew some pictures. Her heart nearly broke when she looked at his simple drawing, which depicted a house in the sunshine surrounded by flowers. Standing in front of it was a stick man and a stick woman. Beside them was a stick dog, and standing in between them, a stick boy was clutching their hands.

'Is that your dog?'

'Yes,' Stevie replied. 'He's called Benji. My nana's looking after him. That's my house and my mummy and my daddy…'

His voice trailed off. Carla could see the tears welling up in his eyes and she reached across and took his hand in hers. He smiled at her gratefully.

'Oh, look, here comes the food trolley. Let's eat, shall we?'

'What about Mummy?'

'Let her sleep. She must be very tired.'

Indeed, she was dead to the world. Carla wondered how long it had been since she'd got some proper rest.

Buoyed by the food and feeling relaxed from the wine, Carla said, 'Shall we play a game on the computer?'

She struggled her way around the entertainment system for a few minutes until eventually their screens and controllers were working in tandem. The pair of them giggled as they played, with Carla conceding colossal defeat. The excitement of their game had taken its toll and Stevie was clearly now struggling to keep his eyes open.

'I know, let's wrap this blanket round you to keep you warm while you have a nap,' said Carla. 'We've still got a long way to go.'

Stevie smiled, closed his eyes and quickly drifted off.

Outside, Carla could see nothing but fluffy, white clouds and blue sky. She glanced back at the sleeping boy. He reminded her so much of James, who'd been loving and attentive towards her at that age. They'd remained close as he reached adulthood, and he had even taken her to Tenerife when his mate cancelled at the last minute, having gone down with mumps. It was a fabulous holiday, but it was also the start of things going wrong between them. Her mind drifted back to the fateful day he'd met Melissa.

They were relaxing by the hotel pool when a young woman glided by. She was wearing a long, flowing beach dress that was almost transparent in the sunlight, revealing her gorgeous, bikini-clad body underneath. Carla saw James's head turn in her direction, his gaze following her graceful movements as she floated by. He watched her spread out her towel and take off her dress, before settling on her sunbed and removing a book from her beach bag. She seemed completely oblivious to the fact she was being watched.

'Don't let me cramp your style,' said Carla with a smile. 'I'm quite capable of looking after myself.'

James grinned at her and leapt up from his sunbed. Surreptitiously, Carla observed her son's awkward body language as he struck up a conversation with the beautiful young woman. At first, Melissa had looked surprised at the interruption, but before long she had invited him to join her on the empty sunbed next to hers. They seemed to be getting on like a house on fire, and so Carla lay back and closed her eyes, enjoying the morning sunshine.

When James returned, he was buzzing with excitement. 'Mum, I've just met the girl I'm going to marry!' he announced.

'Whoa! Who knew you were as impetuous as your father? Does she know this yet?'

'Not yet, but honestly, she's amazing. Her name's Melissa, and she's beautiful and funny and clever. She's here on holiday with her parents, and she's studying English literature at university. After that, she's going to train as a teacher. She was telling me about the book she's reading called *The Grapes of Wrath*, which tells the story of a family's awful journey along Route 66 in America. Wait, I'm babbling, aren't I?'

'Yes, you are. You're clearly very taken with her!'

'I am, I really am.'

James's face clouded over.

'What's the matter?'

'There was this one weird thing. She asked me what I do for a living, and I told her how I'd ditched my accountancy job to work as a ranger with the National Trust. She assumed you must have been upset at me taking a lower paid job, and she even seemed a bit jealous when I told her you and Dad just want me to be happy. Then I asked her to come out with me tonight, but she said her mother wouldn't allow it. At first, I thought she was making excuses, but then she suggested we meet here tomorrow morning. I can't work out what's going on.'

'Oh dear. It sounds like she has an overprotective mother,' said Carla. 'Be careful. If you do marry her, you'll be marrying the family too, and the collateral damage from an overbearing mother-in-law might not be pleasant.'

Carla took no pleasure in being proved right. When James had met Melissa's mother Andrea later in the holiday, she had been nothing short of obnoxious, and Melissa's father was clearly embarrassed by her bullying tactics. As James and Melissa's relationship deepened back in the UK, Andrea had done her best to split them up. She may have failed at that, but she had succeeded in getting James to give up his beloved job and climb back onto the corporate ladder in accountancy in order to 'properly provide' for her precious daughter. Carla had to stand by and silently watch her beautiful son lose his zest for life while shouldering the responsibilities of marriage and fatherhood. To add insult to injury, Melissa's father had grown tired of all the drama and moved back to his home town in Wales, leaving Andrea to focus all her attention on Melissa and her family.

Away from the confines of home, Carla was starting to think more clearly. Now she wondered whether James had actually been selfish towards her, or was he just so busy trying to deal with his own problems that he'd failed to notice hers?

She glanced at Stevie, who was now leaning against his mother. The pair looked so peaceful in sleep. Carla hoped they would hang onto their strong bond over the years to come.

Carla passed the remainder of the flight reading her Route 66 notebook and the travel guide she'd bought in the departure lounge. Then came an announcement from the pilot. 'Ladies and gentlemen, we will be coming into land in approximately twenty minutes. Please fasten your seatbelts.'

Stevie stirred and turned to Carla. 'Boys too?'

'Yes, boys too.'

Just then, Stevie's mother woke up, looking dazed. 'Did he just say we're landing?' she said to Carla, suddenly aware of her surroundings.

'Yes, he did.'

The woman looked horrified. She leaned over and hugged her son. 'I'm so sorry, Stevie, I don't know what came over me.'

'It's alright, Mum. I've been playing computer games with Carla, and I won.' His little chest puffed out with pride, and he seemed to grow a foot taller.

'I'm so embarrassed, what must you think of me?' said his mum. 'Thank you so much for taking care of him.'

'He's told me a little bit about what's happened, and trust me, I know exactly how it feels,' said Carla. 'You obviously needed that sleep, and he's cheered me up no end, haven't you, Stevie?'

The boy nodded, grinning from ear to ear.

'He's a delightful young man, and I'm sure you are very proud of him.'

The woman ruffled her son's hair and, blushing slightly, said, 'I am. I really am.'

The sleep had done the woman the world of good and

although she still looked tired, there was a sparkle in her eyes that had been missing at the start of the flight.

After they landed, Carla watched mother and son as they made their way along the airport corridor towards the immigration hall. Hand in hand, they chatted animatedly to each other, laughing. Carla felt sure they would be OK.

CHAPTER 11
Chicago, Illinois

Carla's guidebook told her Chicago O'Hare International was the sixth busiest airport in the world, and it seemed to her that its eighty million annual passengers had all arrived on the same day, and most were practising for a place in the Chicago Bears football team. She followed the signs to the arrivals hall and ended up in a long line, which snaked its way to the immigration booths. Finally one became available, and she was beckoned over.

A uniformed officer looked at her coldly and drawled, 'Passport please, ma'am.'

Nervously, she handed it over.

What is it about immigration officials? she thought to herself. *They make you feel like a drug smuggler just by looking at you.*

Even so, Carla decided she wouldn't have minded being strip-searched by this hunky man in uniform. She wondered what on earth had got into her.

'Right thumb.'

She awoke from her reverie and placed her thumb and then her fingers on the fingerprint machine. After repeating the exercise with her other hand, she presented her eyeballs for a photo. She was tempted to ask the officer if he wanted a bum print, too, but thought better of it. She was aware that immigration officials generally don't display a sense of humour while on duty, and that to Americans, a bum is a tramp. She quickly ruled out saying 'fanny', that was just wrong, and 'butt' and 'ass' didn't sound much better either. She decided to keep her jokes to herself.

'Business or vacation?'

'Vacation,' she said with a weak smile.

'Where are you staying?'

Why, do you want to meet up with me later?

Had she just said that out loud? No… NO!

'Club Quarters,' she mumbled, her face beetroot.

'Well, you have a great vacation.'

He handed back her passport and flashed her a gorgeous smile that sent her weak at the knees. She scuttled out of the airport, certain she'd drunk too much wine on the plane and promising herself she'd exert more self-control in future. She hailed a bright yellow taxi, elbowed a pushy queue-jumper out of the way and then climbed into the back seat and sat quietly for the short journey to downtown Chicago. After checking into her tenth-floor room, she collapsed on the bed and was asleep within seconds.

She awoke two hours later, feeling groggy and jet-lagged. What time was it? 5pm. Good, that meant there was plenty of time for a walk around Millennium Park and along Lake Michigan's shoreline before dark. Then she would head to Giordano's for a proper Chicago-style deep pan pizza pie, before having an early night, ready to start her holiday in earnest.

* * *

Waking early, Carla thought she must still be dreaming. And then she remembered that she'd actually done it – she'd jumped on a plane and was about to start her dream trip. Excited about her impending adventure, she leapt out of bed and dashed to the window. It was raining, but she wasn't going to let a bit of precipitation dampen her spirits, especially as it was a perfect day to indulge in some shopping.

After breakfast, she hurried the few blocks to Macy's, a glorious emporium in North State Street. Carla's trusty guidebook told her it was built in the early 1900s, when it was known as Marshall Field's, and the iconic clock outside became famous as a meeting point. She wondered briefly how many hearts had been lost beneath it, before determinedly marching into the store. Two hours later, she emerged empty handed, but not because she hadn't been able to find anything. Her credit card was hot to trot, and the sum of her purchases was on its way back to her room at Club Quarters, along with two smart new suitcases.

Now, that's service for you! Carla thought to herself.

She finally knew what the term retail therapy meant. She'd felt like an artist with a blank canvas as enthusiastic sales assistants brought item after item to the fitting room for her to try on. They knew what suited her better than she did, and she'd come away with brightly coloured dresses, floral-print skirts, well-fitting jeans and T-shirts, cashmere jumpers and classy underwear. She'd bought flats, high heels and kitten heels, and, in preparation for varying weather conditions and every eventuality, casual jackets, smart jackets and warm jackets. To complement each outfit, she'd splashed out on matching accessories – jewellery, scarves and gloves, and make-up too. Finally, she'd treated herself to a sensational dress in azure crushed velvet that she didn't need but just had to have. She decided that before moving on, she'd dispose of her old travel bag and all the clothes inside it. If she was going to have an adventure, she wanted to look and feel like a new woman.

Next, she went to a hairdresser to rid herself of her stray grey hairs and restore her natural auburn. Lastly, she popped into the T-Mobile store to buy a new phone. All set to go, she congratulated herself on an excellent morning's work and rewarded herself with coffee and cake at the Intelligentsia coffee bar.

By the afternoon, the rain had disappeared, and the clouds had scuttled away, transforming the city's drab streets into a vibrant metropolis. Carla took full advantage of the brightening weather, determined to see the tourist hot spots of Chicago. She started at Union Station, where a scene from one of her favourite crime flicks, *The Untouchables*, had been filmed. She imagined the Mob's gangsters exchanging gunfire with Eliot Ness's band of men, while the baby's pram bump-bumped down the giant staircase. The station and its colossal pillars had provided the backdrop for one of the most memorable scenes in cinematography, and this time, Carla wasn't just seeing it on a screen.

Next, she went to the Willis Tower and took in the fabulous view over Chicago from the 108th floor. Then she hot-footed it to see the chewing gum whiteness of the Wrigley Building before taking a walk along Lake Michigan's shoreline. It was hard to believe she was in a landlocked state and not a seaside resort; the water stretched as far as the eye could see and the city's Navy Pier completed the illusion. She returned to Millennium Park to look at its collection of modern sculptures, spending a long moment gazing at Anish Kapoor's *Cloud Gate*, which had been nicknamed 'The Bean' by locals because of its shape. Normally a bit of a philistine when it came to modern art, Carla was awestruck by the shiny, stainless-steel structure.

Later she walked up Adams Street and found the brown and white sign commemorating the start of Historic Route 66. She stopped underneath it and asked a passer-by to take her picture. After he'd snapped her in various poses, he returned her little point-and-click camera, and she gave her thanks.

'Are you gonna drive it?' he asked.

'Yes, all the way to Santa Monica, I hope.'

'Well, you have a great trip.'

Carla walked another two blocks and into the offices of Enterprise, the car rental company she'd researched all those months ago, when she and Tom were going to take this trip together. At the counter, an eager young woman greeted her with a warm smile. Her manner was so welcoming that Carla felt as if she must be her most important customer of the day.

'I'd like to hire a convertible Camaro or Mustang, please,' she said.

The clerk's face fell along with her enthusiasm. Her voice took on the tone of an undertaker as she said, 'I'm sorry, ma'am, we're totally out and you won't find one anywhere in Chicago. There's a convention in Kentucky and every muscle car from around here is heading that way.'

Carla's heart sank. 'Oh no. What do you have?'

'Not much right now, I'm afraid. Let me see. I can do you a good price on a Kia Sportage.'

'It isn't quite what I'd had in mind, but I suppose it will have to do,' Carla sighed.

They completed the paperwork and Carla arranged for the car to be dropped off at her hotel the following morning.

What a start!

Dejected, she wandered aimlessly in the direction of

Millennium Park. She became aware of music playing in the distance and followed the sound. To her delight, she discovered a full philharmonic orchestra playing a free concert to a large and appreciative audience at the park's outdoor auditorium. Families and couples were stretched out on blankets eating picnics and enjoying the music. Carla found an empty spot on the grass and was soon mesmerised by the sounds coming from the stage. When the orchestra exited for the interval to rapturous applause, Carla thought how she must stick out like a sore thumb. She was surrounded by happy families laughing and chatting and eating and drinking like it was going out of fashion.

'Looks like you didn't get yourself organised,' a woman said to her.

'No, I didn't,' Carla admitted. 'I just stumbled on this concert by accident. It's marvellous, isn't it?'

'You don't sound like you're from around here,' the woman said, her bright blue eyes twinkling at Carla.

'I'm from England.'

'Come and join us. We've got plenty to go round, and my husband, Darrell, has already eaten enough to feed a whole army.'

Carla demurred. The idea of accepting hospitality from a stranger made her feel uncomfortable.

'I insist. Get yourself over here, honey, and get stuck in.'

Realising she'd been foolish and somewhat rude for turning the woman down, Carla moved onto the blanket. Having not eaten since her cake at Intelligentsia, she gratefully accepted everything that came her way.

'I'm Robyn. What's your name, honey?'

'Carla. This is really kind of you, thank you.'

'Aw, it's nothing.'

Just then, the orchestra returned to the stage for the second half of the concert. Night had fallen, and bright lights blazed from a cluster of imposing skyscrapers. Carla craned her neck skywards. The tower blocks silhouetted against the glowing Chicago skyline, the intensity of the music and the friendliness of the people all combined to chase away Carla's blues, leaving her with a renewed sense of purpose for the journey ahead.

When the concert drew to a close, everyone packed away their things and gradually milled out of the park. To Carla's immense relief, Robyn and her husband didn't ask her any questions. They simply gave her a big hug and wished her luck.

* * *

On her way back to the hotel, Carla spotted an unkempt woman camped in the doorway of a boarded-up retail store. Her clothes were tatty, but a surprisingly clean face peered out from beneath an oversized floppy hat. She appeared to be of a similar age to Carla, though it was hard to tell.

On impulse, Carla stopped to talk to her. 'Is there anything I can get for you?' she asked.

The woman looked at her suspiciously.

'My name's Carla. I'm a tourist from England. I'm not going to hurt you. Can I get you anything to eat or drink?'

'Could you get me a sandwich and some coffee, please?'

'Of course. I won't be a minute.'

A few minutes later, Carla returned with a chicken and bacon melt and two Americanos.

'Mind if I sit with you?'

'Go ahead.'

Carla sipped her coffee and waited in silence while the woman ate her sandwich. Then she said, 'Tell me to mind my own business if you want. Just because I bought you some food and a drink, doesn't give me the right to pry, but if you want to talk about how you ended up on the streets, I'm a good listener. What's your name?'

'Terri. I don't mind talking; I don't get to say much these days. It all started when my husband left me. I didn't see it coming and I couldn't cope. I had a breakdown and struggled to recover. In the end, I lost my job and couldn't make the rent, and I was kicked out of my apartment. So, here I am.'

'I'm so sorry, Terri.'

There but for the grace of God...

'I've got some clothes you can have if that would help.'

'Sure, thanks.'

'I'll just go and get them. My hotel is only round the corner.'

Carla fetched the clothes she'd brought with her from England and handed them to Terri. 'Here's fifty dollars. It's all I have on me, but I can get some more from the bank tomorrow when it opens.'

'I appreciate it,' said Terri. 'Listen, I don't wish to be rude, ma'am, but you need to go now.'

Carla was stunned at the harshness of her words. Terri retreated into the shadows, but Carla could just make out the outline of the woman's body pressed against the door. She saw that she was hunched over, her arms wrapped tightly around her body, staring at the ground. Her changed demeanour told Carla their conversation was over. She wondered if she had been over-enthusiastic in her manner and had made Terri feel uncomfortable, or maybe she just wanted to be left alone. Whatever the reason, Carla knew she had outstayed her welcome. She said goodnight and hurried back to her hotel, aware the streets could be dangerous at this time of night.

The following morning, Carla passed the doorway on the way to the bank and, to her horror, saw that Terri and all her belongings were gone. She wondered if it was her fault. Had she embarrassed the poor woman, causing her to disappear into the night rather than face her in the morning? She had been so busy playing Lady Bountiful, thinking she was being so helpful, that it hadn't occurred to her Terri might not want her charity and had moved on to keep her pride intact. She hoped to God that her attempt to help hadn't made Terri's life more difficult.

CHAPTER 12
Wrendale, Missouri

L eaving Illinois and driving into Missouri, Carla's mood was low. She had nothing against Illinois; in different circumstances she would have enjoyed the state and its agricultural countryside, little towns and Route 66 tourist landmarks – especially the Gemini Giant at the Launching Pad drive-in in Wilmington. The green-clad, thirty-foot spaceman cradled a silver-coloured rocket ship and wore a face covering that looked suspiciously like a welding mask. It was a sight to behold.

If Tom had been with her, they would have stopped and posed for photos, taking it in turns to stand between the man's giant, fibreglass legs and laughing like children. They would have browsed the antique stores, Carla wanting to buy something they didn't need and Tom eventually convincing her they'd have nowhere to put it. They'd have visited the museums along the way, and Carla would have been engrossed in every single detail, while Tom would have got bored after fifteen minutes and waited outside, taking the opportunity to have forty winks in the car. By herself, Carla couldn't raise the enthusiasm for any of it, and she drove on, her despondency rising in direct proportion with the increasing mileage. In the right car, it would have been different: in the Kia, it seemed like she'd dropped the kids off at school and taken a wrong turn on her way home. She felt sad, lonely and tired.

After a couple of hours of driving, and with no improvement in her mood, she decided to stop for the day. She parked outside a tourist information office that proudly displayed the American flag from its rooftop. She'd read that public buildings always fly the 'Stars and Stripes', and that where there's a public building, more often than not there's a public toilet to go with it, for which she was especially in need at that moment, an unwelcome reminder of her advancing years.

She climbed out of the air-conditioned car and immediately broke into a sweat. The humidity was oppressive, and she was glad to get inside. After visiting the restroom, she browsed through the leaflets advertising places to stay, and a quaint, old-fashioned hotel with a swimming pool caught her eye. The thought of lazing by a pool for the afternoon cheered Carla up no end. She approached the woman at the reception desk and showed her the leaflet.

'Hi. Could you tell me the way to the Golden Sunlight Hotel, please?'

Almost imperceptibly, the woman's eyebrows rose. 'Sure. Drive onto Main Street, follow the road until you leave town, take a left at the red barn and continue for five miles until you reach Wrendale. Then take a right into Truman, carry on for about a half-mile and it's on your right. You can't miss it.'

'Thank you.'

The woman opened her mouth as if to say more, but changed her mind and closed it again. Carla thought little of it and thanked the receptionist once again, before returning to her car and following her detailed directions.

* * *

Wrendale was a small town in the middle of nowhere. Main Street was past its early twentieth-century heyday, but considering it was in the back of beyond, it was surprisingly busy. It wasn't typical of the small towns Carla had already driven through, many of which were almost devoid of life, the streets lined with empty, dilapidated stores. Most of these towns had suffered from the opening of the freeways and successive economic recessions. Somehow, though, Wrendale had avoided the same fate.

Carla parked up and walked along the pavement, or sidewalk, as she was now beginning to think of it. Even in her internal dialogue, she was trying to use the local lingo. She noticed most of the shops were 'alternative' stores. Many of the passers-by seemed dreamy, and she guessed they lived a hippy lifestyle outside of normal convention. She spotted a grocery store and went inside, finding it surprisingly bright, clean and well-stocked. She placed a cooked chicken, a baguette, a small tub of potato salad, a packet of crisps, some apples and a handful of magazines into her basket and made her way to the till. By now, she was used to the delightful ultra-politeness of Americans, so she was surprised to encounter a sullen cashier at the checkout. He barely looked at her, rang up her groceries and grunted the total at her. She paid and left without saying anything to him.

Some kind of commotion was going on in the building next door, and as she walked by, she peered in through the open door to see a dingy bar packed with drinkers already the worse for wear, despite the early hour. She shrugged, climbed back into her car and wondered if she should cut her losses and leave town. It would be the smart thing to do, but she was exhausted and worried she wouldn't be safe on the road if she continued her journey. She drove the short distance to the Golden Sunlight Hotel and her first impression of the property was a good one, though the outside walls could probably use a lick of paint. The hotel was presentable otherwise and the grounds were well kept. She parked up outside the lobby, strolled in and rang the bell on the reception desk. A minute or so later, a woman with glassy eyes appeared from the back office and greeted her with a toothy grin.

'Can I help you?'

'Have you got a quiet room for tonight, please?'

'Yes, ma'am. I've got a double with a shower for seventy dollars or a larger room and a bath for eighty. Breakfast is an extra eight dollars.'

'I'll take the larger room and breakfast, please.'

She let herself into her room and was delighted with its quirkiness. Just as the lobby and corridor had been, the original décor was all from the 1930s and 1940s. In line with the old-time feel of the hotel, there was no phone or TV in her room, and Carla looked forward to a relaxing, peaceful time. She sniffed the musky air and was reminded of her grandma's house. It was an intriguing place, decorated with lovely old cabinets filled with antiquities, dusty pictures, lace curtains, brass lamps with frilly lampshades and floral vases. The wooden floorboards in the corridor creaked underfoot. While it all added to the retro atmosphere, Carla thought the hotel could do with a little TLC, but at the cheap price, she decided it would do just fine.

After changing into her new, red, halter-strap swimsuit, Carla made her way down to the pool, where she settled herself on a sunbed and ate the lunch she'd bought at the grocery store. Satiated, she lay back, enjoying the peace and quiet of the hotel grounds. She read a magazine, until the warm sunshine and her full belly sent her into a deep sleep.

Carla dreamt she was in the pool, drowning. As she thrashed around, Judith stood at the edge, telling her everything would be alright. But her arms were flailing uselessly, and she could feel herself going under. Judith stripped off her clothes and dived in to rescue her.

Carla awoke with a start, disturbed by a splash of cold water landing on her legs. She opened her eyes and, to her horror, found the area now resembled a public swimming pool. It didn't take long to work out these people were not hotel guests; she was surrounded by freeloading drunks and deadbeats from the town.

Really?

Some of them were dive-bombing into the pool, while others were swigging back beer or smoking cannabis. Carla couldn't believe what she was seeing. She jumped up and strode over to the hotel's entrance, where she found two chain-smoking staff members rooted to a swing seat that was gently rocking backwards and forwards. They were bitching and moaning about their private lives in colourful language and ignored her arrival. The women only stopped talking when they realised Carla wasn't going away.

'I'd like to speak to the owner, please.'

'He's not here.'

'When will he be back?'

'Don't know, he's in Florida.'

'Of course he is.'

Carla sighed and went back to her sunbed.

When the cat's away the mice will play,' she thought to herself.

Eventually, the interlopers ran out of steam and fell asleep. Peace had returned. From the poolside, Carla surveyed her not-so-immediate surroundings. A row of cabins situated to one side of the main hotel piqued her interest. She wondered if they were little shops, but if so, they were all closed. The sign on the first cabin read, *Janey's Collectibles*. Intrigued, Carla thought she'd have a browse later, should it be open for business. As if reading her mind, a woman opened the shop door.

Janey?

Leaving the store unattended, the woman strolled over to the pool, accompanied by a little boy. She lay down on a sunbed, seeming not to care whether she had customers or not. A while later, Carla saw a man go into the shop. 'Janey' returned to the cabin and closed the door behind her. Concerned for the boy's safety, Carla kept a close eye on him. He didn't seem at all concerned by his mother's absence and happily splashed around in the pool. He was a good swimmer, and Carla was relieved her rusty lifesaving skills would not be called upon. It was some time before the man left, a satisfied smile on his face.

Maybe I won't go for a browse after all, Carla concluded.

Troubled by the day's experiences, she wondered whether it would be wise to venture into town for dinner, but not wanting to spend her evening alone in her room without even a TV for company, she pulled on her new jeans and a cerise shirt, braced herself and headed out. She found a nice little bar-restaurant and ate a tasty Reuben sandwich comprising layers of thinly sliced corned beef, Swiss cheese, sauerkraut and Thousand Island sauce, grilled between rye bread and served with fries.

When the server came over to clear her plate away, he said, 'If you don't have any plans for the evening, we're having a trivia quiz. Fancy joining in?'

'Why not,' said Carla, 'though I doubt I'll know many of the answers.'

She didn't, but then neither did anyone else, and to her surprise, she won, her paltry score boosted by a lucky guess on reptiles, an educated guess with Monet and a random Lone Ranger answer. Her prize was a free glass of cold beer. The locals were indifferent to her presence, and in the absence of any further entertainment, Carla decided on a much-needed early night. She'd get a good night's sleep, shake off the remaining jet leg and, hopefully, wake up feeling far more enthusiastic about hitting the road again.

* * *

Back at the hotel, peace and quiet reigned – apart from the poolside sounds of an out-of-tune singer plucking away at his guitar. Thankfully, the racket ceased at ten o'clock, when the pool was locked up for the night. Carla was just about to get undressed when someone banged on her door. She cautiously opened it; outside stood a strange-looking man wearing a top hat and a bright blue jacket.

'I need to speak to Jake,' he said in an urgent voice.

'There is no Jake here, you've got the wrong room.'

Carla closed the door, locked it, and slid on the chain. She'd just got out of the bath and into her night clothes when she was disturbed by some further loud knocking. Sighing, she opened the door, careful to leave on the chain.

This time it was the handyman.

'You're flooding the lobby,' he barked.

'I only half-filled the bath. It's not my fault if your pipework's dodgy,' she said, slamming the door shut.

What was this place?

Carla climbed into bed. It was uncomfortable, but she was

too tired to care and was soon asleep. An hour later, a loud humming noise woke her up. It took her a few minutes to work out what it was.

Surely not?

She looked out of the window and peered into the darkness. She could just about make out the figure of a man. From what she could see and hear, she was sure he was strimming the grass around the pool's perimeter.

What the hell?

Throwing on her dressing gown, she marched downstairs. There was no one in reception so she went outside, where she found two women sitting at a table. They were smoking weed and sipping from bottles of beer.

'Do you work here?'

'No, but we might be able to help.'

'What on earth is he doing?'

'That's the gardener, he's trimming the grass. He has to do it at night when the pool is shut,' the woman said, as if this was perfectly normal behaviour.

'What, at this time of night?'

'Just chill, lady. Sit down and have a drink with us,' she slurred.

'I don't want a drink; I just want to sleep.'

In hindsight, she should have accepted the woman's invitation, on the basis that if you can't beat them, join them. Instead, she stomped over to the gardener, dressing gown flowing in her wake. He saw her coming and switched off his strimmer.

'What do you think you are doing at this time of night?'

'I have to do it when the pool is shut. The owner don't like me doing it when it's open, in case I flick stones in people's eyes.'

'Can't you see this is totally inappropriate? There's a sign in the hotel telling the guests to be quiet after 10pm. I came here to relax, not to listen to you making a racket in the middle of the night. And what about the neighbours, what do they think?'

That was a daft question, they are probably stoned or drunk, or both, Carla thought.

'Do you want me to stop, then?'

'Yes please, that would be good.'

Carla returned to bed, totally bemused by the whole affair. She dropped off to sleep and was immediately awoken yet again. It was after 2am, and this time the noise was coming from outside her window, from people laughing and talking. A small crowd had gathered by the swing seat, just below her room. They appeared to be having a party.

I don't believe it! Who cares about the paying guests as long as the locals are happy?

Unwilling to get involved in a confrontation with several drunken and/or stoned strangers, Carla covered her head with her pillow until, utterly exhausted, she finally drifted off to sleep.

She awoke the next morning feeling tired and grumpy. She was convinced the staff and locals were deliberately trying to sabotage the hotel's business. It must be hard enough to attract people here in the first place, but to treat the guests with such disdain was appalling. Carla went down for breakfast, and, to her surprise, it was tasty, though her fellow guests were as strange as everyone else she'd encountered here. Most of them were pyjama-clad octogenarians lacking a full set of teeth between them, and every one of them was away with the fairies. Had she stumbled into a lunatic asylum rather than a hotel? Or was she going to find herself on one of those Saturday night entertainment programmes, where tricks are played on unsuspecting victims? She could not think of any rational explanation for this debacle.

Upon checking out, Carla lodged a complaint to the desk clerk.

'I'm real sorry, ma'am. I'm horrified the gardener has gone and done it again. I've told him before not to. The folk outside were just the security guy and the staff from the bar in town letting their hair down after work.'

'So, this is a regular occurrence?'

'Yes, ma'am,' the woman said, her tone indicating she couldn't see what all the fuss was about.

'I asked you for a quiet room. Why didn't you put me at the back of the hotel, then I wouldn't have been disturbed by all this nonsense?'

Carla was trying and failing to keep the exasperation out of her voice.

The dippy-looking woman's response was nothing more than a blank look. Then, remembering her manners, she tried to smooth things over. 'I'll speak to the owner about it when he gets back,' she said. 'I hope you'll give us another chance.'

'I'm not likely to be passing this way again,' said Carla, before picking up her cases and heading back to her car.

Hell would have to freeze over before she returned to this weird town.

CHAPTER 13
Springfield, Missouri

C arla wasn't a fan of fast food, but when needs must, fried chicken sufficed. She sat in a boring KFC diner, in a boring street, looking at her boring car in the boring car park. Ostensibly, she was on Route 66, but this section, like many others, had been paved over and lost in the annals of time. Traffic flowed past on the four-lane highway, which was lined with every fast-food joint you could think of, as well as the banks and corporate retail outlets you could find anywhere in the US. If only she could be bothered to get her guidebook out of her car, she would look up Springfield's tourist hotspots, but with her exhaustion getting the better of her, she continued staring out of the window, her thoughts turning to the past.

Where had it all gone wrong with Tom, and when?

Carla racked her brain. She couldn't think of any seismic shift in their relationship and struggled to think what might have driven him away.

Had *she* become boring?

Yes, that was it! But hang on, so had he come to that, and she hadn't felt the need to run off with anyone. How long had it been since they'd had a really good laugh together? A couple of years, she guessed. Even though they were both busy when she was working, they'd always managed to find time for each other. They'd get into mischief and lead each other astray. Carla smiled at the memory of some of their antics, and her mind drifted even further back…

Not so many years ago, they went for a drink in their local, which they noticed was unusually quiet. They left at closing time, three sheets to the wind, only to discover a winter wonderland. Everything in sight was covered in virgin snow, which was a rare thing in their part of the world. It dulled all sound, and even though it was dark, the whiteness lit up the landscape. The street outside the pub was deserted. Clearly, everyone else had seen the weather forecast and wisely stayed at home. They started walking home, hand in hand, feeling a childish sense of wonder.

'Isn't it beautiful?' said Carla.

'Yes, it is. Look behind us, see our footprints?'

'What about them?'

'No one else has been out. We have a blank canvas to play with.' Tom grinned mischievously. 'Watch this.'

He'd then proceeded to walk into someone's garden, his footsteps crunching in the snow as he sneaked up to the front door. Then he walked backwards, carefully stepping into the footprints he'd already made.

'I'm the Invisible Man, disappearing into thin air,' he declared. 'That'll get them scratching their heads when they open the door tomorrow.'

Carla laughed and said, 'Watch this.' She allowed herself to fall backwards, arms and legs akimbo. 'I'm a starfish, I'm a starfish,' she chanted.

Tom pulled her up and Carla admired her handiwork.

Next, they approached a neat terrace of houses, the gardens separated by low hedges.

Tom lined up in the first garden and said softly, 'And the favourite for today's Grand National is… Tom's Delight.'

He galloped up to the first hedge and leapt over it, then the second and the third, somersaulting over the last one and landing in a crumpled heap. Helpless with laughter, they'd continued in the same vein all the way home.

Walking to the newsagents the next morning, a now sober Tom realised that if anyone was upset by their antics, they would know they were the culprits just by following their wavy set of footsteps to their front door.

Even now, the memory of it made Carla smile.

At least that episode had been harmless, unlike their Tenerife escapade, which almost cost them their lives. *No entry* signs were like red rags to a bull for Tom; they had to be ignored and what was behind them investigated. On a coastal path, they climbed over a locked gate and enjoyed a pleasant walk, wondering what all the fuss was about. But as they progressed, the path got narrower and narrower until, suddenly, they found themselves clinging onto the side of the cliff, staring down at the raging waves crashing against the rocks below. Carla panicked and was rooted to the spot.

'It's just a bit further and we'll be there,' Tom had reassured her. 'Come on, hold my hand and don't look down.'

They inched their way across the cliff face, Carla's heart in her mouth. They had almost made it to the end when her foot slipped. How she didn't fall and take Tom with her she would never know. Somehow, they managed to cling on and work their way along the edge to safety, letting out a huge sigh of relief when their ordeal was finally over. It would be nice to blame it on their youth, but that was only six years ago. Carla shuddered at the memory.

They should have learnt their lesson, yet their stupidity knew no bounds, and the following year they got themselves into another pickle. For such a strong-minded woman, Carla couldn't believe how easily led she was, even in the face of danger. During their holiday in the Lake District, Tom suggested they walk up Helvellyn, the third highest mountain in England. They set out on a beautiful, sunny morning along the clearly marked footpath, wearing nothing more than trainers and light jackets and carrying an apple in one pocket and a bottle of water in the other. The need for checking the weather forecast, taking a map and compass, wearing sturdy footwear and informing someone where they were going didn't even occur to them. After a steady climb, they found themselves in thick fog, unable to see three feet in front of them and with only sheep for company. An eerie quiet had descended on the mountain. Nevertheless, they ploughed on until the path divided in two.

They couldn't see any signposts to direct them, but instead of doing the sensible thing and turning back, Carla had said, 'Which way shall we go?'

'I don't know,' Tom replied. 'Let's toss a coin for it. Heads for right, tails for left... OK, right it is, then.'

On they went, both confident they were fit enough for the challenge. As the mountain became steeper, they could just about manage to work out where the path went, and their breathing became more laboured with the effort of the uphill climb. Then the path gave way to loose scree. They did their best to scramble over it, but it was tough going. Carla shivered, more from fear than cold.

'Do you think we should go back?'

'We'll be alright,' Tom replied, not altogether confidently. 'Let's stop, have a rest and eat our apples.'

They found a rock to sit on and reflectively chewed the

fruit. There was nothing to see – the thick fog blanketed the mountain.

'I think we should cut our losses and claim this as our summit, even though it isn't the actual one,' Carla suggested. 'We can't be sure we're still on the right track.'

It was the first bit of common sense that either of them had uttered all day.

'You're right. I do feel like a quitter though.'

They heard voices in the mist and two fit young things came bounding up the path into sight. They were the first humans that Tom and Carla had seen since the fog came down.

'You can't quit now, you're nearly there,' they said as they shot by. 'Follow us if you want.'

Easy for them to say. They soon disappeared into the mist, never to be seen again. Tom and Carla would have liked to say it was all worth it for the view, but there was no view; they could barely see their feet.

'At least we know we've done it, and I think we should be proud of ourselves for such an achievement,' Tom said.

'Don't you think we should know better than to do crazy things like this at our age?' said Carla. 'And we've still got to get back down.'

They began their descent, picking their way down and successfully negotiating the most difficult part of their journey, despite the lack of visibility. At last, the fog lifted, revealing Red Tarn way down below and a stupendous view of the Lake District. Far from being entranced, Carla paled and bile rose from her stomach.

'Oh my God, Tom, look up! We could have fallen off the side of this mountain and rolled down into the lake. How on earth we've got to this age without killing ourselves I don't know. Why do I let you talk me into these things?'

She was being disingenuous. She knew that he knew that

deep down she enjoyed the thrills as much as he did, albeit after the event. She wouldn't change her Tom for the world.

So why had they stopped doing these things? She'd got busy chasing around after the family, and he'd got busier at work – but which one of them had broken the spell first? There was no point dwelling on it. Whatever the reason, Carla was not about to blame herself for Tom's betrayal.

CHAPTER 14

Kansas

W ELCOME TO KANSAS read the state line sign.
    LEAVING KANSAS, COME AGAIN.
What!

Somehow, Carla had driven the eleven-mile stretch through the state without noticing anything in it. Her planned route had included a visit to the Mining Museum in Galena, a sandwich at the Old Riverton Store, and the Marsh Rainbow Bridge – a single-span, concrete arch bridge that was the last of its kind along Route 66. She'd driven straight past them all and seen absolutely nothing.

Sorry, Kansas, it's not you, it's me.

CHAPTER 15
Oklahoma

Carla pulled into a roadside diner and switched off the engine. The Kia was really annoying her now. This wasn't how it was supposed to be. She should be cruising the open road with the wind in her hair, the sun on her face and Tom by her side, enjoying the freedom of the countryside. Living the dream. The Kia would be great for a supermarket run, but after so long behind the wheel, the car was starting to feel like a prison cell.

She was beginning to bitterly regret her impulse to escape her problems by jumping on a plane. Who was she kidding? Being on the other side of the Atlantic wasn't going to solve anything. In fact, it seemed to have made things worse. She felt Tom's absence more keenly than ever. Apart from the horror story that was Wrendale, she had barely taken anything in since Chicago, and her brain hadn't registered any of Kansas, so what was the point? She may as well pack up and go home. Feeling utterly miserable, she climbed out of the car and walked into the diner. Apart from a couple of old men sitting at the counter drinking coffee, it was almost empty. She found a booth in the corner and slid across the red leather bench seat to the window. The waitress, a friendly, middle-aged woman, bustled over.

'What can I get you?'

'Just coffee, please.'

'Can I tempt you with a piece of my warm apple pie and ice cream? It's fresh in this morning.'

Something in the waitress's face made Carla feel it would be rude to say no. Just a couple of minutes later, she was sipping her coffee, the untouched pie in front of her. What had she been thinking, running away like that? Carla remembered the excitement she'd felt when she'd boarded the plane. All she felt now was disappointment. Disappointment in Route 66, disappointment in Tom and, most of all, disappointment in herself. This was not how she'd envisaged her trip.

'May I sit here?'

Carla looked up to see a little old lady standing at her table. She couldn't have been more than five feet tall, and she looked frail, as if a mild breeze might blow her over. Her hair was tightly permed and she wore little round spectacles, through which she peered at Carla with penetrating blue eyes. Why, with all these empty tables, did the old lady want to sit at hers?

Despite her irritation, Carla's innate politeness won over. 'Yes, of course.'

There was a short, uncomfortable silence, then the old lady said, 'My name's Nancy, what's yours?'

'Carla. Pleased to meet you.'

'Oh, I love your accent. Are you from Australia?'

'No, England.'

Carla was amused by how the old lady had managed to confuse two wildly different accents, but she managed to maintain a straight face. She decided Nancy had probably never left Oklahoma, let alone travelled the world.

'Are you going to eat that?' Nancy asked.

'No, I'm not hungry.'

'May I?'

'Of course, be my guest.'

Carla watched Nancy devour the pie and wondered when she'd last eaten. If she was hungry, that explained why she had wanted to sit at Carla's table. She certainly didn't look homeless, so maybe she lived alone and couldn't be bothered to make meals for one. Carla wondered whether this would be her in a few years' time.

Oh, for goodness' sake, she suddenly thought to herself, *this is too big a pity party, even for you.*

The smiling waitress came over to their table. 'Can I get you anything, Ms Taylor?'

'Just some coffee, please, Betty. I've just eaten some of your apple pie, which was delicious as usual, so I won't need anything else. I had breakfast early today and we've got Merle's favourite pot roast for lunch, so that pie will keep the hungry wolf at bay until then.'

'My goodness, Ms Taylor, I don't know where you put it all, let alone keep that trim figure of yours. I've only got to look at a pie and I put on a pound.'

Betty laughed, poured Nancy's coffee and topped up Carla's.

I couldn't have got that more wrong, could I? Carla thought to herself.

It soon became clear that Nancy was delighted with her captive audience, and she launched into her life history. 'I come here every day and always sit in this booth,' she said. 'Everyone here is real friendly, and they all look out for me. If I didn't turn up one day, I swear they'd send out a search party. I've lived in Oklahoma all my life —'

Got that right, then!

'—and I'll be here until the day I die. I live at a farm about five miles from here. Merle and I are too old to work on it now, so Matthew, our nephew, has taken over, and he does a great job. He's a good boy and he's made life a lot easier for us. He'll inherit the farm someday, as Merle and me weren't blessed with children. I was sad about that for quite some time, but Merle said God didn't give us children because we love each other so much we wouldn't have had enough love left over for them. I think he's probably right about that. I guess you think that's crazy, don't you?'

Carla shook her head, the bitter memories of her parents arriving, unwelcome, into her head.

Finally, Nancy stopped to breathe. 'So, what brings you to our little town? You're a long way from home.'

'I'm driving Route 66.'

'On your own?' said Nancy, a note of shocked admiration in her voice. 'You're either brave or one crazy lady. You know, we worked so hard on the farm that we promised ourselves that when we retired, we would drive Route 66, but you never retire from farming, it retires you when your old bones can't do it no more. By the time that happened, there was no way we could cram into a car and hit the road. Merle isn't in the best of health. He's enjoyed too many of my pot roasts and apple pies over the years. The doctor keeps telling him to change his ways, but he just says, "Doc, I got this far, and I ain't eating no lettuce leaves to please you or no one else. When my time comes, I'll be thinking of Nancy's cooking, not some darned rabbit food."'

She giggled as she mimicked her husband's voice. Despite herself, Carla threw back her head and laughed too.

'You know, you look pretty when you laugh. Have you planned where you are staying tonight?'

'No, the only hotel I booked was in Chicago when I first

arrived. After that, I decided to take each day as it comes and stop when something interests me. To be on the safe side, I always make sure I find somewhere to stay before dark. I'm not on a schedule so I can do as I please.'

'So, you haven't made a reservation for tonight?'

'No, I'll just see how far I get.'

'In that case, come and stay the night with me and Merle.'

Carla demurred in true buttoned-up, British style. 'Oh, I couldn't possibly.'

Nancy looked hurt at Carla's reaction to her offer of hospitality. She pressed on. 'You said yourself that you have no plans. We've got plenty of food to go round, and I know Merle would love to meet you. In any case, if you don't mind me saying, you look tired and in need of a break from all that driving.'

'I'm sorry, Nancy, I didn't mean to be rude,' Carla said. 'It's just an automatic response us Brits tend to have; we're not very good at accepting favours from people we don't know.'

On second thoughts, Carla decided that Nancy was being genuine, and she was right about her being tired.

Decision made, she gratefully accepted her offer of a bed for the night.

* * *

After waving Betty a cheerful goodbye, Carla and Nancy left the diner. As she watched Nancy climb into an enormous pick-up truck, Carla wondered how she would manage to drive it and why she would want to.

Only in America! she thought.

Nancy wound down her window. 'Follow me,' she called. 'We'll just drive into town, then it's four blocks along Main

Street, right along Lincoln and then left into Brownwood Farm.'

Barely giving Carla enough time to get into the Kia, Nancy pulled onto the highway and roared off. A sheriff, who was sitting in his patrol car opposite, just shook his head and grimaced. Carla kept to the speed limit and by the time she turned into Brownwood Farm, Nancy was nowhere to be seen. The road to the farmhouse was nearly two miles long. This was no dirt track; Nancy and Merle clearly weren't poor farmers. She pulled up in front of the property and was taken back to her early teenage years. The two-storey, wooden-clad building reminded her of the house in her favourite TV programme from that time, *The Waltons*. Best of all, just like in the show, the house had a veranda, or did they call it a porch out here? She could see a swing seat on it, along with two wooden rocking chairs upholstered with flower-patterned cushions. A big bear of a man filled one of them. Nancy was standing at the front door talking animatedly to him. She beckoned to Carla, who nipped up the porch steps to greet Merle. He eased himself out of his seat, expanding like foam in a cavity wall. He must have been six feet tall and at least 250 pounds, and he towered over his petite wife. The pair looked mismatched, yet Carla could see the chemistry between them and she felt a pang of envy.

'Welcome, welcome,' said Merle in a surprisingly gentle voice. 'Please sit.'

He gestured to the other rocking chair, and Carla took a seat, finding it deliciously comfortable. She rocked herself gently back and forth, feeling more relaxed than she had done for a long time. Nancy brought out some freshly made lemonade.

Carla thirstily gulped her drink. 'This is delicious,' she said, 'so cool and refreshing. Thank you.'

'I'll get the lunch on,' said Nancy. 'I'll call you when it's ready.'

Seeming to sense that Carla didn't want to talk about herself or her trip, Merle took the opportunity to regale her with tales of the farm. His stories kept her entertained while cooking smells wafted through the screen door and made her tummy rumble.

'Come in and get it!' Nancy called to them.

As soon as she walked inside, Carla clapped her hands in delight. 'Your kitchen is beautiful,' she said, 'a proper farmhouse kitchen.'

The pine table in the centre of the room groaned with food. Merle's favourite pot roast was surrounded by all sorts of colourful, mouth-watering sides, including green beans, carrots, broccoli, buttered potatoes and cornbread. There was even some macaroni cheese. The range cooker, pine dresser and well-used copper pans hanging from the ceiling completed the country picture. Carla sat down at the table and smiled, her spirits continuing to lift. Merle said grace and the clattering of spoons began as the food was shared out in earnest.

'Mac 'n' cheese?' Merle asked Carla, passing the dish to her when she nodded.

They ate in comfortable silence, concentrating on every delicious mouthful, and washed the meal down with sweet iced tea. When they were done, they all sat back, full and satisfied.

'Would anyone like dessert?'

'No thank you, Nancy. I've eaten too much already.'

'Me too,' groaned Merle, rubbing his ample belly with contentment.

'Let me help you with the dishes,' offered Carla.

'Certainly not. Guests in my house are precisely that, so I'll have no more talk of it.'

'OK,' said Carla, suitably chastised.

'Go and get your luggage and I'll show you to your room.'

Carla retrieved her suitcases from the car and Nancy took her up the narrow staircase to a bedroom at the back of the house.

'I hope you'll be comfortable in here.'

'It's lovely, so cosy,' said Carla. 'The bed reminds me of that John Denver song, "Grandma's Feather Bed", and look at this beautiful quilt. Did you make this?'

'Yes, I did. It's a rite of passage for us country women, and for most of us it becomes an obsession. I've made lots of them over the years. This one is my favourite.'

'I love the lacing around the edge, it's so intricate. You have such talent; I can just about sew a button on a shirt.'

Despite Nancy's attempt to look nonchalant, two pink spots appeared on her cheeks, revealing her pleasure at receiving Carla's compliment. 'I'll leave you to unpack,' she called over her shoulder as she left the room. 'Bring your laundry down.'

Carla knew better than to argue with her. She stood at the window and gazed out at the fields, seeing mile upon mile of wheat stretching as far as the eye could see. It swayed gently in the breeze under the vast blue sky. To some, it might not seem much of a view, but to Carla, the huge expanse of open countryside was special. The room was perfect, and something about it made her feel safe. It had a kind of magic she could not explain, almost as if it had been awaiting her arrival; almost as if she was supposed to have come here.

Rousing herself, Carla took her washing downstairs, where Merle pointed her in the direction of an outbuilding in the yard. She walked in and her eyebrows shot up in surprise. The room was like a fully equipped laundromat. Nancy was doing the ironing while watching a giant, state-of-the-art TV, which was attached to the wall in front of her.

'You might not think it from looking at the house, but our domestic and farm equipment is all from the twenty-first century,' she said. 'Leave that with me and go and rest.'

Doing as she was told, Carla stretched out on the swing seat and relaxed. The heavy lunch, warm air and gentle swaying of the seat soon sent her to a much-needed sleep.

* * *

After supper, Nancy and Carla sat on the porch swing, which Carla had learned was the American term for a swing seat. She would crack this American language one day. They chatted amicably about nothing in particular. Darkness had fallen, the stars twinkled, and the only sounds came from the grasshoppers in the fields, the fireflies flitting around the porch lights and the faint squeak of the seat as they rocked back and forth.

'Are you ready to talk about the reason for the sadness in your eyes?' said Nancy.

Carla was, and the whole sorry saga came tumbling out – Tom, the children, her parents, her friend's behaviour, the breakdown, her despair, and her hopes for the trip.

'I thought it would liberate me, give me a purpose, show me the way forward,' said Carla. 'But instead of a shiny muscle car, I ended up with a crappy Kia. I miss Tom, and I don't see any point in carrying on the route.'

She burst into tears. Having opened the floodgates, she could not stop. She sobbed uncontrollably, her body heaving up and down.

Nancy quietly passed her a handkerchief. She let Carla cry her heart out, and when her sobs subsided to a whimper, she reached out her hand and clasped Carla's, squeezing it gently to offer comfort. It was the first time Carla had cried since Tom left and she felt purged. She hadn't realised how much tension had built up inside her. The release of all that emotion had rid her of it, as well as her deeply ingrained unhappiness. They sat there like that for a long time, and Carla was grateful for Nancy's silence. She didn't need her sympathy or advice. She was just glad she'd had the opportunity to bare her soul to someone who seemed to understand her.

The quiet was broken by the screen door crashing open; Merle lumbered onto the porch. 'What's going on here?'

Nancy shot him a look, but he carried on regardless. 'I know what she needs. Stand up, young lady.'

Carla rose obediently. Merle advanced on her, wrapped his huge arms around her and gave her a bear hug. 'Better?'

'Better.'

'Come on, let's get you tucked up in bed. You look washed out,' said Nancy. 'You go on up. I'll be there with a cup of hot milk and honey in a couple of ticks.'

Carla changed into her pyjamas and clambered into bed, which was so comfortable she felt cocooned. It made her feel safe and secure, as though she belonged here.

Nancy came in with the hot drink and said, 'I guess it's the first time anyone's tucked you in since you were a child.'

'Actually, I don't think it's ever happened before in my whole life,' Carla replied, casting her eyes down.

She drank the milk and settled down under the covers. Nancy switched off the light and Carla was dead to the world within seconds.

* * *

When Carla awoke, she was shocked to find it was ten o'clock. She climbed out of bed and quickly washed and dressed before making her way downstairs. Nancy was in the kitchen cooking breakfast.

'Good morning.'

'Morning, Nancy. Sorry I overslept. I can't believe I was out for more than twelve hours. The bed was so comfortable, and the room so quiet and dark that I didn't stir all night. It was heaven.'

'And how are you feeling now?'

'Do you know, I feel on top of the world, thanks to you.'

'I'm glad to hear it. Now, let's get some breakfast inside you.'

'Where's Merle?'

'He always has his breakfast at seven, though I'm surprised the smell of bacon hasn't brought him in for a second one. He's in his barn tinkering with something or other. We'll go over and see him after you've eaten.'

'You've been very kind, but I don't want to outstay my welcome. I should leave and let you get on.'

'I won't hear of it. You need another day to recover before you set out again, and in any case, I'm enjoying fussing over someone other than Merle for a change.'

Carla held up her hands in mock surrender. She sat down to a hearty breakfast of sausage, bacon, hash browns, fried eggs and pancakes.

'Do you want maple syrup or blueberries with those pancakes?'

'Blueberries, please. Are you trying to fatten me up?' Carla said with fake outrage.

'Just getting rid of those hollow cheeks and the dark rims around your eyes.'

After breakfast, they walked through the yard at the side of the house towards a huge, red barn.

'Merle also has a Carla,' Nancy confided. 'I thought I was the love of his life, but I'm sure he thinks more of her than he does me.'

Carla was shocked and speechless. She stopped walking and stared at Nancy, unable to compute what she'd just heard.

Nancy looked back at her mischievously and called out, 'Merle, where are you?'

'Over here,' came a muffled voice from the far corner.

Carla looked around and gasped. The barn was full of cars – big cars, small cars, jalopies, classics and trucks. There was even an old yellow school bus.

'Wow, how many are there?'

'Heaven knows. Merle's been collecting cars since he was a boy, but most of them are junk. He swears there are people out there ready to pay big bucks for them, but as he'll never sell a one a them, we'll never know. He does have a few nice ones, though. What have you been doing in here, Merle?'

'I've been moving some of these little beauties around so I can get Carla out.'

The penny dropped, and Carla turned to Nancy. 'That wasn't fair.'

'I know, but I couldn't resist my little joke.'

Carla must be precious to Merle, Carla thought. *She's the only car in the barn protected by a cover.*

She was curious to find out what was underneath it.

With great ceremony, Merle announced, 'Ladies and gentlemen, I give you Carla!'

He whipped off the cover to reveal a Roman red, soft-top Corvette with ermine scallops trimmed with chrome fittings. Carla squealed with genuine delight. 'Oh, Merle, it's my dream car!' she said. 'I've hankered after one of these since I saw one exactly like it at a car show in England. What year is it?'

'1960.'

'I knew it! I love the red colour and matching interior.'

'Yep, everything's original, and she's my pride and joy.'

'Oh, she's beautiful, Merle, I absolutely love her.'

'I thought we could take her out for a spin this afternoon. What do you say?'

'Oh, yes please! I'd love to have a ride in her. Is she really called Carla or are you both pulling my leg?'

'It's true,' said Nancy. 'When you told me your name, you could have knocked me down with a feather. It was one of the things that drew me to you – as well as your sad eyes. You might think it, but I don't really believe in coincidences; things always happen for a reason. We were meant to meet, and I'm sure glad we did.'

'Me too.'

* * *

After lunch, Merle parked Carla the Corvette outside the farmhouse. He'd been busy all morning cleaning and polishing 'his other woman', and now the car looked stunning: the bright red paintwork and chrome fittings gleamed in the bright sunshine.

'OK, hop in,' Merle said, grinning from ear to ear.

Carla opened the passenger door.

'Not that side, this side. You're driving.'

'Me? Oh, I couldn't possibly, she's far too precious.'

'You got a driver's license, ain'tcha?'

'Well of course, but...'

'No buts. I can't drive on the road no more 'cause my

eyesight ain't what it used to be. Nancy won't drive a stick shift, so if you take me, you'll be doing me a favour.'

'What if I crash it?'

'Do you make a habit out of crashing cars?'

'No. I've never had an accident in my life, but there's always a first time.'

'Enough of your lily-livered protests, get in and let's go.'

Somehow, Merle managed to squeeze into the passenger seat and Carla got into the driver's side. She adjusted the seat and mirror, checked out the controls and turned the key. Carla roared into life. Even when it was idling, Carla loved the sound of a V8 engine, and she couldn't wait to get the car out onto the open road. She drove sedately through town, attracting whoops, hollers and waves from the locals, who were curious to note that Merle was out in his pride and joy with a younger woman, and that *she* was the driver. Carla noticed the sheriff she'd seen yesterday was watching them cruise by, an expression on his face she could not fathom. Concerned he might follow them, she looked in the rear-view mirror and was relieved to see him crossing the road, presumably heading for the diner.

Carla soon gained her confidence and cruised along the road, enjoying the wind in her hair (she was thankful for the shorter cut she'd gone for in Chicago) and the sunshine on her neck. This was just how she'd imagined it when planning the trip with Tom. The sound of the engine rumbling under the bonnet made her giggle with excitement. She couldn't remember the last time she'd felt so alive. A long, straight, traffic-free stretch opened out in front of them.

'Hell, woman, this baby's got 275 horses in there. Maybe you should think about using some of them,' yelled Merle.

Carla looked across at him and he nodded.

'OK, on your head be it.'

She pressed her foot down harder on the pedal and effortlessly increased the speed. The needle on the odometer quickly moved clockwise until it reached the hundred mark. They both cheered and yelled, loving the exhilarating twin feelings of fear and excitement. The Corvette held the road like glue, and Carla felt she could drive like this forever, although common sense prevailed, and she eased her foot off the throttle, allowing the car to slow at its own pace until they were cruising back within the sixty-five mile an hour speed limit. She pulled into a layby to catch her breath and switched the engine off.

'Oh, Merle, that was incredible. I've never felt so scared and excited in my life. Weren't you terrified I might crash?'

'No, honey. I wanted to hit a three-figure number just one more time, and you made it happen. If it had been the last minute of my life, I'd have died a happy man. I'm not sure Nancy would have been too impressed though.'

Carla stared at him aghast. Merle chuckled. She started the car again and waited for a long line of traffic to pass before she could pull out onto the highway. It was odd: the road was empty when they raced the Corvette, yet there was a lot of traffic now. Concentrating on her driving, she thought no more about it.

* * *

Back home, they found Nancy sitting on the porch. 'Did she do it?' she asked.

'Yes, she did!' replied Merle.

'So, you knew your husband would ask me to drive fast?' said Carla.

'Of course I did. Merle was quite a hell raiser in his day. He fancied himself as a regular James Dean and spent more than one night in jail after outrunning the cops on 66 in that very car you've just driven in. His daddy was none too pleased with him; the car belonged to him in those days.'

They all laughed, and Carla collapsed on the porch swing, her heart still pounding with elation. She couldn't quite believe she'd had the courage (or was it stupidity?) to drive any car at that speed, let alone a rare and expensive classic car, risking not only her own life but Merle's as well. And yet, she'd had a strange sensation that someone was watching over her, keeping her safe. Silly, she knew... yet comforting all the same.

Nancy returned with two glasses of lemonade and sat next to Carla. 'How are you feeling?'

'Oh, Nancy, I feel incredible. I can't believe what you've done for me over the past twenty-four hours. You seem to know what to do, what to say and when to say it. I feel as though you know me better than anyone else... better than I know myself, even.'

'Well, maybe I do,' Nancy said, her eyes twinkling.

She went back into the house, returning a few minutes later with a book, which she handed to Carla.

'Have you heard of this novel by John Steinbeck?'

'*The Grapes of Wrath*? Yes, I have, though I've never read it.'

'Most people these days travel 66 for sentimental reasons because they have childhood memories, real or imagined, of family vacations in their big station wagons or, if they were lucky, big-finned Chevrolets. Or maybe they just want to wallow in some nostalgia, thinking of how things were in the 1950s heyday and trying to live the American Dream. They love the little towns and rail against their destruction or dereliction, complaining that I-40 ruined Route 66, while happily using the freeways everywhere else in the USA. What most people don't get is that Route 66 is so much more than that. Mr Steinbeck didn't call it the Mother Road for nothing.

It represents the beating heart of the American people and what this country is made of. It's not just a cute road for vacations. There's been so much heartbreak too, especially for us Okies, as the Californians cruelly called migrants during the Great Depression, and we feel the darker side of Route 66 more than most.'

'I've read some American history, but I didn't know that,' said Carla.

'Forget your troubles for now. Carry on your journey; see the beautiful scenery and the quirky landmarks. Most of all, feel the history. Picture the dust bowl that was here in the 1930s. Imagine losing your farm or your job and being forced to leave your home and most of your possessions behind to drive a jalopy to California, and that was if you were lucky. Then, if you actually made it to the Golden State, finding it wasn't the land of milk and honey you'd been led to expect. As if it couldn't get any worse, you were probably turned back at the Californian border, or if you did get in, you were treated like a bum. I want you to really feel the hardship and the pain of the people who travelled the road before you, as well as enjoy the scenery and the freedom that Route 66 has afforded more fortunate folk.

'I'm not trying to make light of your distress. You have some difficult decisions to make and problems to overcome, but for now, you need to step back a little, forget about your issues for a while and make the most of your time here. Then you'll be able to put things into perspective and find the best course of action to take.

'Stay a little while longer, stretch yourself out on the porch swing and read this book. Mr Steinbeck's tale is heartbreaking and heartwarming in equal measure. The human spirit, even in the face of terrible adversity, is strong, and I want you to feel it.'

'Thank you, Nancy. If you really don't mind, it would be wonderful to stay another day.'

'We would love to have you, and it'll give me one more day to make a fuss of you.'

* * *

After a delicious supper, they all retired to the porch to relax and enjoy the evening air. Carla listened to Merle and Nancy's tales of old times. They'd led a simple life, notwithstanding Merle's driving habits, and were obviously content and in tune with each other. Carla felt a little envious.

'Do you know, I've hardly ever left Oklahoma,' said Nancy.

Carla frowned, inadvertently giving away her feelings.

'Don't feel sorry for me, young lady, I've had a wonderful life. I was brought up on this farm, and my ma and pa were the best parents in the world. They loved me and my sister, Olivia, with all their hearts, and they always did their best for us. Money was tight and life wasn't easy – we were even put to work in the fields. At seven, I could drive a tractor.'

Carla didn't doubt it.

'This life wasn't big enough for Olivia, so she left and went to art school in Los Angeles. She had no desire to come back to Oklahoma, and when she tired of California, she moved to New Mexico. But moving away wasn't for me; I had everything I ever wanted right here. I knew as soon as I locked eyes on Merle at school, when we were five years old, that I wanted to marry him, and my wish came true —'

'My wish came true too,' butted in Merle. 'My folks were dirt poor, and there was many a time I went to school hungry. I only married Nancy for her farm!'

'Hush now.' Nancy smacked him lightly on the arm,

stared at him with mock hurt in her eyes and pulled a face. 'Merle moved in here with my parents and me after we married, and we all managed the farm together, so he had to work darned hard for his meal ticket. My folks left the farm to us after they passed and, as you can see, we made it our own. We've led a simple life but a happy one. I feel so blessed. And while I admire you for what you are doing, Carla, it's not for us.'

'Yep, everything she says is true,' Merle drawled, looking tenderly at his wife.

'What about the Route 66 trip you planned?'

'We never got as far as planning it,' said Merle, 'it was just a vague idea. Deep down, we knew we'd never retire, and if we'd really wanted to go, we could have made it happen. No, I got my kicks on Route 66 with you this morning, and that's good enough for me.'

They all laughed and then settled into a comfortable silence. Carla was in awe of their contentment, though she knew such a small life would not have satisfied her. She understood why Nancy's sister had moved on.

She looked up and marvelled at the mass of sparkling lights in the night sky. 'I've never seen so many stars,' she said. 'We've got so much light pollution at home that we can only see the bigger ones.'

'Tonight's a good night to see them, the moon isn't up yet,' said Merle. He switched off the porch lights, plunging them into darkness. 'Lie down in front of the porch, let your eyes adjust and look directly above you. Can you see the star that isn't twinkling?'

'I see it.'

'Well, it's not a star, it's Jupiter. Planets don't twinkle. Now, just be patient and keep looking at the sky.'

Sure enough, swirls of stars started to reveal themselves

and illuminate the black sky. The shape of the earth came into focus, and some of the stars appeared to touch it.

'Oh, my goodness, is that the Milky Way?' Carla asked.

'Yes, it is.'

'I've never seen it in my whole life.'

'With all the amazing things you're going to experience, I think you will be saying that a lot over the next few weeks,' said Merle. 'Like we said, me and Nancy didn't go on many vacations, and even then, only for a few days; we were always busy on the farm. We got to travel some when Matthew started working for us. It's a shame you didn't get to meet him; he's visiting his pa, my brother, in Florida, and he won't be back until the weekend. Anyway, since we could trust him with running things here, we got to see some wonderful places, but we left it too late to cruise 66. Such a shame when you think that it runs right past us.'

He glanced at Nancy, betraying a little sadness and regret in his voice.

Hmmm. Carla noted the contrast between what he'd said a little earlier and the trace of remorse he was showing now. So, the relationship was not quite perfect, then. Carla guiltily found this discovery comforting.

Merle let out an enormous yawn. 'I'm off to bed now,' he said, before turning to Carla. 'Thank you for making an old man's wish come true.'

'No, thank you for letting me drive my dream car,' said Carla.

She smiled affectionately at the couple and rubbed her eyes, shattered from the day's exertions.

Later, she fell into bed with a renewed sense of purpose and a newfound readiness to face the challenges to come.

* * *

After sleeping like the dead, Carla got out of bed feeling refreshed. She wolfed down a hearty breakfast and settled comfortably on a rocking chair to read *The Grapes of Wrath*. She got so wrapped up in it that she read it from cover to cover. Occasionally, she found the story so distressing that she had to get up to walk around the yard. She could barely imagine the pain and heartbreak these poor families had suffered. What must it be like to lose everything and have no hope of recovery, to leave the only place you have ever known and put yourself through even more hardship in search of a better life, only to be exploited and oppressed to the point of starvation? The pain of losing so many loved ones must have been unbearable.

Carla was glad Nancy had recommended the novel, and it was true that it had altered her perspective. She would never have to worry about where her next meal was coming from, and she would never have to witness the death of her loved ones in such a cruel and brutal manner. She did not have to live in fear, anger or misery. The time for self-pity was over. She was ready to continue her journey, and this time, she vowed she would stay in the present, forget her own troubles and make the most of this opportunity. At the same time, she would pay homage to the people from Oklahoma and beyond who'd travelled the road before her and suffered so much.

* * *

When the time came for her to leave, Carla packed her suitcases and brought them downstairs to the hallway. She could hear Nancy chatting on the phone in the kitchen. Her ears pricked up at the mention of her name and, remembering the old adage, 'Listeners ne'er hear good of themselves,' she went outside, where she was out of earshot.

'Oh, there you are!' said Nancy as she bustled onto the

porch a little flustered. 'I've just spoken to Olivia. I hope you don't mind, but I've been telling her all about you and your journey. I know, I should have asked you before sharing all your troubles, and I didn't mean to, but my big sister is a master at extracting information from me, however hard I try to keep a secret.'

'It's OK, honestly,' laughed Carla. 'It must be nice to have such a close bond with her.'

'Yes, it is, mostly. Anyway, she's real excited that you will be driving almost past her door, and she is desperate for you to stop by and stay a few days with her and her husband Randy. Can I tell her you'll visit?'

'I'd love to. You're all too kind to me,' said Carla, with tears in her eyes. She hugged Nancy and they held each other for a long moment, until Nancy ushered her into the kitchen for breakfast.

Once again, Nancy had excelled herself on the food front, both in quantity and quality. The three of them enjoyed their final meal together in an atmosphere of contentment tinged with a little sadness.

'I can't thank you enough for your kindness and hospitality,' said Carla. 'I hadn't realised how much I needed company, and you took care of me when I really needed it. I promise I won't let you down and will make the most of my trip.'

'You are so welcome, Carla, we're glad to have had you here.' Nancy handed her a piece of paper. 'This is Olivia and Randy's address and phone number. Give them a call when you get to New Mexico, and they'll be ready for you. Oh, and just to warn you, Olivia's nothing like me, but she is a lot of fun.'

'Thank you. Tell her I'm looking forward to meeting her.'

They went down the steps to the front yard, where Carla

was delighted to see her namesake in all her glory, looking beautiful and shiny.

'Oh, Merle, thank you for bringing Carla out so I can say goodbye to her.'

'No, Carla, it's not goodbye, you're taking her with you.'

'What?'

'Just because me and Nancy are too old to do the trip doesn't mean Carla shouldn't. Take her, with our blessing.'

'I can't, she's your pride and joy. What if she gets damaged or stolen? What about insurance? What about the Kia?' Carla babbled.

'Details, details. My pride and joy is of no use to anyone locked away in the barn. She should be driven – just not at a hundred miles an hour this time.' He winked at her. 'She's fully insured, so if something happens, it happens. When he gets back from out of town, Matthew will take the Kia to the rental company in Oklahoma City, and we'll arrange for Carla to be shipped back from California when you're done. Now, stop whining and go!'

'How can I possibly repay you?'

'You can repay us by having fun and enjoying yourself. Give us a hug before you go.'

The three of them held each other tightly in a group huddle until Carla reluctantly extricated herself.

'I'll put your cases in the trunk,' said Merle. 'The car cover's in there too. Just put it on every evening, but make sure the engine has cooled down first.'

Carla climbed into the Corvette, started the engine and gave a wave. And with that, she was gone.

CHAPTER 16

Texas

Nervous she might damage Merle's car, Carla began the journey with trepidation. Besides, as she drove along Main Street, heading west, she saw the town's sheriff leaning on his patrol car, watching her.

Does that man ever do any work? Carla wondered.

Once out on the open road, she increased her speed a little, gripping the steering wheel so hard her knuckles turned white. Several cars whizzed by. Finally, the ignominy of being overtaken by a truck full of pigs brought her to her senses and she eased the throttle down to a cruising speed of fifty-five miles per hour and began to relax. The glorious sunshine beat down on her neck, and the wind whipping around her head soon cleared away the cobwebs and made her alert to the sights and smells around her. Best of all, without a roof, she was able to see the whole road in front of her. The landscape expanded to the left and right as far as her eyes could see, and the clear blue sky above seemed to be even bigger than usual. This really was a BIG Country. Was she dreaming? She hoped not. The further she drove, the more excited she became. She

was going to have the trip she'd envisaged after all, and she
was going to enjoy every minute of it.

* * *

Exhausted from the exhilaration of the day's driving and
buffeted by the wind, it was time to stop for the night. Not
quite a one-horse town, the unnamed place she'd decided to
hitch up in didn't have much more – just a petrol station, a
saloon bar and a motel, which had clearly seen better days. It
was a typical roadside motel: two storeys high with outside
corridors, rattling air conditioning units, a basic lobby and a
receptionist who was far more cheerful than Carla imagined
she would be in the same job, especially in such a remote place.
Her room hadn't been refurbished in years. To say it was tired
was an understatement. It still had a big, old, clunky TV, and
the bedspread was one of those synthetic, flowery covers she'd
seen on American TV programmes in the '80s. She shuddered.
Dead bodies were found in motel rooms like this one, and
someone like Columbo would amble in and immediately know
who the murderer was. No, that was California. Anyway, she
got her own drift. She didn't dare think of what substances
might be revealed if CSI agents shone their fancy equipment
on it. Nevertheless, the sheets appeared clean, as was the
bathroom, which predictably didn't have a plug in the bath.
Anyway, what had she expected for forty dollars? It was better
than taking her chances with the critters on the road.

Faced with the prospect of dining on potato chips and a
Hershey bar from the vending machine, Carla thought about
going to the bar across the road and getting something to eat
there. From the outside, it didn't look too inviting; single
storey and jerry-built, it was a functional building made even
uglier by a solid, uninviting front door. The only thing to

indicate it was a bar came from the flashing neon signs in the curtained windows advertising beer. Parked outside were half a dozen Harley motorbikes and a couple of Ford pick-up trucks. She wondered if the bar would be haunted by Hell's Angel types. But then, Carla reasoned that nothing could be worse than being stuck in that room chomping on Skittles and watching endless commercials on TV.

Decision made, she decided she may as well make a bit of an effort, so she showered and changed into her new figure-hugging Levi's and a white T-shirt, which she accompanied with a simple black jacket and cowboy-style, black ankle boots. Then she applied a touch of make-up and put in some small diamanté earrings. Checking herself in the full-length mirror, she was pleased with the result. Nancy's cooking had brought back her healthy glow, and her new, shorter hairstyle had shaved a few years off her face into the bargain.

'There's life in the old dog yet,' she said out loud.

Carla had a spring in her step as she headed towards the bar. She was about to cross the traffic-free road when she spotted a small animal. It had a long nose and a scaly, stripy shell.

An anteater? No, an armadillo.

This was the first live armadillo Carla had seen. Plenty of dead ones could be found on the side of the road, but this one was alive and kicking, and stopping periodically for a sniff as it ambled across the road. Carla happily watched it continue its journey, but then she became aware of engine noise in the distance. She peered up the long, straight stretch of road, guessing the vehicle was about a mile away and approaching fast. What should she do? She didn't know anything about armadillos. Could she pick it up like a tortoise? What if it bit her or was poisonous? What if it chased her if she tried to catch it? No, she couldn't risk it. She just had to stand there and wait, and hope. She considered jumping up and down to get the driver's attention, but it was getting dark, and he wouldn't see her until it was too late. The noise was getting nearer. Meanwhile, the armadillo continued its journey, unaware of the danger. Carla held her breath. Then, with only yards to spare, Dilly (she realised how stupid it was to name an animal just as it's about to meet its maker) safely reached the other side of the road and the car roared past. Spooked, the animal stopped and jumped three feet into the air. Seeing its reaction, Carla realised why she'd seen so many dead ones. Recovering itself, Dilly raced off at great speed into the bushes. At least this one had made it.

The whole experience made Carla feel a warm glow inside. This was what the trip was supposed to be about: seeing new things, making discoveries, getting close to nature and having adventures.

But as she approached the saloon, she heard raucous laughter and loud music coming from inside and lost her nerve. She was turning around when the door opened, and a leather-jacketed biker sauntered out. He held the door open for her and said in a deep drawl, 'Come on in, ma'am.'

Surprised by his politeness, Carla decided the clientele was probably OK and that she might get out alive after all. She smiled at him as she breezed by, shoulders back and head held high, stopping just inside the door to scan the room. It was dimly lit, much bigger than it looked from the outside and more welcoming. To her right was a small stage and a good-sized dancefloor. Several booths lined the walls, and to the left, tables were laid out with red and white chequered tablecloths, all set for dinner.

Good, they serve food, she thought.

The centre of the room was dominated by a huge, horseshoe-shaped bar. As she advanced further inside, the few customers turned around to see who'd just come in. They gave Carla a cursory glance before turning back to carry on with the important business of eating and drinking. She noticed the walls were adorned with all sorts of memorabilia, from old war rifles to stuffed fish and other hunting trophies. There was no Route 66 stuff anywhere in sight, so clearly tourists were not expected to drop in here. Having assessed the situation, Carla decided getting a booth or a table on her own could lead to unwanted attention or, even worse, being ignored. She spotted that the person behind the bar was female and plumped for a stool at the end of it.

'My name is Gina. I'm your bar tender for this evening. What can I get you?'

'A beer, please.'

'Draft or well?'

'What's a well?'

'It's bottled beer, honey. I love your accent, are you from Australia?'

Carla chuckled. 'No, I'm from England. I'm Carla by the way.'

'Oh, pardon me. Pleased to meet you, Carla. So, what'll it be?'

'I'll have a draft Bud Light, please.'

Served in an ice-cold glass from the freezer, the beer hit the spot and calmed Carla's jangling nerves.

'Are you eating with us this evening?'

Carla nodded.

'Here's the menu. We have a special today of honey-coated ribs, spicy chicken wings and fries. All for $10.'

Amazing as that sounded, Carla decided it wouldn't be a good match for her white T-shirt, and she played it safe, ordering what turned out to be a good choice: a proper steak burger, fries and a side salad – not forgetting the pickle. She was so busy enjoying her meal and washing it down with a second beer that she didn't notice the band setting up on the stage behind her or the steady stream of customers coming through the front door.

'Is this seat taken, ma'am?'

Carla looked up and involuntarily gasped. The man in front of her was Drop. Dead. Gorgeous. At least six feet tall, with piercing blue eyes and slim hips, he wore jeans held up by an ornate buckle belt and a short-sleeved shirt, which partially covered a nice pair of biceps. He was holding a buckskin jacket and was actually wearing a cowboy hat and boots. Carla thought men only looked like that in the movies, but no, here was a real, live cowboy. Far from being amused, she was blown away by this gorgeous hunk of a man. Thank goodness she'd had a couple of drinks, otherwise she'd be acting like a blushing, tongue-tied schoolgirl, or worse, a jibbering idiot.

'No,' she replied, cool as you like. 'Please, sit down.'

He smiled at her, a Colgate, jelly-leg making smile. If she'd been standing, Carla was convinced her knees would have buckled. She couldn't remember the last time a man had had that effect on her. Oh wait, it was the night she met Tom. Carla quickly put that thought to the back of her mind.

'I'm Curtis.'

'Carla, pleased to meet you.'

'Can I get you a drink?'

'Only if you let me buy you one back.'

Did I really just say that? said the voice in her head. *Yes, you did, you saucy little minx!* it replied.

Curtis turned out to be a real Texan cowboy. Whether or not he was single, Carla didn't ask, and nor did he volunteer the information. She didn't mention her marital status, either. They drank and chatted comfortably, each of them giving away only the barest details about their lives and what had brought them here, until the band struck up, making conversation impossible. Carla looked around and was surprised to see the place now packed with people. Where had they all come from? There wasn't a town for miles, but then again, Carla had already learned that when Americans say something is just around the corner, it could be fifty miles away, and it appeared she had stumbled on the state's hottest venue. The band was an obvious favourite with this boisterous crowd, and it wasn't long before the saloon was buzzing.

Curtis leaned into her, shouting in her ear, 'Come and dance.'

'No, I couldn't,' she yelled. 'I haven't danced for years, and I don't even know how to line dance.'

'There's nothing to it, and no one will be watching you anyway.'

He dragged her onto the dancefloor, where it turned out he was right; it didn't take long to get the hang of it. Emboldened by her new skill, Carla was happy for Curtis to take her in his arms and twirl her around. Somehow, they avoided crashing into other enthusiastic couples, all demonstrating varying degrees of skill. Breathless, they returned to their seats and sank another beer.

'That was brilliant,' said Carla.

'Karaoke next. I've put our names down for a nice little duet.'

'No, definitely not. I couldn't possibly get on stage to sing,' Carla said, aware she suddenly sounded terribly English.

'You said you couldn't dance an hour ago, so a little song shouldn't be too much of a problem. Here, have a drop of Jack. That'll oil your tonsils.'

The first act, 'Elvis', managed a reasonable rendition of 'I'm All Shook Up', complete with a curling lip and swinging hips. He was followed by a group of giggling girls caterwauling to goodness knows what. Curtis and Carla grimaced at each other. Surely their singing couldn't be as bad as that.

'And now it's time to welcome our Texan cowboy, Curtis,' announced the DJ, 'and Carla, a lovely little lady from London, England.'

To polite applause, Curtis dragged Carla onto the stage and into the bright lights. Looking down at the expectant crowd, she was hot with embarrassment. To her surprise, they pulled off a more than decent rendition of the Kenny Rogers and Dolly Parton duet 'Islands in the Stream', finishing to prolonged applause. Either that, or both she and the audience were so drunk they wouldn't know a good tune if it smacked them in the face.

Back at their seats, Carla threw back her head and laughed. 'This is the best fun I've had in ages.'

'Me too.' He gazed into her eyes, suddenly serious. 'We could make a night of it, if you'd like.'

Carla was more than a little tipsy, and she was still on a high from the dancing and singing. It had been so long since she'd felt like this, and she didn't owe Tom anything. This gorgeous man had made her feel special, and it was just what she needed to boost her wounded pride. After all, Tom was cosied up to the 'lovely Jane' right now, so why not enjoy the rest of the night with this fantastic man? She'd never done anything so reckless before, and she was enjoying the moment.

Curtis studied her intently, which made her heart pound even faster and her body tingle. Well, this hadn't been on the agenda when she'd left home. Call it an adventure or late middle-aged madness, but only a fool would pass up this opportunity. Carla beamed at him with what she hoped was her best sexy smile. Swaying slightly, she leant forward. She intended to kiss him, but hesitated and stopped short of his lips.

Looking into his beautiful, blue eyes, she said, 'I'm sorry. I would love to spend the night with you, but it seems my conscience won't let me. My marriage is probably over, and my husband is with another woman, yet my stupid brain won't let me do this tonight, even though my body is screaming at my brain to shut up.'

'That's OK, I understand. I can't say I'm not disappointed, but it has been a fabulous evening, hasn't it?'

'Yes, it has. I certainly won't forget it in a hurry.'

'Well, I'll say goodnight then, pretty lady. Safe travels.'

Carla woke the next morning with a mouth like a wrestler's jock strap. Cozy Powell had taken up residence in her head and was happily playing one of his more enthusiastic drum solos. Gingerly, she lifted her head off the pillow and winced, lying flat again and resisting the urge to be sick. Just how many Jack Daniel's had she drunk? She knew for certain it would be a long time before she had another one. She drifted back into a restless sleep, only to be roused two hours later by some loud knocking.

'Housekeeping!'

Carla looked at her watch. It was eleven o'clock. Clutching her head, she stumbled out of bed and answered the door.

'You look rough,' said the maid.

'You don't look so hot yourself,' Carla replied without thinking.

Seeing the expression on the young woman's face, Carla realised she was being offensive. Unlike her own self-induced, horror hangover look, the teenager's heavy, goth-style make-up was deliberate, and from the withering look she gave Carla, she was proud of it.

'Sorry, I didn't mean to be rude,' Carla said.

'Apology accepted. Not trying to rush you or anything, but you should have checked out an hour ago.'

'Oh, I'm sorry, I lost track of time.'

'Good night, was it?'

'Yes, it was. Worth feeling like this anyway. I don't think I'll be fit to drive for a while. Do you think I'll be able to stay another night?'

'They're not exactly lining up to stay in this dump, so it won't be a problem. Want me to tell them at reception?'

'Yes, please. I think I'll go back to bed for a while, and I definitely won't be needing room service today.'

'OK, cool,' said the maid, grinning as she closed the door.

Carla looked at herself in the mirror and winced. *Thank God I didn't sleep with Curtis*, she thought. *Imagine if we'd woken up this morning and he'd seen me like this!*

She had no regrets about last night. It was the most fun she'd had in ages, her ego had been given a boost and she'd quit while she was still ahead – apart from her dalliance with Jack Daniel's, of course. She should have said no to him at least three shots earlier.

CHAPTER 17

Midpoint – Adrian, Texas

The town of Adrian in Texas marked the halfway point in Carla's journey. Running parallel to Interstate 40 (I-40), it provided a road less travelled, as myriad trucks and cars whizzed by on the freeway next door.

Carla asked a fellow tourist to take the obligatory photo of her standing by the signpost at the exact mid-point between Chicago and Los Angeles. Aside from the occasional diversion and wrong turn, so far, she'd covered 1,139 miles of Route 66. The road hadn't always been easy to follow – sometimes disappearing altogether – but somehow, she'd made it to this point without too many mishaps. After taking a moment to congratulate herself for reaching this important milestone, she wondered if there would be as many adventures waiting for her over the following 1,139 miles. She'd come a long way, both literally and figuratively, and she was looking forward to the second half of her trip.

Carla crossed the road, intending to buy herself a cup of hot chocolate at the Midpoint Café. Outside, a battered old moped with a little trailer attached to the back caught her attention. The trailer was packed to the hilt, and nestled in the middle of the owner's belongings sat a pure white husky. Someone had painted on the side of the trailer #*Walking with Jesse*.

Carla knelt in front of the trailer and whispered to the dog, 'Hello, you must be Jesse.'

The dog pricked up his ears and looked at her. His exquisite blue eyes melted her heart. Certain that Carla meant him no harm, he quickly settled down, comfortable in his home from home. She went inside and spotted a rather scruffy young man with a large bushy beard and a mop of unruly hair. It looked as it was some time since he'd slept with a roof over his head.

She sat down at the table next to him and said, 'Is that your beautiful dog outside?'

'Yes, ma'am.'

'Call me Carla.'

'I'm Jesse, and my dog's called Ona.'

Ah, got that wrong then, Carla thought.

'Pleased to meet you, Jesse. If you don't mind me asking, what's your story?'

'Of course not, but be warned, it's a long one. The short version is that I wanted to see the wonders of this incredible country before I settled down to normal life. I also wanted to motivate young people to get up and get active, so I decided to walk Route 66 with Ona. I left Chicago two months ago, but the journey is taking me longer than I expected. A while back, a guy gave me his old scooter, and that has helped a lot, but it's starting to give me trouble, and I don't think it will run much longer.'

'Where do you stay?'

'Occasionally, we stay in a cheap motel. Mostly, we're

outside under the stars and the moonlight. It's so dark when it's cloudy that I feel like I'm in a cave.'

'Don't you get scared or cold?'

'Sometimes, but it's worth it to feel truly alive.'

'Wow, I'm in awe of you. I'm doing the route in a Corvette, staying in comfortable hotels and with access to good food. I've done a lot of amazing things on my journey, but I haven't got the courage to sleep out under the stars. My goodness, your adventure makes mine seem tame in comparison.'

'It's still a big deal because you're following your dream,' said Jesse. 'Not many people are prepared to step out of their comfort zone and take risks, so be proud of yourself.'

'Thanks, I will. Well, good luck for the rest of your journey.'

'You too.'

On the way back to her car, Carla knelt before Ona and murmured, 'Good luck, little one, take care of Jesse, won't you?'

No doubt she imagined it, but Carla could have sworn Ona winked at her.

CHAPTER 18

Tucumcari, New Mexico

A s Carla trundled into Tucumcari, she passed several restored 1950s motels and felt the atmosphere of Route 66's heyday. She imagined the scene, the two-lane highway full of big, sleek, bright-coloured cars, chrome glistening in the sunshine and purring engines echoing through the streets. They were symbols of the post-war affluence that so many Americans got to enjoy – they'd never had it so good. She could see them stopping at the gas stations, checking into their bright and breezy, neon-lit motels, eating at the Mom and Pop restaurants and living the American Dream. Carla felt the excitement of these holidaymakers, many of whom would have been away from home for the first time.

It made her regret her lack of enthusiasm in the early days of her journey and the missed opportunities to visit iconic landmarks, museums and restaurants, though she doubted the hot dogs at Springfield's famous Cozy Dog Drive In would have suited her English palate. Her guidebook claimed it was the birthplace of corn dogs on sticks. Patronised by enthusiastic diners from all over the country, the allegedly superior quality of one of the nation's favourite foods ensured the restaurant's bucket-list status. Whether she would have enjoyed dining there or not, Carla wished she hadn't wasted her time sulking along the highway, and she resolved to make the most of the rest of her trip and welcome with open arms everything the so-called 'Main Street of America' had to offer.

According to her guidebook, the best and most famous motel on Route 66 was the Blue Swallow, so here she was. Before she checked in, she strategically parked the gleaming Corvette on the forecourt underneath the motel's neon sign. She chuckled at the advertisement boasting how the rooms had 100% refrigerated air and a TV. How times had changed! She was brought sharply back to the present when some of her fellow guests excitedly crowded around to take photos of the Corvette with their very twenty-first-century smartphones.

Once checked in, and having parked up in her room's own personal garage, Carla phoned Nancy's sister.

'Hi, Mrs Tulley, this is Carla Bright. Nancy said I should give you a call when I got to New Mexico. I'm in Tucumcari.'

'Why, hello, Carla. Nancy's told me all about you, and I've been expecting your call. Why don't you come on over? Our ranch is only one hundred seventy miles from where you are, just a little way off Route 66's old Santa Fe Loop.'

Only?

'Thank you, Mrs Tulley, but I don't like driving when it's dark. I've checked into the Blue Swallow Motel, and I'm planning to eat dinner and then have an early night. How about I come over tomorrow?'

'That would be lovely, and please call me Olivia. Tucumcari is a cute little town. It has a nice Route 66 museum, and don't forget to check out the murals before you leave. Did you choose the Blue Swallow on purpose, or was it a happy accident?'

'Yes, I did. My guidebook said it was a fine example of the old-fashioned motels that used to be popular along Route 66, and it really is. The rooms even have their own garages, so Merle's car is safe for the night. I love it here; it makes me feel like I've gone back in time, and the other guests are really friendly. There's nothing like a classic Corvette to get people talking.'

Olivia gave her directions from Route 66 to her home, before adding, 'I'm looking forward to your visit. See you tomorrow.'

* * *

Carla woke early, glad to see she would once again be driving in beautiful sunshine under a clear blue sky. She checked out of the motel and set off for the convention centre at the other end of town. The euphoria she felt from the previous day was smashed to pieces as she drove past empty lots and derelict buildings with broken windows, their doors and roofs missing. It was a harsh reminder of that dark day in 1981 when I-40 opened and took away the town's business overnight. In a rush to get goodness knows where in a lot less time, drivers abandoned Route 66 in favour of the freeway. The golden era was over, and the small businesses were destroyed and replaced with a depressing array of conglomerates conveniently positioned alongside the interstate slip roads. Motorists soon lost their sense of adventure, coming to rely on the predictability of the freeway and its soulless business franchises – not giving a second thought to the road that had once been the backbone of the country. Carla could not help making a tenuous comparison to her own life. One day, it was ticking along nicely, the next – *bam!* – and everything had gone. She only allowed herself a few moments of introspection before rallying at the sight of the fabulous murals she could see painted on the sides of the town's buildings.

At the convention centre, she intended to visit the New Mexico Route 66 Museum. Discovering it in darkness, nevertheless, she pushed the front door and, to her delight, it opened.

'Hello, is anybody here?' she called out.

An old man poked his head out of a broom cupboard. 'Can I help you, ma'am?'

'I'm just passing through, and I was hoping to have a look around the museum. What time does it open?'

'Nine o'clock, but come on in anyway.' He ushered her down the corridor and into the museum. 'Where are you from, I don't know that accent?'

'I'm from England.'

'Do you know the Queen?'

Carla smiled. 'No, not personally, but I have seen her a few times.'

'Well, you just take your time and enjoy yourself.'

He shuffled back to the broom cupboard and left her to her own devices.

Wow, what a privilege! The caretaker was giving her the run of the place – her own private viewing – and she was amazed at his faith in her. For someone less honest than herself, the temptation to steal something could prove too strong. It warmed her heart that some people in the world were still willing to trust others to do the right thing.

Carla spent the next hour wandering around the museum, reading about the history of Route 66 and looking at memorabilia from the golden era of motoring – classic cars (almost as nice as the Corvette), porcelain signs, gas pumps and a juke box. There was even a Route 66 guitar signed by the country singer Loretta Lynn. Carla was particularly taken with a display of photographs by Michael Campanelli, who she learned had travelled the route seventy-five times and taken 40,000 photos, of which 166 were in the museum. From gas stations to water towers, signage to derelict buildings, the exhibition reminded her of the icons she had already seen (some of them subliminally, she realised), and it gave her a taste of the exciting things yet to come.

She was glad of the opportunity to indulge in this nostalgia. Forward-thinking conservationists had fought hard to restore the 'Main Street of America', she learned. They were responsible for the creation of Historic Route 66, which had led to much of the road's past being preserved. In the 1980s, the campaigners even got the Mother Road put back on the map, which gave many towns like Tucumcari the opportunity to retain or recreate much of their original charm. Tourists just like Carla flocked from all over the world for their personal pilgrimages across the USA. She felt sad for the communities for whom it was all too late. When Carla had driven through them, she hadn't fully appreciated the sudden, devastating impact on towns like Glenrio in Texas. As soon as the I-40 bypass opened, it became nothing more than a ghost town. All that was left were tumbledown buildings, an old Texaco garage, 'no trespassing' signs and a ferocious dog barking in the yard of probably the last remaining resident. And yet, these shocking sights added to her experience, providing a poignant reminder of the ups and downs of Route 66's history, and of life itself.

CHAPTER 19
Santa Fe, New Mexico

Leaving Tucumcari, Carla somehow managed to take a wrong turn, and she ended up on a road to goodness knows where. She'd already discovered that Route 66 was poorly signposted through New Mexico, and it was some time before she realised she was going the wrong way. Recognising her error, she pulled over and consulted her woefully small-scale map. The road was generally heading west, and she decided to carry on, only to find the map didn't show all the twists and turns of driving up and down the mountains. She was very much now on 'the road less travelled', even by her own standards. It took her miles out of her way, and she hoped she wouldn't ruin the car's suspension on the occasional bumpy surface she had to contend with.

On the plus side, the scenery was stunning. There were striated sandstone rock formations and grasses all around her, and the road took her to a mesa – a flat-topped ridge bounded by an escarpment that overlooked a vast plain, where she could imagine hordes of charging buffalo in the days before the pioneers and military men arrived. Now, she saw pronghorn antelope and even a roadrunner. Fortunately, she had plenty of petrol in the tank, otherwise she'd have freaked out, not knowing how far she had left to go on a road where she had not seen another living soul for miles. She was well and truly out of her comfort zone, and it was only when she was safely back on Route 66 that she felt glad of her mistake.

Luckily, she found the ranch without any further difficulty. The land was dry and arid, and with no sign of any livestock, Carla figured that Olivia and Randy weren't farmers but had chosen the ranch simply to get away from civilisation. Being only half an hour's drive from Albuquerque, it wasn't as remote as it appeared.

Best of both worlds, thought Carla.

The house was enormous. Built mostly from wood, the shell was constructed from huge, pine tree trunks. From the outside, it looked like a ski lodge, and Carla was soon to discover that it was just as spectacular on the inside. As she parked the Corvette in front of the building, the front door opened and out trotted a woman so opposite in looks to Nancy that it was hard to believe they were sisters. She was the same height as Nancy but twice her weight, and she had long, grey-blonde hair and was wearing a flowing, multi-coloured kaftan. The only familial trait they had in common was their distinctive blue eyes. She rushed towards Carla and hugged her.

'Welcome, welcome. Bring your bags in and come and make yourself at home.'

Carla followed her inside and looked around in awe. 'Oh, it's beautiful, Olivia.'

'Why, thank you.'

'Did you design the house yourself?'

'No, I commissioned an exclusive and very expensive

interior decorator to work her magic and incorporate some of my ideas. It's a bit different to Nancy's house, isn't it?'

'I'll say. Nancy told me you weren't alike, but I wasn't expecting this.'

'We both grew up in Oklahoma, and while she stayed on the farm, I wanted more. So, I moved to California and went to art school. Turns out I was pretty good, and people were willing to pay a lot of money for my paintings. In the end, I got tired of the bright lights of Los Angeles and discovered the radiant light of New Mexico. I decided to follow in the footsteps of the artist Georgia O'Keefe and settle here permanently. Then I met Randy in Santa Fe. He's lived on this piece of land all his life. We demolished his little house and built this one. I'm happy painting and he's happy hunting, so we rub along real well together.'

'Is this one of yours?' asked Carla, pointing at an enormous oil painting that dominated the wall above the giant fireplace.

'Uh huh, it's called *Evening Sun in Santa Fe*. It's slightly abstract, but there's no disputing I painted it here. It's probably my best piece of work.'

'It's marvellous. I expect Nancy wanted you to be a surprise for me, and you certainly are!'

'Come and sit outside on the patio.'

The house backed onto a fast-flowing river, and in the distance, Carla could see a vast mountain range. 'I can see why you moved here,' she said, a note of envy in her voice.

'It's very different from where I'm from, and from LA too, but I feel as though this is where I belong. Randy will be home soon. You mustn't mind him, he's a man of few words; I do enough talking for the both of us.'

Just then, the front door slammed.

'Hey, Randy, come outside and meet Carla.'

Olivia's husband towered above them. A big bear of a man, he could easily have been Merle's brother.

He nodded at Carla. 'Howdy.'

'Hello, Mr Tulley.'

'Randy,' he grunted.

'Lunch will be ready in thirty minutes, honey, if you want to freshen up.'

Carla helped Olivia lay the table on the patio, and the three of them sat down to a simple meal of cold meats and cheeses served with olives and some delicious, seeded bread.

'Do you call this artisan bread over here?'

'Yes, we do. Artisanal bakers are very popular here. Slowly but surely, people are demanding better food, and we are lucky to have some great independent stores in Santa Fe. I'm a bit late to the party for healthy eating, but I'm getting there,' said Olivia, slugging down a large mouthful of wine.

After lunch, they sat contentedly on the shady patio, hiding from the sizzling afternoon sun. A welcome breeze wafted from the river and hummingbirds hovered around the feeders, busily extracting sugar water.

Carla was fascinated. 'I've never seen a hummingbird before,' she said. 'They're so tiny – and look at those colours and their pointy beaks. It's exhausting just watching them flitting between the feeders, and I love the humming noise their beating wings make. How much energy must it take for them to hover like that?'

'They are beautiful, aren't they?' said Olivia. 'I could watch them all day, they mesmerise me.'

Something caught Carla's eye. 'Oh, look, there's something in the water. It's a beaver!' she shouted excitedly.

Within seconds, and close to her ear, Carla heard a click.

And then – *BOOM!*

The beaver leapt into the air and crashed back into the water, dead.

'Vermin,' muttered Randy, before walking back into the house, rifle under his arm. Carla was shocked to the core. She'd never seen a beaver before, nor had she seen a loaded gun, let alone heard one go off. Olivia seemed unconcerned.

'Does he often do that?' Carla asked.

'Only if he doesn't like them,' Olivia replied matter-of-factly.

Carla made a mental note not to mention any further wildlife sightings. She didn't want to be responsible for the death of any more creatures, vermin or not.

'Would you like to visit Santa Fe later?' said Olivia. 'I'm going there to paint, and the evening is a fine time to do it. We could go a little earlier so you can see the Native American artisan market, if you'd like?'

'I'd love to,' replied Carla, glad to have her mind taken off the beaver.

* * *

Santa Fe was unlike any place Carla had seen so far on her journey. It was as if she'd travelled back a couple of centuries and landed in Mexico. The Cathedral Basilica of St Francis of Assisi dominated the skyline, towering over the adobe buildings that stretched across the town below. Carla ambled along the streets and found the market under the portal at the Palace of the Governors. A group of Native Americans had spread colourful blankets on the ground, on which they displayed their handcrafted wares: pottery, textiles and jewellery made of traditional materials such as turquoise, coral and silver.

With so many beautiful items to choose from, Carla

struggled to make up her mind. In the end, she settled on a turquoise and silver pendant with matching earrings, as well as a beautiful dreamcatcher bracelet. Believed by Native Americans to dispel bad luck and protect against nightmares, she was willing to take any help she could get on this journey.

She continued through the streets, drinking in the atmosphere and enjoying the slower pace of life. When she was done exploring, she bought a Georgia O'Keefe biography to read at the rooftop bar where she'd arranged to meet Olivia. It had a prime view overlooking the plaza and beyond. From this vantage point, she could see the town's pueblo-style buildings and the way the rays of the evening sun intensified the warmth and vibrancy of the terracotta-coloured walls. How different everywhere looked at this time of day. She could understand why Olivia had felt drawn to live here. Throw in the sun setting over the mountains and the stunning sky left in its wake, and it was an artist's paradise.

When Olivia arrived, she found Carla engrossed in her book.

'I'm hungry, are you?'

Carla nodded.

'Well, then, I'm going to take you to a great restaurant for dinner. It's an ancient adobe building called The Shed. It was built in 1692, but today it does the best green chilli stew in Santa Fe. You must try it.'

Carla did as she was told, and it was indeed delicious.

* * *

In the backyard of the ranch house, perched close to the river, stood a generously sized hot tub. Olivia and Carla wallowed in the warm, bubbling water, sipping wine and relaxing in each other's company underneath the night sky.

'Do you know, the last time I stargazed I was with your sister in Oklahoma?' said Carla.

'Really? That's lovely. It makes me feel closer to her and connected to you. We only see each other at Easter and Thanksgiving, but at least we get to talk on the phone most days. I do miss her sometimes. Do you have any brothers or sisters?'

'No, I'm an only child.'

Noticing the catch in her voice, Olivia said, 'Do you want to talk about it?'

'Not really. Some things are better left unsaid.'

'And some things are better aired,' Olivia said in a quiet, coaxing manner.

Carla wrestled with her thoughts. She didn't want to spoil the atmosphere, but Olivia's warmth towards her invited the sharing of confidences.

'My parents never intended to have me, and when they did, I was just an inconvenience to them,' she explained. 'I got in the way of their idyllic twosome.'

'Are you sure about that?'

'One hundred per cent.'

Carla recounted the tale of Judith and the dolls' house. 'I've never told anyone about that day, not even Tom. At the time, I had no idea what they were talking about, thank goodness. Once I was a teenager, I understood the significance of the word accident.'

Relieved when Olivia didn't jump in and issue platitudes, Carla continued her tale. 'Even then, I didn't mind. I didn't know there was anything wrong with their indifference until I met Tom and his family. Don't get me wrong, my parents didn't mistreat me or anything. They fed and clothed me properly and bought me beautiful Christmas presents. I never went without anything except love and affection. And I didn't know I was missing out until Tom came along and I discovered that I belonged somewhere, and to someone. I didn't resent my parents' lack of affection for me. It wasn't as though they weren't capable of love, it's just they had so much for each other, and still do, that there wasn't any left over for me.

'That sounds self-pitying, I know, but that's not always how I've felt about the situation. It's only in the last few years that I've become resentful. Since I stopped working, they've expected me to run around after them. They're becoming frail, and I was happy to help, but they act as though I owe them something, when really, I don't think I owe them anything. My father is becoming increasingly brusque with me, and it's got so I dread seeing them now.

'On the bright side, their attitude towards me shaped the woman I am now. I'm self-sufficient, and I've always been independent. That's a good thing, isn't it? They don't know any better and I'm OK with that, but the nastiness and unfair criticism I have to put up with these days hurts.'

Carla found herself blinking back tears.

'And now with Tom gone, it hurts even more?' Olivia gently enquired.

'Yes, it does. I feel abandoned, as though I've been cut adrift from the only person I could depend upon, and now I can't help wondering if it's all my fault and that I don't deserve to be loved.'

'Come on, you know that's not true. Tom couldn't have pretended something he didn't feel for all those years. From what you are saying to me, and what you told Nancy, I'm sure there is something missing from this jigsaw puzzle. When you are ready, you need to speak to Tom and get some answers, so that your life makes sense again.

'As for your parents, it sounds like you've already worked out why they are the way they are, and there's nothing you can do to change them or their opinion of you, so stop trying. It's their problem, not yours. Maybe the deterioration in your father's behaviour is being driven by fear; fear that he may be left without your mother, and you are the only person he can take it out on. It doesn't make it right, but you need to let go of these negative emotions and stop worrying about things you can't change. I think it took a lot of courage for you to leave your home and come to a strange country and meet strange people. Now you're here, let your worries go, sit back and enjoy the rest of your trip.'

'You're right. I have been a lot better since I stayed at Nancy's, although I still find myself struggling at times. Thank you so much for listening to me and for your wonderful hospitality. I'm blown away by how so many complete strangers are stepping forward to help me and give me the most amazing experiences here.'

'Aw, it's nothing. If we can't give each other a helping hand once in a while, then what's the point of being alive?'

Randy lumbered onto the patio and broke the sombre mood.

'ATVs eight o'clock,' he said, before retreating into the house.

'Night, honey,' Olivia called after him, receiving an affectionate grunt in reply.

'What was that all about?'

'We're going on an adventure in the morning on our ATVs.'

'What's an ATV?'

'An all-terrain vehicle.'

Carla was none the wiser.

'It's like a sit-on buggy with fat wheels.'

'Oh, you mean a quad bike.' Carla grinned. 'I'm starting to realise what is meant by the saying we're two nations divided by a common language. Tell me more, it sounds exciting.'

'We'll have an early breakfast, then Randy will take us out to explore the wilderness. Have you ridden an ATV before?'

'No, I haven't, but I'll give it a go,' Carla said, surprised at her enthusiastic reaction. She liked doing different things, but without Tom goading her on, she was often too afraid to try, especially if she thought she might make a fool of herself. She was done with that timidity. She would grab any opportunity that came her way, with the caveat that it didn't involve horse riding.

'You'll need to wear an old pair of jeans and a long-sleeved shirt, baseball cap, sunglasses and a neckerchief to cover your mouth.'

'I haven't got any old clothes,' Carla said, explaining about her shopping spree in Chicago and how she'd given her old clothes to a homeless woman. 'But never mind, I'm not precious about these new ones.'

'I'm sure I've got an old shirt in my closet you can have, from when I was smaller than I am now.'

'Thanks, Olivia, that would be great. I'm chuffed to bits at having the chance to wear my new neckerchief for real instead of it being a fashion accessory.'

'I take it chuffed means stoked. Let's get to bed, we've got a tough day ahead of us.'

* * *

After a healthy breakfast of smashed avocado on wholemeal toast, Olivia and Carla assembled in Randy's garage, dressed and ready to go. Randy showed Carla the controls and patiently explained how to use the bike. She gingerly opened the throttle and was excited to feel the machine ease forward.

Randy guided her around the ranch, getting her used to manoeuvring the weighty machine on the asphalt surface.

When he was satisfied she knew what she was doing, the three of them set off, driving across scrubby terrain and into the wilderness.

With some alarm, Carla noticed that Randy was carrying a revolver in a leather holster around his waist, in full open view. She wondered whether this was legal, or what his reason was for carrying it – to protect them against wildlife or from other landowners? She suspected they may be trespassing, but wisely kept her mouth shut. Gradually, she relaxed into the ride, and they were soon careering around the countryside, a cloud of dust rising in their wake. Carla marvelled at the couple's sprightliness and sense of adventure, despite their advancing years.

After a couple of hours, they pulled up alongside a small lake in the middle of nowhere. Carla neither knew nor cared exactly where they were. They hadn't seen any buildings or signs of life for miles, and it was exhilarating. Carla felt completely free from her worries and had no time to think about anything other than keeping herself upright.

Olivia had thoughtfully brought along water and snacks to keep them going until they got home. The three of them sat in silence, enjoying the peace and quiet, which was broken only by their munching and the occasional bird call. Carla felt enormously fortunate to be witnessing things that many people never get to see. Any regrets she'd had for undertaking this journey were now long gone.

In the distance, the sky was darkening. Randy looked up and frowned. Just then, the first of many spectacular forked lightning bolts erupted from the thick black clouds, illuminating the sky. The flat landscape and the electrical storm encroaching ever closer enhanced the frightening beauty of the powerful strikes as they made contact with the earth.

'We need to get going,' Randy said in a calm, authoritative voice.

Here we go, thought Carla.

Her heart thumped so fiercely she thought it would explode, and her sphincter was dangerously close to loosening to the point of no return. She was terrified of the two-hour journey ahead trying to outrun the storm.

Seeing Carla's white face and grim expression, Olivia said, 'Don't worry, we're not far from home; it's only fifteen minutes away. We've been riding in a loop.'

Thank goodness.

They just managed to get the bikes parked in the garage when the heavens opened.

'See, we made it just in time.'

'I was frightened we would get struck by lightning,' said Carla, still shaking.

'The chances of that happening are next to none, and the least of our worries. When it rains, the terrain turns into quicksand.'

Seeing the look of horror on Carla's face, Olivia said hurriedly, 'It was fine, we weren't in any danger. Randy always has one eye on the weather, which is why we stopped so close to home.'

'That's good to know. Now, if you don't mind, as soon as that storm passes, I'm going to have a long soak in that hot tub of yours and wash my aches and pains away.'

'Be my guest. You go on ahead and I'll fetch you a nice glass of New Mexican Viognier to settle you down.'

* * *

The following morning, Carla and Olivia relaxed on the patio together, drinking coffee, soaking up the sunshine and watching two fishermen on the opposite riverbank casting their lines and successfully reeling in some impressively sized fish.

'You've been so good to me over these last two days. Is there anything I can do for you?' asked Carla.

'Maybe you can. Nancy told me you used to have a good job in finance. Is that true?'

'That's right. I was head of the North American desk.'

'You see, I've built up quite a portfolio of stocks and shares over the years. So far, they've rewarded me well. I use a broker in Santa Fe, but I can't help thinking my investments have gotten too big for a small-town man to handle. I was wondering if I should move to a bigger firm. Would you take a look at my portfolio and tell me what you think?'

'Well, I'm a little rusty. I haven't watched the markets since I left the bank. I tell you what, I'll spend the morning surfing the net and catching up on what's going on, and then I'll have a look at your investments after lunch.'

'Would you? That would be great.'

It felt good to exercise her mind, and Carla felt the familiar buzz she'd had when faced with a challenge at work. By the end of the morning, she was confident she could look at Olivia's finances and give her some advice. Eschewing the usual lunchtime glass of wine, she hid in Olivia's office and pored over the large file of paperwork. After a couple of hours, she called Olivia in to join her.

'I'm pleased to tell you all your stocks and shares look very healthy. Your broker knows what he's doing, and you should hang on to him. If I'm going to make one criticism, I'd say your investments are spread too thinly, which leaves you vulnerable if something unforeseen should happen to affect the market. If, for instance, something bad were to happen to the travel industry, you'd take a hit on the value of a big chunk of your shares. On the other hand, should home improvements suddenly become a thing, you'd make a killing on those shares. What you need to ask yourself is whether you're a big risk taker. If you are, what you've got is fine. If not, I suggest getting your broker to spread the load a bit more.'

'So, are you saying that if something like 9/11 were to happen again, people would stay at home?'

'Maybe. We live in a global economic marketplace, and without a crystal ball, we just can't tell what the future has in store for us.'

'Thank you, Carla, you've put my mind at rest. It's reassuring to know I am in good hands with Arnold, and I will ask him to diversify a little. I hope that spending the day doing this wasn't too tedious.'

'I enjoyed it. I'm glad my brain still functions in the real world.'

'Do you miss your job?'

'No, I don't. I loved the cut and thrust of it when I was there, the respect it generated from my colleagues and, of course, the money, but I've no desire to go back. Any doubts I may have had about leaving my professional life behind have been put to bed on this journey. I've just got to sort out what to do with the rest of my life.'

'I'm sure you'll work it out.'

'I hope so,' Carla replied, with a hint of a smile.

* * *

That evening, Olivia and Randy attended a meeting in their community hall to help organise the forthcoming Independence Day celebrations. Carla took the opportunity to soak in the hot tub, sip wine and stargaze. She thought about her earlier conversation with Olivia. Had she really meant everything she'd said? Now that she was retired, she had the freedom to live her life the way she wanted to and, looking up at the mass of stars shimmering high above her in the galaxy, it was obvious her career was unimportant in the grand scheme of the universe. Yet, she also remembered how important it had been to her, from the time she'd left school until the time she'd left it all behind.

She knew she was part of a lucky generation of women. The trailblazing feminists before her had successfully fought for equal pay and employment rights. Her generation was the first to benefit from that. Even so, in the early days of her career, it was necessary for her to choose between work and marriage. Employers were not enlightened enough to let married women get on the corporate ladder. She'd willingly chosen a career – she didn't even like children, and she doubted she'd ever meet a man she'd want to settle down with. How wrong she'd been! As she'd described it to Olivia, she'd really loved her independence, the respect she commanded and the generous salary, which allowed her to wear stylish clothes, live in a nice flat in London and drink champagne whenever she felt like it. She was living the dream, or so she'd thought.

Meeting Tom had changed all that. She fell for him so heavily that it was inevitable she would marry him. Her colleagues were astounded at the change in her. They'd had her down as being married to her job, and although they all liked Tom, they couldn't see what it was about him that had changed her mind about matrimony. His spectacular chat-up line had certainly caught her attention, but it was the fact he loved her with all his heart that had sucked her in. She'd never been unconditionally loved before, and it didn't take long for her to return the feeling.

It was only after she'd accepted his proposal that she worried her precious career advancement would be halted as soon as she told her boss the news. Luckily, by then she was a valued member of the firm and attitudes were changing. Her company was at the forefront of creating genuine equality in the workplace, and she found being a wife and mother was not too much of a barrier to progression. Sometimes, when exhausted from trying to juggle all her commitments, she did wonder if she had it all. On balance, she thought she did. She wasn't cut out to be a traditional housewife, and she knew she would have hated it. She counted her lucky stars for being given the opportunity to keep her independence, use her brain and still get to experience the joys of marriage and motherhood.

Years on, unlike some of her colleagues, she hadn't felt diminished by her redundancy. She had seen it as an opportunity, a chance to do something different. So how had she allowed herself to become everyone's dogsbody instead of finding a new purpose for herself? She shook her head in disbelief.

Guilt, that's what it was.

She hadn't had it all, had she? Because of her commitment to her job, she had subconsciously believed she wasn't quite good enough as a mother, daughter or wife. So, when she finally had free time, she'd slipped into the role of being everyone's carer, feeling the need to make it up to them for putting so much emphasis on her career. What had happened to that feisty woman Tom had fallen in love with, the one so full of ambition and sparkle? Oh God, it was true, she had become a boring, middle-aged (fast heading towards old age) woman. No wonder Tom had run off with his fancy woman.

Wow, Carla, you're really good at this self-pity lark. Listen to yourself.

No, she wasn't boring. Preoccupied maybe, trying too hard to please and allowing herself to be side-tracked. Well, if she learnt nothing else from this trip, she knew that when and if she went home, things were going to be different.

* * *

Early next morning, the Corvette was packed and ready to go.

'Here's my cousin Martha's phone number,' said Olivia, handing Carla a bit of paper. 'She lives in Malibu, and she's expecting you to get in touch when you reach the end of the route. You will call her, won't you?'

'Of course. I can't wait to meet her. Being around your family always involves drama, I can't imagine what she'll have in store for me!'

'I've got to run some errands in Albuquerque this morning. Follow me. I'll slow down and wave when you need to turn off.'

Olivia roared away, with Carla following her into the distance.

Damn, what is it with this family and their need for speed? she thought to herself.

Olivia tooted her horn and gave her a wave. Carla was alone once again.

CHAPTER 20
Gallup, New Mexico

C arla continued her journey through 'The Land of Enchantment', taking in the fabulous views around her. On Olivia's recommendation, she took a detour from Route 66 and drove for two hours to the Jemez hot springs. Olivia had told her how the springs were once occupied by ancient tribes, who considered them to be sacred. From the 1800s, they had become a tourist attraction, with stagecoaches bringing travellers up from Albuquerque to relax and enjoy the healing powers of the restorative waters. Like them, Carla fancied a few hours of rest and relaxation. She immersed herself in the turquoise pools, drinking in the beauty of the landscape and enjoying the peace. Then, with her eyes closed, she listened to the babbling river and felt the warm spring water loosen her muscles and calm her mind.

Fully refreshed, she decided against her original plan to continue the Santa Fe Loop to Albuquerque and then re-join the main Route 66, much of which paralleled the noisy interstate. Instead, she chose to head west along the quieter Scenic Byway, enjoying the beauty all around her as she went.

Back on Route 66, she realised she'd lost all track of time. The light was fading as she approached the outskirts of Gallup. A vague memory popped into her head, and she pulled over to retrieve her travel guide from her suitcase. She was right. It recommended a stay at the Sunshine Lake Bed and Breakfast, which was described as 'an independently owned house in a superb location with a mouth-watering breakfast'. The reviewer said it was the best accommodation in New Mexico and was worth the expense. It sounded perfect. A couple of miles and a few wrong turns later, she found it.

When Carla rang the doorbell, there was no reply. She tried again and was about to give up when she heard footsteps in the hallway. The door opened, revealing a dishevelled-looking woman with unbrushed hair and mismatched clothing. She appeared to be in her late forties and her eyes were red-raw from crying.

'Yes?' she said, without enthusiasm.

'Hello, I was wondering if you have a room for tonight?'

'Sorry, we haven't got any vacancies.'

'Oh.' Carla's shoulders sagged. 'Can you recommend anywhere around here?'

'There are plenty of motels in town, just off I-40.'

Carla couldn't help but feel disheartened. After all the fun she'd had over the last few days, she wanted to continue it with something more than a bog-standard room, and she didn't relish driving on the freeway in the dark.

'Thank you for your time.'

Head bowed and body limp with disappointment, she turned to leave. She was halfway down the steps when the woman called out to her.

'Wait, I'm sorry. Things are difficult here right now, but I do have one room available if you still want it.'

Seeing the woman was deeply troubled, Carla said, 'I don't

want to cause you any bother, but if you're sure, it would really help me out.'

'Yes, I'm sure. Come on in.'

Ten minutes later, Carla was settled in a beautiful room at the top of the house. Tiredness washed over her, and she had a quick shower and put on her pyjamas. She needed an early night, and this quiet room was perfect for that. She was just nodding off when there was a loud knock on her door. The woman, whose name – she now knew – was Pandora, was standing in the doorway looking distressed.

'I am so sorry to bother you, Ms Bright, but my son Jacob cut himself on a kitchen knife while I was sitting with my grandpop. You'd think at fourteen he could make a simple sandwich without any drama, wouldn't you? My husband is at work, and I need to take Jacob to the ER and get him stitched up. Grandpop Bill can't be left alone, and I know I shouldn't ask you, but please would you sit with him while we're out?'

'Of course. I'll just grab my dressing gown. Go!'

Carla crept into Grandpop's bedroom and found a frail old man asleep in his bed. She flopped into the chair next to him and studied his skeletal head and wizened face. His skin was pallid, and only his wheezing breath told her he was still alive. As if sensing her presence, he suddenly woke up and peered at her through rheumy eyes.

'Who are you?' he croaked.

'Carla Bright, I'm a guest here. Pandora had to take your great-grandson to the ER.

'What's the matter with him?' asked the old man urgently.

'He cut his hand. It's nothing serious. They'll soon sort him out, don't worry.'

The man relaxed. He looked at her intently, seeming to analyse her. 'You English?'

She nodded.

'Thought so. I was in England during the war.'

'Really? Where were you based?'

'I was with 306th Bomb Group at Thurleigh Station 111. Do you know it?'

'Know it? It's only twenty miles from where I live! What a coincidence!'

At this news, the old man brightened and appeared stronger, more alive. Carla could see his mind ticking over, drifting back to old times – over seventy years ago.

'I was one of the lucky ones. I was only nineteen when I was posted to England, and as I wasn't as smart as the aircrew, I was allocated to ground personnel. Every day I watched those big ol' B-17s take off and fly away in a massive formation, heading to occupied Europe and Germany on bombing raids. What a sight they were!

'Those heavy bombers were kept in the air by four massive engines. We used to call them Flying Fortresses, but they weren't impregnable. When they were due back, all of us ground crew stared into the sky with fear and dread in the pits of our stomachs, willing them to come into sight, desperate to hear the droning noise in the distance and praying they would be safe. It was a dangerous business. Between '42 and '45, we had over three hundred successful raids, though we lost one hundred and forty-one aircraft and seven hundred and eighty-seven men, including my buddy, Doug. Our bunkmates called us "Bill and Doug, the mighty men of Michigan."'

He looked pensive, and Carla saw a single tear roll down his cheek.

'What happened?'

'It was October ninth, 1943. We waited for the plane, but it didn't come back. We found out much later that the Krauts attacked it on the return journey. Doug was hit in the chest and died instantly. The plane came down in Samso, Denmark.

The surviving crew were sent to Germany and spent the rest of the war as prisoners.'

He shook his head, anguish showing on his face; time had not diminished his pain.

'Even though we were billeted in freezing cold concrete huts with tin roofs and given terrible food, it wasn't all bad. I met my wife at a Land Army dance at the Corn Exchange in Bedford.' His face lit up at the memory. 'The aircrew were more glamorous than us groundcrew, and they got all the purdy girls... well, all except for my Peggy. She was the purdiest of them all, yet she chose me over all the other men. She never did tell me why, but I was sure glad she did.'

He was silent for a while, lost in his memories. Carla didn't want to interrupt his chain of thought; she could see he was in a happy place.

'Peggy was born in London, you know. She had to leave when her house was bombed out. It was too dangerous to stay, so she joined the Land Army girls and went to Thurleigh. She worked the fields doing the men's work while they were away fighting. The hard work and fresh air sure did give her rosy cheeks. I couldn't believe my luck when she agreed to marry me after the war. She came back with me to Michigan, and I was so proud of her, my chest was fit to burst. I was glad she never got homesick like I thought she would. We wanted to visit England again one day, but our daughter got sick and then she got sick...'

'I'm so sorry.'

'Don't be. She was the love of my life, and I treasure the years we spent together. Better to have happy memories of the past than be unhappy with the wrong person in the present.'

'True.'

'Did you know I'm dying?'

'No, I didn't.'

Though I'm not surprised to hear it, Carla thought to herself.

'Are you sure?' she asked.

'Yes, I am, though my granddaughter won't accept it. I'm ready to join my wife and daughter. I keep asking Pandora's permission to go, but she keeps saying no.'

'I don't understand, how can she stop you?'

'I won't be happy to pass on without her blessing, and so I keep going even though my body is failing and I'm in a lot of pain. Will you talk to her and try and make her understand?'

'Well, I'll try, if that's what you want, though I can't see her listening to me, given that we've only just met.'

'She trusted you to take care of me, didn't she?'

'Yes, she did.'

Carla didn't have the heart to tell him there was no one else available at such short notice.

'I've had enough. You will tell her I need to go now?'

'Yes, of course.'

He gave a satisfied smile, closed his eyes and went back to sleep.

Shortly afterwards, Pandora and Jacob returned from the ER. They hurried into the bedroom, panicking at the sight of Grandpop's ashen face.

'It's OK, he's just asleep,' Carla whispered.

They both sighed with relief.

The old man's eyes opened. 'Hello, my GG, the cleverest boy in the whole world. How are you?'

'I'm fine, GG. My hand slipped on a knife is all.' Jacob held up his bandaged hand for inspection.

'I am so proud of you and your mom; don't you ever forget that. Come over here and give your old GG a goodnight hug.'

Jacob did as he was told and then took himself off to bed. Bill nodded off.

'GG?' asked Carla.

154

'It's short for Great-Grandson and Great-Grandpop. Jacob started it when he was only three; it's less of a mouthful. How's Grandpop been?'

'Lucid actually, and very interesting to talk to. He wanted me to speak to you.'

Carla recounted their recent conversation. Tears filled Pandora's eyes.

'You know you need to let him go, don't you?' said Carla, squeezing her hand.

'Yes, I know it, but it's so hard. He's been living here with us since before Jacob was born, and I shall miss him so much. I lost both my mom and Grandma in '95, then my dad in 2000, and Grandpop is the only person I have left from the past. I'm being selfish, aren't I?'

'No, you care, that's all.'

'Will you stay with me?'

'Of course I will.'

They sat quietly together until Grandpop's eyes blinked open. He looked at them both and raised his eyebrows.

'Yes, Grandpop, you can go now.'

'Thank you, my darling. I'm so proud of you and GG. Thank you for taking care of me. I love you.'

'I love you too, Grandpop.'

Pandora kissed him on the forehead, and they clutched hands. Then he closed his eyes, smiled and gently slipped away.

* * *

The next morning, Carla found Pandora cooking up a storm – scrambled eggs, fresh muffins, pancakes and strawberries. The meal was served on the patio, from where Carla admired the fabulous view. The lake before her was teeming with wildlife, and beyond the vast expanse of water, miles of open wilderness stretched into the distance.

'This breakfast is exquisite, Pandora. You didn't need to go to all this trouble, though – you've got enough on your plate.'

'It's no trouble, I just wanted to show you my appreciation. You helped me come to my senses. I feel a strange sense of elation from knowing that I was with Grandpop at the moment he chose to pass.'

Carla was comforted by the strength of the human spirit. She'd witnessed the old man controlling the time of his death and she was in awe of it. She ate her food in silence and was glad to have been with the family in their time of need.

CHAPTER 21
Arizona

C arla was driving the Route 66 she had anticipated in her dreams. Quirky landmarks like the Wigwam Hotel in Holbrook made her smile. Standing on the corner in Winslow, Arizona, hugging a statue of Glenn Frey from the Eagles was a highlight. But best of all was the mile upon mile of lonely, straight highway surrounded by scrubland and blue sky. The freedom, the wonderful aromas and the beautiful panorama filled her heart with joy. The railroad tracks and telegraph poles lining the highway reminded her of the trailblazers seeking out the West on 'Iron horses', long before Route 66 was born. She loved it all, and the icing on the cake was the burbling sound of 'Carla's' engine. Even the feel of dust in her hair and grit in her mouth could not dampen her mood.

She noticed that the needle on the fuel gauge had slipped below the halfway mark. As she was so far away from civilisation, she didn't want to risk running out of petrol, so she stopped at the next gas station. A twenty-something James Dean lookalike ran his eyes approvingly over Carla: the car not the woman. She was amused; it was a long time since a young man had salivated over her like that.

'Nice ride!'

'Thank you.'

'It's my dream car. Can I sit in it?'

'Why not?'

She got out, and in he hopped. If he drove off now, there was nothing she would be able to do to stop him, but somehow, she had faith in this stranger. It hit her that since embarking on this trip, she'd let her innate cynicism go. The kindness of all the people she'd met while traversing this wonderful country had clearly made a lasting impact already. Rightly or wrongly, she was becoming more trusting, and it felt good.

'Will you take my picture?' the man said, handing her his phone.

'Of course.'

He put his hands on the steering wheel and looked up at her with earnest blue eyes and a rapturous look on his face.

This one is going to break a few hearts, Carla thought as she snapped away.

'Thank you, ma'am,' he said as he clambered out. 'It's the best thing that's happened to me all week.'

'Call me Carla.'

'Ryan. Happy to meet'cha, Carla!'

She watched him climb into his battered pick-up truck and drive off, before filling her car and going inside to the cashier's desk. She paid thirty dollars for the petrol and bought a Coke and a packet of Doritos for the onward journey.

* * *

Before moving on, Carla consulted her map.

158

'I was right,' she said, not caring if anyone thought she was crazy for talking to herself; it wouldn't be the first time.

Her memory was correct. Paul Preston's monument was nearby, and as she had nowhere she needed to be, she decided to take a little diversion to see the most famous resident ever to emerge from Staverley. So little had ever happened in her village that he was regarded as a legend for his pioneering spirit and for crossing the American West, even though it ultimately led to disaster.

A mile down the road, the brown signpost she was looking for came into view. She turned onto a narrow asphalt road, which was steep and winding and challenged her driving skills. It was taking longer than expected to get there. She consulted her map again.

You idiot, Carla, of course it is.

One day, she'd learn how to read a map properly. Tight squiggles were not good news. She couldn't turn back as there was nowhere to turn.

Oh well, it would have to be onwards and upwards – quite literally!

Five minutes later, she'd reached the top of the hill and parked in a shady layby.

There he was, Paul Preston, the person whose name appeared everywhere in Staverley. There was a Preston Avenue, a Preston Bridge and a Preston Common. Even a new housing estate had been named after him. Here, the huge bronze statue of the explorer dominated the top of the hill. He was cupping his eyes with his right hand as he stared into the distance. Carla stood next to him and followed his gaze to the vast expanse of wilderness. She saw patches of green pinyon pines nestled amongst scrubby sagebrush and vegetation, which had adapted to survive in this harsh climate, spreading out like a vast blanket across the arid earth towards the distant hills. Above, the cloudless, azure sky stretched out as far as the eye could see.

Carla was completely alone, with only birds and insects to keep her company. She sat on a rock and listened to the little noises they made and the sounds of the leaves rustling in the trees behind her. Completely at peace and in tune with the world around her, she was proud of how far she had come. Before The Day That Tom Left, she'd have lacked the courage to do anything like this, but the American pioneering spirit was having a positive effect on her, and she felt invincible.

The beads of sweat forming on her forehead alerted Carla to the increasing heat of the sun as it rose high in the sky. It was time to move on. She patted Paul Preston and strolled back to the car, smiling with contentment.

Oh no!

Her stomach lurched and nausea overtook her as the unmistakable smell of petrol hit her nostrils, evidenced by the rivulet of liquid emerging from the car and coursing its way down the hill. As the gas evaporated in the heat, a shimmering haze rose above it.

'Oh God, what am I going to do?'

She opened the bonnet and gazed at the mysterious paraphernalia in front of her. She was clueless about anything mechanical, but the one thing she did know was that in the unlikely event there was anything left in the tank, it would be too dangerous to start the car with all that petrol underneath it. Realising it was pointless to stare any longer, she shut the bonnet and sighed. Miles from anywhere on a lonely road high up in the hills, she hadn't got a clue what to do next.

'OK, calm down. Breathe. Think.'

You're talking to yourself again, Carla, said the voice in her head.

'Who cares? No one is going to hear me, more's the pity,' Carla replied to it.

It was so hot now; the temperature must have been ninety degrees and rising. At least the car was protected by the shade, and she had a good supply of water in the boot.

'Phone. Find the phone. Here it is.'

The battery was dead.

'How could you be so stupid, Carla? When will you ever learn?'

Who was she going to call anyway?

Think, Carla.

Her head was spinning, her thoughts jumbled.

Focus!

She would have to start walking, but it was so hot, and once she left the shade, there would be no tree cover for miles. On the other hand, if she waited, it might get too cold in this high desert, and it could be dangerous after dark. She might fall over the edge, and who knows what wildlife was out there waiting to get her? Panic threatened to overwhelm her. So much for striking out on her own. Who did she think she was kidding? She looked up at Paul Preston, who now seemed to be smirking at her.

'And you can wipe that smile off your face, you ungrateful so and so,' she said to him. 'I'm probably the only person who has come to see you in years. And who do you think you are anyway? When you planned to leave our beautiful village and sail the bloody Atlantic to seek your fame and fortune, why the hell didn't you prepare for it properly? If you had, you wouldn't have died up here all on your own, and I wouldn't be stuck up here with you. Did you think about your wife before you buggered off and left her? It's a good job she was independently wealthy and wasn't left a penniless widow. What I'd like to know is this: did she arrange for you to be immortalised in bronze because of a broken heart, or to tell the world of your folly?'

She wondered who'd found him. And if *she* died up here, would anyone ever find *her*? She suddenly felt very stupid.

'Looks like we're both crap at exploring,' she growled at the statue.

'Calm down. Everything is going to be fine,' said a familiar voice.

Carla whirled round, expecting to see Judith, but she was all alone.

'The sun must be getting to you, woman,' Carla said, but this time to herself.

She knew she was letting her imagination run away with her. Nevertheless, she felt strangely comforted, and she did calm down, just as the voice had told her to.

* * *

A faint engine noise in the distance disturbed the silence. Carla's ears pricked up. She was sure the sound was getting louder. Yes, it was! A few seconds later, a battered old pick-up truck came juddering to a halt beside her. The driver jumped out, looking every bit the hero. And boy, was she glad to see him.

'What are you doing here, Ryan?'

'I could ask you the same question, Carla.'

His gaze moved to the Corvette. 'Looks like she's run out of gas, or should I say, the gas has run out of her.'

He laughed, pleased with his little joke.

'Forgive me if I don't join in with the hilarity,' said Carla severely, but the corners of her mouth were twitching, and Ryan wasn't fooled.

'Let me take a look under the hood,' he said.

After a few moments of humming and hawing, he added, 'It looks like you've got a split fuel line. I'll call my buddy and he'll bring his recovery truck up here.'

'What, on this road? He'll never make it.'

'You don't know my buddy. He could get his truck through the eye of a needle.' Ryan spoke rapidly into his phone. 'He'll be here in a half-hour. So, what are you doing here?'

'I drove up to see this statue. Paul Preston came from my village back in England, and he's a bit of a legend. As I was in the area, it seemed like a good idea to come and visit him. Not such a great idea, as it turns out. What made *you* come up here? It doesn't look like many people visit this spot.'

'I come every year. Look at the inscription and you'll see that today is the day Paul Preston died, some hundred and fifty years ago. After my pa passed, I used to come up here on my motorcycle when I needed someone to talk to. I felt like Paul Preston listened to me, so I've come here every year since to pay my respects. Sounds crazy, I know.'

'Well, thank you, Paul Preston, and thank you, too, Ryan; I thought I might die up here with him.'

Ryan stood next to Paul Preston and followed the man's gaze, just as Carla had done not half an hour earlier. She thought how, if she'd been forty years younger, she'd have found him very attractive indeed. She guessed his age put him bang in the middle of her two children, and her heart went out to him.

She caught the faraway look in his eyes and said gently, 'I'm sorry about your pa. You must have been very young when he died.'

'I was sixteen.'

'Do you want to talk about it?'

Ryan's sad eyes met hers and he nodded.

'It must have been really hard losing your father at such a young age.'

'Yes, it was. He was an amazing guy; he was my hero…'

The words caught in his throat, and he was unable to continue. Carla watched him surreptitiously and waited for him to recover himself.

He blinked back tears and breathed deeply. 'My pa was so dependable, big and strong. He taught me so much and he made me feel special. I thought he would live forever… and then he died.'

'What happened to him?'

'He just keeled over, right in front of me and Ma. I think he'd gone even before he hit the deck.'

'How old was he?'

'Thirty-nine. It was so unfair; he was such a good man. He didn't deserve to be taken from us.'

'My God, what caused his death?'

'The autopsy said he had a massive heart attack due to an undiagnosed heart condition. It was out of the blue: there was no history of it in the family. But I tell you, it was all the government's fault.'

'How come?'

'My grandpa fought in the Vietnam War, and he was there when they were spraying Agent Orange. Have you heard of it?'

'Yes, I have. I don't know anything about it, though.'

'It's also called dioxin, and it's a potent weed killer. Millions of gallons of it were sprayed to kill the foliage in the jungle and expose the enemies' hiding places. My grandpa survived the war, but years later he got cancer. After a big fight, the veterans got some justice when the government finally admitted Agent Orange caused serious health issues for the soldiers in 'Nam. On top of this, lots of people think the veterans passed on birth defects to their children, and one of them is heart disease. My pa was a bit overweight, and he had type two diabetes, which also might have been caused by Agent Orange, but we can't prove it.'

'I'm so sorry to hear that. I can't imagine what it's been like for you and your mother.'

'It was hard, Carla, so hard. I was sixteen years old and suddenly I had to be the man of the house. Luckily, my pa left us well provided for, so at least we didn't have to worry about money. I knew I had to be strong for Ma and my little sister, Lucy.'

'What do you do now?'

'I'm a garage mechanic in Flagstaff. I earn a reasonable living and I have the time to fix up the house and anything else Ma needs doing.'

'What would you have done had your dad lived?'

'I was a grade A student, and my teachers told me I could easily get a place at Stanford University to study engineering. But I couldn't leave my ma and sister, so I didn't apply.'

'Did you tell your mother this?'

'No. Things were bad enough already, and she needed me to take care of her and Lucy.'

'Did she say that?'

'Well, no, but I knew it was my duty to protect them.'

They were silent for a few minutes before Carla ventured some advice. 'You do know it's not too late to follow your dreams, don't you, Ryan?'

'What do you mean?'

'I'm sure your mother would be mortified if she knew you'd turned your back on your ambitions for her sake. Have you ever spoken to her about your plans or your decision to take on your father's role?'

'Well, no, it was just the right thing to do.'

'You are a wonderful human being, and if you were my son, I would be so proud of you, but, even if my heart was breaking, I wouldn't want you to put your life on hold for my sake, and I'm sure your mother wouldn't, either. You need to talk to her about it. I'm sure she'll slap your backside – metaphorically, of course – and tell you to apply to that university right away.'

'Ya think?'

'I think!'

Ryan looked thoughtful and then a huge smile spread across his face. 'Thanks, Carla, you talk a lot of sense. I'll speak to Ma about it and see what she says.'

* * *

Ryan was right. His friend Chris arrived without issue and expertly loaded the Corvette onto his trailer.

'Hop in.'

Carla wasn't about to complain about the bone-shaking ride down the mountain in Ryan's old pick-up. They soon arrived at Chris's place, which in Carla's opinion resembled a scrapyard. She knew better than to say so. When a piece of machinery dies in the West, it stays there. Not for the Western man do the words, 'I wish I'd never sold that car, pick-up, tractor, motorcycle...' apply. Everything is kept, just in case, to be fixed up sometime in the distant future.

'Hang on,' said Chris. He disappeared for a few minutes and returned with a length of rubber hose. 'We'll soon get you fixed up and on your way.'

An hour later, it was all done.

'Where are you headed next?' asked Chris.

'I know it's off Route 66, but I can't travel through Arizona without detouring to the Grand Canyon, can I?'

'Too right, you must visit. It's best to go in via the east entrance. Get a room in Cameron for the night before you go. Shall I call them and make a reservation for you?'

'That would be great, thank you.'

Chris disappeared into his office. 'All done,' he announced when he returned a few minutes later. 'It's called the Grand Canyon Motel, and it's at the Cameron Trading Post on the Navajo Nation reservation. From the outside, the rooms look pretty standard, but inside there are genuine Navajo furnishings. Make sure you have dinner there, and don't forget to try the fry bread. It's worth clogging your arteries up for! Get up early and get into the park as soon as the sun starts to rise and before the crowds arrive.'

'I will. Now, how much do I owe you for the repair?'

Chris frowned and said, 'If I can't help a lady from the old country in her time of need, then I'm not much of a man. Off with you.'

He shooed her towards the car.

'Thank you so much for your kindness, both of you. I really appreciate it.'

'Take my card and call me if you get into any more trouble,' said Ryan.

'Thanks. Hopefully that's the end of my dramas.'

As the Corvette rumbled out of the yard, Carla looked over her shoulder and waved.

And then she was gone.

CHAPTER 22

The Grand Canyon, Arizona

C ruising the highway once again, Carla mulled over her lucky escape. She shuddered to think what might have happened had Ryan not turned up. She debated whether she should ease off and be more conservative in her travels. But she couldn't shake off the strange feeling of having a protective barrier around her, and buoyed by that sensation, she resolved to make the most of her new-found freedom and carry on with her adventures, whatever the consequences.

Leaving the highway near Flagstaff, Carla soon reached the Navajo Nation reservation, entering territory belonging to a people she knew nothing about... not their way of life, their laws or their culture. Having been brought up watching old Westerns, where the Indians were always the baddies, it would have been easy to let her imagination run away with her and believe herself to be at risk. However, as an adult, she knew some of the history of the United States and how badly Native Americans were treated in their homeland when the pioneers pushed west and claimed all the valuable land. The movie industry had never let truth get in the way of a good story, and in any case, she reasoned, she'd watched films about Al Capone, and that hadn't stopped her walking the streets of Chicago!

Away from I-40, Carla became aware of the vast remoteness of the reservation. She followed the asphalt road north. To her right and left, the tracks leading to the houses were dusty and unpaved, and she noticed how most of them had pick-up trucks in their yards. She imagined these vehicles were a necessity when rain fell, turning the dirt tracks into a quagmire. All she could see for miles was useless red soil. She wondered if there was fertile land to be found elsewhere on the reservation, and she couldn't help thinking how the tribe had been given a rough deal, after being driven from their rightful homes by soldiers and politicians. However unfair that seemed, she reasoned that life was complicated. Human nature dictates that there will always be some who want to conquer other people's land, who are prepared to stop at nothing to get it. But for every avaricious parasite, there are many others just trying their best to provide a better life for their families, and who wouldn't want that?

Carla's maternal grandparents had died before she was born, and she reflected on the hardships they had endured. From the perspective of her own more than comfortable lifestyle, it was hard to believe her grandfather had been sent down a coal mine at thirteen, was in the trenches in Flanders at nineteen, and had survived to bring seven children into the world. Her grandmother had tragically died at the age of just forty-two, in no small part due to their poverty, and her grandfather had passed away soon after – of a broken heart and a broken body – leaving Carla's own mother an orphan at the tender age of eight. No wonder she didn't know how to be a loving parent herself. Who knew what horrors she'd contended with after the death of her parents or what privations she had suffered while they were still alive? In a rare moment of candour, Janet had confided in Carla that her mother had often gone hungry to keep her children's bellies full, and they had gone to school with cardboard stuffed in their shoes to cover the holes in their worn soles. Within two generations, everything had changed. Carla's extended family had benefited from the work ethic instilled in them, and for having the good fortune to be born in the second half of the twentieth century, allowing them to take advantage of the opportunities that era presented. It was another reminder to Carla of how lucky she was to be here.

She managed to bring her attention back to the here and now just as she reached Cameron Trading Post. Chris was right. The décor in her room contained original Navajo hand-carved furniture, artefacts and blankets. From her balcony, she spent some time watching the Little Colorado River flow beneath her on the final part of its journey to the Grand Canyon before it converged with the daddy of all rivers, the Colorado River.

There's nothing like a little local knowledge, and Carla was glad of Chris's recommendation for dinner. Never mind the food, the stupendous view through the restaurant's enormous picture windows of the Little Colorado Canyon was worth the price of dinner alone. Tearing her eyes away from it, she drank in her surroundings, admiring the Native American rugs, clothing, basketry and pottery, as well as the local art adorning the walls. This was her favourite restaurant so far, she decided. She wondered whether the food, when it arrived, would elevate the restaurant even higher or bring her opinion crashing down to earth. Fortunately, it was the former. She chose a Navajo Taco, which comprised fry bread, chilli beans, lettuce, cheese, tomato and green chilli. Mouth-watering didn't cover it; the fry bread was to die for, and the whole meal was sensational. She could almost feel her arteries hardening with every bite, but it was so delicious that she ordered some to take with her for lunch the following day. Her server advised her to put honey on it for extra flavour. She couldn't wait to try it.

The only downside to the evening was that the reservation was an alcohol-free zone, which Chris hadn't thought to mention. Carla decided that a sober night wouldn't kill her.

* * *

As Chris had instructed, Carla got up early and trundled the Corvette through the east entrance of the Grand Canyon National Park. She drove straight to the car park at Desert View and walked the short distance to the lookout. There it was! How was she ever going to describe this moment to anyone else? She could hardly process it herself. All she knew was that it was a sensation she would never, ever forget.

All alone, surrounded by silence, the spectacle of the Grand Canyon was incredible. She was moved to tears by the sight of this vast gorge cutting through the mountain, and by the rising sun extracting the beautiful colours from the canyon wall. The striated rock, formed over millions of years, created a rainbow effect, and far, far below, the Colorado River appeared to be no bigger than a turquoise stream. She had never felt such an intense reaction to one of Earth's wonders.

'Are you OK, ma'am?'

Startled, Carla turned around and saw a park ranger, identifiable by his neat khaki and green uniform.

'I'm fine. It's just all of this...'

Lost for words, she spread out her arms to indicate what she was referring to.

'It sure gets to you, doesn't it? No one ever forgets their first glimpse of the Grand Canyon. The only thing that comes close is watching the sunset here. If you've got time, there's been a couple of cancellations up at Bright Angel Lodge by the visitor centre. You could check in there for the night, then hop on the park's free shuttle bus to Hopi Point. Trust me, the view up there is even more breathtakingly beautiful than this one, and you'll catch the sunset, too.'

'That sounds like a wonderful idea, thank you.'

And it was. At first, though, the evening hadn't looked promising. A rare fog had descended, obliterating the view, but Carla, along with several other tourists, optimistically set off on the park bus anyway. Carla found a quiet spot, away from the others, in front of a forest of pine trees, where she could enjoy her surroundings in peace. Fingers crossed, she'd chosen a good spot to view the sunset, if only the fog would lift. She silently waited and was rewarded with visits from a variety of wildlife. She was used to seeing squirrels, but the pinyon jay bird was a new one on her, as was the cute little chipmunk. She heard a rustle in the trees and there, no more than two feet away, stood a baby deer. The spitting image of Bambi, it was a sight guaranteed to soften even the hardest of hearts. Carla stared in awe until another rustle spooked the little creature and sent it scampering off into the forest.

Carla got excited when the fog cleared, only for fast-moving clouds to take its place. They floated towards her, enveloping her body before disappearing into the forest. The eerie atmosphere heightened her senses and the mesmerising clouds kept coming, almost hypnotising her. Then, just as she thought the sky was clearing, an enormous rolling cloud came straight at her before miraculously parting to reveal the most magnificent view of the north side of the canyon and the sheer drop below. The rays from the rapidly setting sun reflected on the canyon walls, and an orange glow filled the sky. Carla was overwhelmed and thankful for the opportunity to witness such an incredible spectacle. Two unforgettable experiences in one day – how lucky was she? As the sun disappeared behind the mountain, she reluctantly returned to the bus, feeling such an affinity with nature that she didn't want the day to end.

Happy as she had believed herself to be before Tom left, she now realised she had been treading water and drifting any which way the current had taken her. For the first time in her life, she felt completely in control of her own happiness and confident that outside forces would take care of her destiny. Would this feeling last? Probably not, but for now, she was part of the earth and the sky and everything in between.

CHAPTER 23

Oatman, Arizona

Arizona ticked all Carla's boxes for what the modern experience of Route 66 should be. If anyone were to ask what state to drive if you could only choose one, for her it would be Arizona. She was sure the poor migrants back in the 1930s wouldn't have agreed. The contrast between her experience of driving a fancy car and staying in a luxury lodge in the Grand Canyon National Park and the near starvation and endless troubles the Oklahomans encountered as they moved west in search of a better life was not lost on her. The further she drove through the Arizona desert, the more she felt their presence. The drive up the steep and winding Sitgreaves Pass from Kingman was tricky enough in the Corvette. She couldn't imagine how difficult it would have been for all those desperate people.

Just before she reached the summit, Carla pulled into a layby. She'd spotted a narrow, dusty and well-worn footpath going into the scrubby little trees and decided to follow it and see where it went. Only a few yards in, the bushes ended, and the trail brought her to the cliff edge. The landscape opened out in front of her, the big skies dominating the panorama. Down below stretched a vast expanse of high desert. To see so much land devoid of human habitation must have been devastating for all those poor travellers passing through this barren territory. They wanted nothing more than a small patch of farmland to grow their own food, survive the harsh life and regain their sense of self-worth. Instead, the gods were laughing at them, tantalising them with the sight of so much land yielding so little. Carla sat on the cliff's edge, her legs dangling over the side, trying to ignore the feeling of anxiety the sheer drop below was causing her. The fear heightened her awareness. She could sense the ghosts of the troubled souls who had been part of the 'wagon train' of Oklahomans and farmers from other Mid-Western states who had struggled up that mountain, their jalopies coughing and spluttering and overheating from the effort. And they were the lucky ones. So many vehicles and precious belongings had already been abandoned by then as, one by one, their machines broke down after sustaining irreparable damage. Their occupants were forced to continue their journey on foot. Hungry, thirsty and with diminishing hope, they no doubt remembered the days when they worked their own little farms, up until their land had been turned into a dust bowl by the cruel winds and years of drought.

As if that wasn't bad enough, there was to be no rainbow at the end of their journey. Guards were waiting at the Californian border ready to turn them back. Should they be allowed through and manage to survive crossing the harsh conditions of the Mojave Desert, there was little or no work waiting for them in the Californian fields. They had travelled all that way, and for what? It would be easy to condemn the

176

Californians for being heartless, but Carla knew that was too simplistic. If the migration had continued unchecked, the volume of people would have destroyed the fabric of life for the people already living there. The real culprits were the landowners and their agents. They arrived in Oklahoma to spread lies about a land of milk and honey to desperate people, thus facilitating the misery that was to follow. It was nothing more than a ruse to drive down wages to starvation levels.

Carla sighed. History continued to repeat itself. She thought of all the asylum seekers making their way to England after being promised the world, only to find themselves effectively enslaved by the criminals who brought them over to pay back the cost of their passage. Then they faced months, years even, of trying to obtain refugee status.

Carla had set out on her journey for no other reason than to escape her troubles for a while and postpone the decisions she would have to make about her future. When she left home, it hadn't occurred to her that her journey would become not just a distraction but a voyage of self-discovery. The kindness of strangers, the desperation of people from the past and the sights and sounds around her had all combined to show her the way. Nancy had suggested she needed to get some perspective, and she had certainly got some now. Would that stop her feeling sorry for herself in the future? She doubted it. But for now, she appreciated every little thing she had.

Time to crack on. Few cars had passed her, it seemed to Carla, so driving into Oatman, just a few miles up the road, was a shock. From a lonely landscape, she'd arrived at a hectic tourist trap. The town was straight out of a Western movie, with mock gunfights and, somewhat weirdly, donkeys roaming the streets. The *burros* were smart enough to stand around looking pretty and accept the carrots fed to them by the holidaymakers, which were conveniently on sale in the many souvenir shops. Carla laughed at the incongruity of it all. So, it was true that you could get your kicks on Route 66, especially if you got too close to the hind legs of a donkey!

CHAPTER 24
Amboy, California

Crossing the bridge over the Colorado River, Carla entered California, the final state on Route 66. Now it was time to cross the infamous Navajo Desert. Luckily, it was a cool morning and she was able to enjoy the drive, savouring the miles of open desert and pootling through interesting little towns, including a living ghost town called Amboy, which had a population of just four. It was a familiar tale of a once-thriving route stop destroyed by the Interstate Highway. Only the post office and Roy's Café and Motel (no gas, no overnight guests) remained open for business. Carla entered the café and was delighted to see its '50s décor. She grabbed a stool at the counter and ordered a root beer, somewhat unsure of the taste.

The young man on the stool next to her said in an English accent, 'Alright? Is that your beautiful car parked out there?'

'If you mean the Corvette, a very good friend of mine lent it to me.'

'Wow, I wish I had a pal like that. What year is it?'

'1960.'

'Thought so,' he said, looking pleased with himself.

Earlier in her journey, Carla had found that question irritating, but she had come to realise it was either intended as a conversation opener or, as in this case, a quiz question that petrolheads loved to guess. Either way, she was glad it had given her the opportunity to chat to so many interesting people along the way.

'Is that a Liverpudlian accent I hear?'

'Right first time. Do you mind if I take some photos of your car for the blog I'm writing about my Route 66 trip?'

'Fill your boots.'

'Can I be cheeky and ask you to move it so I can get Roy's sign in the background?'

'No problem.'

She repositioned the gleaming red Corvette, recognising how much it lent itself to a photoshoot. The backdrop of Roy's iconic boomerang sign towering above the motel's deserted cabins and the barren mountains rising to the blue sky in the distance presented a prize-worthy photo opportunity. Immediately, a mass of Route 66 pilgrims converged like ants, frantically taking photos while they had the chance.

'Now look what I've started,' said the scouser.

'It's fine. I love seeing everyone smile when they see the car. It reminds me how lucky I am. Anyway, I'm going to have to love you and leave you.'

'Ta for the photos and ta-ra for now.'

Carla drove off with a wave. Only then did she realise that she hadn't asked the man his name.

CHAPTER 25

'J-Tree', California

Taking a detour along Highway 29, Carla headed for the Joshua Tree National Park in the Mohave Desert. She was excited by the sight of the Joshua trees, knowing this was one of only two places in the world they can be found. From the yucca family, these unusual-looking trees were dotted randomly across the desert, their upright trunks spreading out into gnarly branches and topped with clusters of spiky leaves pointing heavenwards. Back in the '80s, when she'd played her U2 album, *The Joshua Tree,* so often it was in danger of wearing out, little could she have imagined that one day she would actually get to see its namesake. She was here in homage to the music and to the group that had played such a big part in her younger years. Now she understood how the band had found inspiration in this wondrous desert landscape, and she gave thanks for the opportunity to visit such an amazing place. She was also reminded of the time she'd listened to U2's music whilst in labour, hoping it would take her mind off the agony.

Carla was on her way back to Route 66 when her attention was caught by a signpost. She slowed down to read it – *Blue*

Angel Falls. Puzzled, she stopped the car. She couldn't remember reading anything about the place in her guidebook and nor could she find it on her map. Nevertheless, it sounded rather good. Curious to know more, she turned off and drove along the traffic-free road. Was it the Dalai Lama who'd said, 'The road less travelled can lead to a greater wisdom?' Or was it Shakespeare? She had no idea, but she liked the sound of it and pressed on. A little way in the distance she could see a stationary silver-grey car. A bulky young man sporting a bushy beard and an unruly mane of brown hair was standing at the roadside, frantically waving at her. Building on her new-found trust in people and ignoring the voice in her head of cynical Old Carla, she drew the Corvette to a halt. She noticed his bulging, panicked eyes and quickly jumped out of the car.

'Please, ma'am, can you help us? My car is bust, and my wife has gone into labour two weeks' early. I don't think it will be much longer before the baby comes. My buddy, Gary, is on his way, but I don't know when he'll get here.'

The man looked at her pleadingly. Noticing her car only had two seats, his face fell.

He hesitated, then said, 'Please can you take her to the hospital?'

Carla peered through the windscreen and saw the poor woman's discomfort.

Her clothes were clinging to her body from sweat and her long, lank hair was stuck to her crimson face. She held her enormous belly as a wave of pain overcame her, and though she valiantly tried to suppress it, she couldn't help crying out in agony.

Carla handed the Corvette's keys to the poor woman's husband. 'You take her, your wife needs you to be with her. I'll stay with your car and wait for your friend, and then I'll come to the hospital as soon as we get your car fixed. Which hospital is it?'

'JFK Memorial, Palm Springs. I can't thank you enough. I'll take care of your car, I promise.'

He helped his struggling wife out of their car, manoeuvred her into the Corvette's passenger seat, ran round to the driver's side and jumped in.

'Don't worry about the car, you just take care of your wife!' Carla called after him as he sped away.

Inside, she was thinking, *Yikes, if he doesn't calm down, they won't make it to the hospital, and how will I explain to Merle how his car got wrecked?*

She hoped it wouldn't be too long a wait; it was hot enough to fry an egg on the road and she'd left everything except her handbag in the Corvette. Thirty minutes later, she saw a truck heading towards her. Thankfully, it was the man's friend. Seeing the worried look on his face, Carla quickly explained the situation.

'Thank the Lord. I thought I might have to deliver that baby myself! Let's find out what's wrong with this car.'

After a couple of minutes checking over the Prius, Gary shook his head and laughed.

'What a dope, he's only run out of gas! What man in his right mind doesn't keep a full tank when his wife is expecting a babe? Good job I've got some spare in my trunk.'

Gary poured petrol into the fuel tank and said, 'There you go. There's enough in the tank to get you to the hospital. Tell him he owes me one.'

Carla jumped into the Prius and drove hell for leather to the hospital, not really knowing why; the timing of her arrival wasn't going to change the outcome, but it seemed like the right thing to do.

* * *

In the hospital car park, Carla spotted the Corvette and parked the Prius in the next bay. Relieved to find Merle's pride and joy intact, she dashed inside and breathlessly told the receptionist behind the admissions desk who she was and why she was there.

'Oh, hi, ma'am, we've been expecting you. Mr and Mrs Wilkinson only just made it in time. Go on up to the maternity ward. They can't wait to see you.'

Reunited with the Wilkinson family, Carla watched the man and wife gazing gooey-eyed at the new arrival, a seven-pound baby girl. When Mr Wilkinson spotted her, he jumped up and gave her a massive hug.

'I don't know how to thank you for your kindness and for putting your trust in us.'

'Don't mention it.'

Carla decided it was not the moment to tell them it wasn't her car she'd entrusted them with.

'This is our precious little daughter. She arrived safely, thanks to you. Would you like to hold her?'

'I'd love to.'

Carla made herself comfortable and took possession of the precious little bundle. Clasping the baby protectively to her body, she took in her perfect little face and doll-like features: the cute little snub nose, the downy fluff on her head, her dinky ears and her tiny hands and fingers. Inhaling her sweet smell, she marvelled at the delicacy of a newborn. The child appeared to be staring at her in a knowing fashion, her gorgeous, cobalt-blue eyes penetrating Carla's, as if she'd been on this planet before. A lump rose in Carla's throat, and she choked back tears.

'She's beautiful.'

'What's your name, ma'am?' asked Mrs Wilkinson.

'Carla.'

'That's a perfect name for our baby girl, isn't it, Bobby?'

'Yes, it is,' he agreed.

Carla broke down, tears of joy streaming down her face.

And then there were three – her, the Corvette, and now this perfect little addition to the universe.

'Welcome to the world, Carla Wilkinson,' she whispered.

Recovering herself, she heard Bobby Wilkinson say, 'I thought it was a mirage when I saw you coming. What made you go off the beaten track like that?'

'I wanted to see the Blue Angel Falls.'

Bobby roared with laughter. 'You know we're in a desert, right?'

'Of course, but it sounded like somewhere special.'

'I see. Well, it's just a tiny town of a few houses and nothing else. I guess the founder was a homesick Hawaiian or a Californian with a sense of humour. There are no waterfalls to see, just desert!'

'Oh well, it's good to know I didn't miss anything. Anyway, I wouldn't have seen this little darling if I'd been thinking straight, would I?'

'No, you wouldn't, and I thank the Lord for sending you to us in our hour of need.'

Whatever or whoever had drawn Carla down that road, she didn't know, but it felt like serendipity.

CHAPTER 26

Palm Springs, California

After leaving the hospital, Carla retraced her route to a fancy hotel just outside Palm Springs. It stood alone in the desert, its magnificence incongruous against the arid landscape surrounding it. She decided she'd earned herself some luxury for the evening. The building was elegant in design, and a set of marble steps ascended majestically to two giant doors that framed a grand revolving door. It seemed doubly impressive when compared with some of the small but functional motels that Carla had stayed in over the last few weeks. It was time to spoil herself for a change, and this place was just what the doctor ordered.

Her grimy, windblown hair and crumpled outfit had seen better days. Driving the open road in a convertible was not conducive to looking glamorous, let alone running around on mercy missions. Never mind, her money was as good as anyone's. She mounted the steps, her shoulders back and her head held high, as if daring anyone to stop her. The red carpet beneath her feet might discourage someone more timid, and while it was certainly designed to keep the riff-raff out, she would not be intimidated by the grandeur. At the top of the steps, a snooty-looking doorman in full regalia, his body as straight as a ramrod, stared down at her.

Here we go, Carla thought.

She braced herself and was pleasantly surprised when the man touched his hat and opened the door for her with a cheery, 'Good afternoon, madam.' He spoke with what she swore was an English accent, not unlike the butler's in *Downton Abbey.*

'Thank you,' she said, before strolling through the doorway and stopping dead. Where she was standing could hardly be called a lobby. The hall opened out beneath a magnificent high ceiling, painted in the style of Michelangelo. Then she noticed the marble floors and marble columns. In fact, there was marble all over the place, including several 'Roman' statues that would have looked at home in the British Museum. As if this wasn't enough, an enormous chandelier hung from the ceiling, lights twinkling through exquisite glass. The effect was totally over the top, but it worked. Carla didn't care if she looked like some country bumpkin who'd stumbled in by mistake; she wanted to stand here, drink in the opulent surroundings and admire the décor, the paintings on the walls, the huge leather chairs and the chunky glass coffee tables. It was such a contrast to the last few weeks. She had loved the wilderness and beauty of the spectacular landscapes she had driven through. The remoteness of the little towns she'd stayed in had swallowed her up and made her feel she belonged there. This was her country, her habitat. While this hotel was at the other end of the spectrum, she wasn't in awe of it entirely. She'd stayed in smart hotels while working, but she'd never really looked around, appreciated the splendour, or understood how lucky she was to stay in them. Those hotels were just places to sleep in between business meetings and 'networking', an activity she'd always detested and certainly didn't miss. Well, she damned well would appreciate her good fortune tonight. Carla vowed to relax and enjoy every aspect of the grandeur.

'Can I help you, madam?'

Carla was startled out of her reverie by the concierge, who had noiselessly approached.

'Yes, please. I'd like a room for tonight if you have any vacancies?'

'Of course. I'll take you to the check-in desk and Susan will assist you.'

As Carla approached, 'Susan' looked up from the counter and gave her a broad smile. Carla was immediately struck by the dark-skinned woman's beauty. She had never seen such a combination of facial features before: ebony skin and piercing blue eyes. It gave Susan an ethereal look; she was exquisite yet seemed to be totally unaware of her impact on the people around her.

Five minutes later and five-hundred dollars lighter, Carla stood in the elevator as it cranked its way up to her seventh-floor junior suite, while a bellhop retrieved her luggage and a valet parked the Corvette in the 'safe parking garage'. Carla permitted herself a wry smile, remembering some of the less salubrious places she had spent the night during her travels.

She'd felt a strange connection with Susan she couldn't fathom. Their conversation at the check-in desk had been business-like and impersonal, but when their eyes met, somehow there seemed to be an empathy between them and a feeling of having met before. Carla couldn't put her finger on what it was about Susan that had made such an impact, other than her obvious beauty and penetrating blue eyes. When Susan looked at her, she seemed to be peering into her soul, as if she knew her thoughts and deepest feelings, in the same way identical twins have a deep understanding of each other. They certainly didn't look alike, and Susan was at least ten years younger, but there definitely was a connection. She shook her head and decided she'd spent too much time alone in the sunshine. The open air and solitude must have addled her brain.

Carla stepped into her accommodation and stopped dead for a second time. This was no junior suite – this was a senior, superior, double-plus platinum one. For anyone from Carla's walk of life, five hundred dollars was a lot of money to pay for a room, but no way was this a five-hundred-dollar room, it was more like a five-thousand-dollar one. Whatever it cost, it reminded her of a royal palace back home. She was blown away by the Regency furnishings (reproduction, obviously), the attention to detail in the sitting room and the plush four-poster bed. An enormous bath with vintage-style fittings dominated the centre of the cavernous bathroom. It was perfect: every mod con and all the toiletries anyone could possibly need were ready for her to enjoy. She found a hidden fridge inside a Regency-style cabinet. It was stocked with snacks and a whole array of soft drinks and beverages, as well as a tempting half-bottle of champagne.

There was a knock at the door. Outside stood a bellhop with her luggage.

'There must be some mistake,' Carla blurted. 'I only paid for a junior suite.'

'There's no mistake, ma'am,' the young man replied with a cheeky grin. 'Ms Archer thought you would like this room better.'

'Like it, I love it, but…'

'No buts, ma'am. Enjoy your stay.'

Speechless, Carla scrabbled in her bag, fished out a twenty-dollar note and handed it to him.

'Well, thank you, and please thank Susan for me. I really appreciate it, and I will have a great night here.'

Dazed, Carla moved to the window. Below, the golf course looked out of place: emerald greens, lush fairways and a large lake at its centre – it was an oasis in the desert. The view seemed unreal, and so was this room. Would she wake up if she pinched herself?

Carla couldn't help wondering why so many people had been so exceptionally kind to her. She'd arrived in Chicago feeling downhearted and cynical about mankind, and yet, time after time, perfect strangers had given her so much without expecting anything in return. Gradually, her heart had become lighter, her positivity had returned, and she was grateful for everything she'd experienced so far.

Tom would have loved this hotel, she thought with a pang.

A small knot appeared in her stomach.

Oh, Tom, I miss you.

It was the first time she'd thought about him, or home, for several days, and she was cross with herself for allowing him into her head at that moment, just when she had been given this special treat and an opportunity to spoil herself rotten. She knew she was going to have to face the reality of her broken life soon, but not yet. She wasn't about to let Tom or anyone else spoil this precious time, so she forced her thoughts about him to the back of her mind and relaxed in a warm bubble bath.

Afterwards, swaddled in the fluffy, white robe she'd found hanging on the back of the bathroom door, Carla dried her hair and curled up on the comfy sofa with a cup of rich hot chocolate. It felt good to be clean, with all the grit and grime from the open road well and truly washed out of her hair. Her eyes drooped and she fell into a deep sleep.

* * *

She awoke with a start two hours later to the sound of the ringing telephone.

'Hello,' she answered, drowsily.

'I'm sorry to disturb you, Ms Bright. Our restaurant is almost fully booked for this evening, and I wondered if you required a table?'

'Oh, yes, I do.'

'Seven o'clock suit you?'

'Wonderful, thank you.'

How thoughtful. Carla wondered if Susan had been behind it. She realised she hadn't eaten since breakfast, and she was famished. She had an hour to get ready, which was plenty of time. She was thrilled to have the opportunity to wear the azure, crushed-velvet dress she'd bought from Macy's. It had long sleeves, just reached her knees, and fitted her perfectly, accentuating her good figure without making her look like mutton dressed as lamb. At the time, she'd thought she was crazy for buying such an expensive item of clothing, never dreaming there would be a suitable place for her to wear it, and now she was glad of her recklessness. Time had definitely been kind and her adventures had done her body no harm at all. Her make-up carefully applied and barely noticeable, her hair glossy, her sparkling diamanté jewellery, stiletto heels and matching black patent leather handbag made Carla feel like a million dollars. She had no qualms about dining alone in a fancy restaurant; she had always been good at warding off unwanted attention. She had dressed to please herself and was satisfied that her look, whilst flattering, was not suggestive in any way. She could handle herself, but she would rather avoid any misunderstandings.

* * *

Before making her way to the restaurant, Carla went to the check-in desk and was disappointed to discover that Susan had already gone home. She hoped she would have the chance to thank her in person the following morning.

As expected, the enormous restaurant was every bit as grand as the lobby. It was furnished with matching chandeliers and plush carpets. The tables were covered with crisp, white linen tablecloths, decorated with small vases filled with tiny pink roses, and laid with silver-plated cutlery and cut-glass wine goblets. The lighting was dipped to create an ambient atmosphere. She was thrilled to see a live band playing soft jazz on the stage. She loved jazz, and the music made her feel even more comfortable. The maître d' welcomed her warmly and took her to a delightful table near the stage, close enough to watch the band, offset enough for her not to stick out like a sore thumb. She ordered a large glass of Chablis and sipped it while studying the extensive menu.

Vegetables! Much as she'd enjoyed eating in roadside diners and small-town restaurants, Carla had been appalled at the lack of fresh vegetables on offer. She never thought she would crave steamed broccoli, but her mouth was watering at the prospect. Although the Chablis was delicious, she decided to pace herself, alternating the wine with iced, sparkling water. It wouldn't do to wake up in that glorious bed with a raging hangover.

Carla chose a scallops appetiser followed by a medium-rare fillet steak with pepper sauce, dauphinoise potatoes and a selection of vegetables. The meal was every bit as delicious as she'd hoped. The wine had her feeling mellow, as did the fabulous tunes emanating from the young, up-and-coming band members. She sat back contentedly, enjoying her coffee.

Then, for the first time that evening, she turned around and saw the restaurant was full. She became aware that, three tables away, a middle-aged man was staring at her. He looked like a typical, entitled businessman. In the short time she looked at him, she saw his face had the reddish hue caused by imbibing too much alcohol on a regular basis. She quickly turned her head to the front of the room. She'd met his type on many occasions and knew it would take little encouragement on her part for him to descend and give her the benefit of his wisdom and charm.

A few minutes later, a waiter appeared at her table carrying a glass of champagne on a silver salver. 'Excuse me, ma'am,' he said. 'The gentleman on the table over there sent you this drink with his compliments.'

Without looking round, Carla looked up at the waiter and said coolly, 'Thank you, but I've had my quota of wine for the evening. If he gives you any indication that he is intending to join me, please inform him I wish to remain alone.'

'Of course, ma'am.'

Looking embarrassed and uncomfortable, the waiter shuffled away.

Carla kept her gazed fixed forwards and did not see how the man reacted to the news. Her spirits sunk a little. She had done nothing to attract his attention, let alone give out any signal that she was available. In fact, it had been quite the opposite. Why did some men believe that any lone woman must be in need of company? She knew any new relationship had to start somewhere and that it must be hard for men to make the first move, but this guy was clearly a predator looking for easy prey. No doubt he would go home to his long-suffering wife and complain about his tough business trip. Well, she'd met his kind before and knew how to handle herself. Determined not to let this man ruin her evening, Carla settled back in her chair to enjoy the music, clapping enthusiastically at the end of the show along with the other guests, most of whom had stayed behind after dinner. Carla was relieved to see the man wasn't one of them. She rose from her table, left a generous tip for the waiter and headed for the lobby.

* * *

At the unattended concierge desk, Carla browsed the tourist information booklets looking for ideas for the following day. She didn't know anything about the area and wanted to explore it a little before moving on. She picked up several leaflets, intending to look at them in the morning. By now, the lobby had cleared, and when she walked over to the lift and pressed the button going up, the door opened immediately. She stepped in and was just about to ascend to the seventh floor when a pudgy hand grabbed the doors just as they were about to close.

In stumbled the predator.

Carla darted to the front of the lift to get out, but he blocked her exit and the door closed behind him. Her heart pounded against her chest and blood pumped furiously around her body. She swayed, fighting the urge to pass out.

He leered at her. 'Well, look who we have here.'

At full height, he was bigger than he looked in the restaurant, and meaner. She was right. He was a heavy drinker, and tonight was no exception. Glassy eyed and slightly unsteady on his feet, his face was puce with rage and his voice scornful; Carla realised she was in serious trouble. Screaming would be pointless. The noise from the elevator's heavy mechanism would probably cover any sound she made, and the predator would likely grab her and cover her mouth to silence her. On the other hand, there were no avoidance tactics she could employ; looking away and pretending he wasn't there wouldn't help. He must have hidden out of sight to wait for her. She was his target, and now she was trapped.

Oh, the irony.

All those nights she had spent in rough motels with equally rough-looking guests, and never once had she felt threatened, let alone *been* threatened, and yet here she was in one of the most exclusive hotels in the country with a 'respectable' businessman who clearly had every intention of harming her.

'Who do you think you are, you stuck-up bitch?' he slurred.

Even though he was swaying from the effects of the alcohol, he was sober enough to bar her way from the control panel with its alarm button. Carla remained silent: she didn't want to add fuel to the fire. He'd got her where he wanted her. His ugly personality and sense of entitlement shone through; he was clearly used to getting his own way. She needed to act smart. The chances of anyone being at the lift entrance on the seventh floor were slim to none at this late hour. She guessed he would lunge for her when the lift stopped, and she hoped he hadn't thought his plan through, in which case she'd have a chance to escape.

The lift stopped, the bell pinged and, just as the doors opened, he pounced, hands raised, aiming to cover her mouth. Carla hurled the leaflets in his face, grabbed him by his lapels and brought her knee up, smack into his groin. He wouldn't be making his crown jewels public now. Her dress cushioned the blow, but the connection was still powerful enough to make him yelp and bend double.

He stood up, his face contorted with pain and anger. 'You fucking whore. You'll regret this,' he yelled.

Frantically, Carla opened her bag and removed something.

Then, as her attacker lunged at her, she raised her hand and discharged a canister of pepper spray at him. Screaming, he clutched his face and collapsed onto the lift floor. Carla pressed the button for the lobby, clambered over the crumbled mess in a suit and felt the relief flood through her as the lift doors closed.

Once inside her room, she locked the door and called reception.

'Good evening, this is Claude speaking. How may I help you?'

'Hello, it's Carla Bright here, room 705. The elevator in front of you will be arriving any second. You will find a man in a heap on the floor. He tried to attack me and lost. I'll leave you to deal with him in any way you see fit. Good night.'

She replaced the phone in its cradle and let out a long, slow breath. Then she opened the cabinet in the corner of the sitting room, poured herself a large brandy and took it over to the window. The moonlight glistened on the lake, and eerie shadows on the fairways created a magical atmosphere on the golf course below. A lone man was walking his dog, but otherwise the hotel grounds were devoid of people and traffic. The peace and quiet restored Carla's equilibrium.

Far from spoiling her evening, the incident had empowered her. It had proved she could take care of herself and had been right to go on with this adventure. She was satisfied she had taken revenge on this creep and was certain he'd preyed on many women dazzled by his obvious wealth and smooth talk. He was angry, she believed, because he had misjudged her, but not because she had rejected his advances. In the absence of younger, 'better' material, he'd probably convinced himself that, rather than spend the night alone, he would slum it and settle for the old spinster/divorcee in the corner who had at least made the effort to look good and would be glad of his attention. Carla was proud of herself for her presence of mind, and if she'd removed just one man from the prowl, her actions had been a success.

She finished the last drops of brandy and realised she was desperately tired. She took off her clothes, dropped them on the floor, dragged herself into the huge bed and went straight to sleep.

* * *

Carla was unaware of the sunlight streaming into her bedroom until she awoke at eight o'clock, feeling fully refreshed and ready to face the day. She showered and put on smart black jeans and a flowery top. Ravenous, she headed to the breakfast room. As soon as she exited the lift, Susan rushed over to greet her.

'Ms Bright, I'm so sorry you had such a nasty experience in our hotel last night.'

'Call me Carla. Don't worry, it wasn't the fault of any of the hotel staff, and I'm sure you've heard that I dealt with it quite effectively.'

'We didn't just hear. The night porter took pictures of that drunken fool. We've all seen him slumped and crying in the corner of the elevator surrounded by travel flyers.' She raised her hand for a high five and Carla duly responded.

'What happened to him?'

'Claude called the cops, and they took him away to the city jail. Talking of which, a police officer wants to speak to you. She's coming at nine o'clock if that's OK with you?'

'Yes, of course, but I need to get some breakfast first. I'm starving.'

'Sure thing. Follow me.'

They went to the breakfast room and Susan spoke to a waiter.

'Please make sure Ms Bright is served immediately, Marco.'

'Of course. Follow me to your table, Ms Bright.'

Carla devoured a plateful of scrambled eggs, bacon, sausage, grits and pancakes with maple syrup, all washed down with some excellent coffee. She returned to the lobby and saw a beefy male police officer and a petite policewoman chatting to Susan.

She went over and introduced herself. 'I believe you want to see me?'

'Yes, ma'am. I'm Officer Lena Rock and this is my partner, Jim Beck. Is there anywhere quiet we can go, Susan?'

'Yes, of course. Please come through to the office.'

They all trooped in, and Susan asked the office clerk to leave.

'Please, sit. Would you like some coffee?'

The police officers' eyes lit up. 'Yes, ma'am, and if you can stretch to it, a little something to eat? We've been on shift for hours and could use a little sustenance.'

'Coming right up.'

She returned a few minutes later with a plate of pastries and a pot of hot coffee. She smiled reassuringly at Carla, then slipped out of the room, closing the door behind her.

'We arrested Robert Waters at 12.30am for public intoxication and intimidation, and we've kept him overnight in the city jail. The night porter told us he attempted to assault you. Is that correct?'

'Yes, he did.'

'Please tell us in your own words exactly what happened.'

Carla wasn't exactly sure who else's words she would use, but she didn't voice that thought. Instead, she recounted the story from when she entered the restaurant to the phone conversation with the night porter. She neither embellished the tale nor left anything out.

'Well, ma'am, you seem to have dealt with him rather satisfactorily,' Lena Rock said, a note of admiration in her voice. Officer Beck didn't look quite so sure, but then again, Carla mused, he was probably visualising being kneed in the nuts and his eyes stinging from being pepper sprayed.

'For the record, Mr Waters woke up this morning with a very bad head, and he appears to be contrite. Whatever happens, he won't be allowed to forget his actions anytime soon. An anonymous person phoned his wife and told her everything in great detail. She phoned us from New York and told us to tell him that unless he checks himself into an addiction clinic, she is going to divorce his sorry ass and take him to the cleaners. And judging by the look on his face when I told him this, she means it, too. Do you want to press charges?'

The officers waited patiently while Carla mulled it over.

'Has he been accused of anything like this before?'

'No, ma'am.'

'To be honest, I reckon I was probably the first person to make him angry, not that I think it is my fault in any way. I imagine he believed he'd lowered his standards by targeting a woman older than himself, and he probably considered he was doing me a favour, so when I rejected him, his pride was more sorely tested than if I'd been a bright young thing.'

She shifted in her chair and smoothed imaginary creases in her jeans, momentarily distracted from the memory of the previous evening's events. She brought her mind back into focus and continued with her explanation.

'I'm not excusing his behaviour by the way; I'm just thinking it is probably the first time he has overstepped the mark. If he'd been well practised at it, I wouldn't have been able to overpower him so easily. It sounds like his wife is going to punish him pretty harshly, and if he's definitely going to get help with his alcohol addiction, I don't think it is necessary for me to take it any further, but if you think I should, I will. I would hate to think another woman could suffer if I don't. What do you think?'

She aimed the question at Officer Rock. Officer Beck wisely remained silent.

'Well, when he sobered up, Waters did appear to show genuine remorse, so with your permission, I will recommend he's released from jail this morning, as long as he commits to rehabilitation.'

'Permission granted,' Carla said, secretly relieved she could put the whole thing behind her and move on.

* * *

Seeing Carla exiting the office, Susan approached her.

'Everything OK?'

'Yes, fine. I've agreed not to press charges. His wife is likely to give him the worst punishment unless he agrees to go to rehab, though how she found out about it, I don't know.'

The tension in Susan's face dissolved. She looked relieved; Carla realised the publicity for the hotel might have caused a problem for the management.

'That would be Claude. He was so mad that it happened on his watch that he looked up Mr Waters' home phone number and called his wife. He should be reprimanded, but secretly we all agree with what he did. I'm really sorry you had to go through this experience at our hotel. We are having a staff meeting later, and I shall be putting procedures in place to better protect our lone female guests, starting with instructing our waiters not to take unsolicited drinks to anyone.'

'You?'

'Yes. Pardon me for my subterfuge, I'm actually the hotel manager. I put myself on the frontline from time to time, so I can keep abreast of things.'

'Ah, that explains how you were able to give me that wonderful upgrade, but not why.'

'Oh, that's simple. You walked into the lobby, and I saw you stop and gaze around in wonder. I could tell from your face that you had a deep appreciation for your surroundings. You are the first guest I've seen here in a long time to really look at our fabulous hotel. People are usually so busy, rushing here and there, demanding this and that. They're so secure in their sense of entitlement that they see no need for manners. The master suite was vacant, and I knew you would love it. When your eyes met mine at the desk, I could sense your kindness – and a sadness too – so I decided you deserved a break and let you have it.'

Perhaps there is a telepathic connection between us, Carla thought to herself.

'Thank you so much for your generosity, Susan, the room was fabulous. Anyway, I'd better go and pack, it's nearly time to check out.'

'There's no hurry. The suite is vacant again tonight. After everything that's happened you must stay an extra night, compliments of the management. Unless you have somewhere to be today?'

'No, I've nothing planned. If you're sure, that would be wonderful.'

'Of course. I finish at four. How about I take you out and we'll have something to eat, a few drinks and, with luck, some fun too?'

'I'd love to.'

'OK, meet me in the lobby at four-thirty and we'll go into Palm Springs and paint the town red.'

* * *

Susan took Carla to a sports bar, where they slid into a booth in a quiet corner. Carla was surprised at her choice of venue, and it must have shown on her face.

'You can have too much splendid food and fancy surroundings,' Susan explained. 'Plus, they serve the best ribs and wings in town.'

They ordered cold beers and the special of the day.

'Are we expecting company?' Carla asked, when the platter of ribs, wings, corn cob, baked potatoes and onion rings arrived.

'No, this is just a typical American meal!'

They worked their way through the mound of food until they were fit to burst. As soon as they'd finished, the waitress came over to clear the table.

'Can I get you a dessert?'

Susan and Carla looked at each other, rolled their eyes and groaned.

'No thanks, just a couple more beers please,' said Susan.

They lapsed into a comfortable silence for a few minutes, both lost in their thoughts.

Uncharacteristically forthright, Carla said, 'I don't know anything about you, so tell me about yourself.'

She nodded at the gold band on Susan's left hand. 'I can see you're married.'

Susan smiled wryly and looked at her wedding ring.

'Widowed.'

Carla willed the floor to open up and swallow her.

'I'm so sorry, how clumsy of me.'

'Don't be. I'd like to talk about it. It feels like I've known you forever, and even though we've only just met, it's like we are kindred spirits somehow.'

'That's funny, I feel that connection too. What was your husband's name?'

'Morgan. We were high school sweethearts, got married when we were nineteen. We had our first baby, Lori, a year later, quickly followed by Ben. I know it sounds crass, but it really was a marriage made in heaven. He was a good man, a great husband and a wonderful father. We were truly blessed to be married for twenty years. Of course, we had fights like any normal couple, and it wasn't always easy between us.' She paused, tears pricking her eyes. 'He was killed in a car crash on his way home from work five years ago. It was a drunk driver, who walked away from the accident without a scratch on him. There isn't a day that goes by when I don't think about Morgan.'

'I can't imagine what it's like to lose the one you love so suddenly.'

As she said this, Carla realised that she *did* have some idea how it felt. The pain she'd experienced when Tom walked out was still raw, but it was true that she couldn't envisage how much worse it would be to have lost him in such a brutal, permanent way. What must it be like to kiss your husband goodbye in the morning and for him not to come home in the evening, not because he didn't want to, but because a selfish idiot had taken his life? Carla felt tears welling up in her eyes and instinctively took Susan's hand.

Susan smiled and continued. 'I won't deny it's been really hard coping,' she said. 'But luckily, I have my children, my work and my faith. I have to keep going for Lori and Ben's sakes. My work keeps me busy, and God has given me the strength to carry on.'

Carla had yet to get used to the open way Americans spoke about their faith, which was so opposite to the British way of avoiding the serious issues of politics, religion or earnings. Carla was no exception to the rule, though she was glad that Susan drew comfort from her faith.

'Are your children still at home?'

'Oh no, they've both finished college. Lori is in New York at a publishing company and Ben is in Fresno, doing something techie I don't understand. He's doing well, and he enjoys his work. They both offered to come home after college, and although I would love to have them around, they needed to spread their wings, so I said no.'

'Is it lonely on your own?'

'I don't have time to be lonely. I was pretty much a stay-at-home mom until Morgan passed. Though while the kids were teenagers, I did go to evening classes in hotel management. Not too long after I was widowed, I was lucky to get a job as a desk clerk – I think the recruiter took pity on me. Even so, I worked real hard and had some good ideas about how to improve the running of the hotel. Before I knew it, I was in charge. I love my job, and the long hours suit me. When I work late, I stop over in a little apartment in the attic, so it's all good. Nothing will ever bring Morgan back, but I'm living the best life I can. I'm not ready to date yet, but you never know, I might surprise myself one day.'

'I'm in awe of you. To pick yourself up after such a tragedy is incredible, and your positive outlook is so inspiring.'

Susan leaned forward and caught Carla's gaze. 'So, girl, spill. What's the sadness in your eyes all about?'

Carla hesitated. If this were a game of top trumps, she'd already lost. Her problems paled in comparison to Susan's.

Then again, everything is relative, and she *was* feeling the pain of losing the life she'd had, or thought she'd had. Susan listened carefully while Carla recounted the whole saga from the minute Tom had said, 'I'm going', to the moment she arrived at the hotel.

Afterwards, Susan blew out her cheeks and hooted with laughter. 'Wow, that is some adventure!'

'Yes, it does sound a bit crazy, doesn't it, now I've said it out loud? I promise you, it's all true.'

'I don't doubt it. I know the reasons behind you coming here are sad, but wow, just wow; some people would kill to do what you've done.'

'You're right, I hadn't thought of it that way. It has been quite a trip, hasn't it? I wish Tom was with me, though. It would have been our adventure, and we'd have created memories together.'

'Something doesn't add up here,' said Susan. 'You're a smart woman, and you're empathetic and seem to be in tune with the needs and characteristics of your family. I can't believe you've gotten it so wrong about them. You can't possibly have been that deluded about being in a happy family. Sure, it won't have been perfect, but surely if things were as bad as all that, you would have sensed something was up. I can't help thinking that some wires have been crossed, and that things aren't what you think.'

'But he left without saying anything!' said Carla defensively, 'and he didn't even call to see how I was. And no one else even noticed I was in trouble.'

Carla watched as Susan wrestled with her thoughts.

'OK. We've just become friends, and I hope we can stay friends, but I'm going to go out on a limb here, and if I offend you, I'm sorry. I'm not going to sit here and say, "Poor you." It would be wrong of me not to speak out. You've come a long way since you've been here, but you've still got a little way to go, so I'm going to try and help you get there. I'm blunt, and this won't be pretty, but just hear me out. First, it sounds like it's your own fault that your children are the way they are with you.'

Carla flushed and opened her mouth to defend herself. Seeing an unfamiliar, stern look cross Susan's face, she closed it again and continued listening.

'You obviously love your children, but you were tied up with your career, and that made you feel guilty. So, every free moment you had, you lavished your attention on them and expected nothing in return. Am I right?'

Carla nodded.

'Then after you finished work, you didn't plan what you wanted to do with your life and instead allowed everyone else to fill that time for you. You were culpable in this takeover because it meant you didn't have to look inside yourself and find out what *you* really wanted. It also eased the guilt you were still feeling for, as you saw it, abandoning your children when they were young. Is that true?'

Carla nodded again. 'I hadn't articulated it, but yes, you're right. I did overcompensate for being at work, and I never made many demands on them.'

'Exactly. It's not that they don't care about you – you are their rock, and they can always rely on you to be there for them. They're not consciously selfish, it's just that you have allowed them to be that way. I'll wager you've never displayed any weaknesses in front of them or expected them to take any responsibility. You've been so busy being the glue that holds the family together that you haven't left room for anyone to take care of *you*, or to feel the need to give you any consideration. Does that make sense?'

'Yes, it does.'

'You didn't need to feel guilty about being a working mother. Just because I chose to stay at home with my children doesn't make me a better mom, it's just a different way of parenting. Don't beat yourself up. You clearly love your children, and they know it – that's all that matters. My kids are oversensitive towards me because they lost their dad, and they are constantly trying to protect me. It can be annoying at times, though I do appreciate why they do it. I know if Morgan were still alive, we probably wouldn't hear from them much. They're young, and you remember what it was like at their age, when all that really matters is yourself. I wish they hadn't had to grow up so quickly, but there it is. I can't change it, so I move on the best I can.'

Seeing Carla's mortified look, Susan continued, 'Don't feel sorry for me, Carla, and don't think your problems are insignificant compared to mine because they're not. If my life helps you to get a bit of perspective, then that's all good. In any case, I'm guessing your children won't take you for granted again, you crazy woman!'

Carla grinned at Susan; the mutual fan club was still intact.

'You know your parents are not going to change now. It is what it is, and nothing you do or say will make any difference. So, you need to have a good long think about a level of contact that will sooth your conscience without dragging you down. And as for that girlfriend of yours, she's never been a true friend to you, has she? Why did you start hanging out with her in the first place, let alone hang on to her?'

'Oh, I don't know. I suppose I felt sorry for her when I met her, and if I'm honest, I thought it would make me seem normal if I had a friend.'

'What on earth do you mean by that?'

'I don't really have any friends; I've never felt the need for them. Don't get me wrong, I'm sociable. I've always got on well with my work colleagues, and Tom and I have plenty of people we go out with. It's just I've never felt the need to share my innermost thoughts with anyone. Having Sally as a friend gave me the illusion I did have someone. I've always been self-contained, and Tom and the kids were all I needed.'

'Until now.'

'Yes, until now. And here I am baring my soul to someone I've only just met. Already you feel like a lifelong friend.'

'I feel that way too. It's funny how you meet some people and know instantly it's meant to be. I knew the day I met Morgan I was going to marry him, and he felt the same way about me, or so he told me years later. I sometimes wonder if there was something that drew us together at such a young age, so we still got to spend lots of precious time together before he was taken. Was it love at first sight for you and Tom?'

'Pretty much, and it came out of nowhere. I was pursuing a high-flying career, single and single-minded. I had no intention of getting married, let alone having children, and then he walked into this pub where I was having after-work drinks with some colleagues. He asked me to marry him before he'd even said hello. And the rest, as they say, is history.'

'Can I give you some more advice, Carla?'

'OK,' Carla replied, though she was doubtful.

'You need to call him.'

'I can't.'

'Why not? You clearly still adore the guy, and I can't believe he's fallen out of love with you. You would have had an inkling of it if he had. And if nothing else, you need answers to the questions rattling around in your head. You are nearly at the end of your journey, and at some point, you're going to have to make some decisions about what to do next. How are you going to do that, when so much of your life is unresolved? Talk to him.'

'What about Jane?'

'What about Jane? It can't be any worse than you think. If it turns out she's bewitched him and is the new love of his life, then at least you'll know. And if he really is a coward who ran away with another woman and can't even face his wife to tell her, you'll see he's not the man you thought he was. You will rage and cry until you have no more tears left, and then you will be ready to move on. But you will never move on if you stay in this limbo. And what if it turns out to be just a fling, a midlife crisis, and the guilt and shame made him go? If so, I bet he already regrets it and wants to come home. Of course, you've got every right to be mad at him, but if he still loves you just as much as you still love him, can't you find it in your heart to forgive him? Call him.'

'I'll think about it,' Carla replied, almost in a whisper.

'OK, that's a start. You still have the chance to talk to Tom. I wish I could speak to Morgan, but anyway, enough of this doom and gloom. I said we were going out for some fun, so let's go and find some.'

They left the sports bar and walked to another bar, which was rowdy with people shouting at the TV.

'Hey, Susan,' called one person after another.

'Hey, everyone, this is Carla,' she replied, trying to make herself heard above the noise.

They pushed past the throng to get to the bar and, miraculously, found two empty seats. Susan ordered two beers from a dumbstruck barman, seeming not to notice his discomfiture. Carla chuckled inwardly. How was it possible that Susan was oblivious to the effect she had on people? Heads had turned as she glided through the doorway, her shapely body swaying from side to side. With her silky-smooth ebony skin, high cheekbones and bewitching blue eyes, how could she not know she was one of the most beautiful women on the planet?

'Don't worry, it'll quieten down in a couple of minutes,' Susan said.

Suddenly, there was a cheer. The game was over, and there was a stampede for the door as the sports fans headed home, leaving the bar empty.

'Well, Susan, you sure know how to show a girl a good time!'

'Patience. A new crowd will be in soon. It's karaoke night.'

'What is it with you Americans and karaoke?'

'This one is different, you'll see,' said Susan, piquing Carla's interest.

As promised, the bar soon filled, and Carla was amazed to see the line of people waiting to sign up to sing. At karaoke nights back in England, the DJ spent most of the evening begging for volunteers to get up and strut their stuff. It was only when they were paralytic that anyone would come forward, and if they didn't fall off the stage, they were so legless they couldn't read the song lyrics properly. Then at last orders, a fight would break out over the microphone when everyone wanted to sing at the same time.

The first act took to the stage, a muscular man, who Carla guessed was in his mid-twenties. The music started, and a respectful hush filled the room as he began to sing. This was definitely not like karaoke in England.

Carla stared at Susan in amazement and said, 'He's got the voice of an angel! If my eyes were closed, I would swear it was a woman singing.'

The haunting song came to an end and the audience cheered. Both Susan and Carla fought back tears.

'That was beautiful,' said Susan.

'Yes, it was. Do you know him?'

'No, I don't know many of these singers. They come from out of town.'

The man was heading their way.

'Excuse me,' Carla said.

'Yes, ma'am?'

'That was amazing. You've got a beautiful voice.'

'Thank you,' he replied, looking pleased.

'I didn't recognise the song. What was it?'

'It's called "Wings of a Dove".'

'Wow, you are so talented. Congratulations.'

'Thanks again. I'm just hoping I can make a career out of it. I'm on leave from the Marines based in Pendleton, and I heard this bar was a great place to hang out, so here I am. I'm auditioning for *America's Got Talent* next week, and if that doesn't work out, maybe someone else in LA will spot me.'

'Good luck, you deserve it,' Carla said, before turning to Susan. 'Well, I've never heard anything like it. The rest of the singers are going to be a let-down after that performance.'

'I doubt they'll reach those dizzying heights, but I think you'll be pleasantly surprised.'

And Carla was. They sat at the bar, giving each act their full attention, and dishing out well-deserved applause. After a while, Carla became aware that the performers were looking over at her expectantly. She gave each one the thumbs up and clapped.

One woman came over and said, 'How did I do?'

'Er, yes, you were great, thank you.'

The woman moved on, beaming.

'Excuse me, ma'am,' said another burly Marines type. 'My pal and I do a mean "Piano Man". Would you like to hear it?'

'Um, yes, I'd love to, thank you.'

And they did indeed do a mean rendition of the Billy Joel hit, all of it directed at Carla and Susan.

'How was that?'

'Fantastic,' Carla replied. She was starting to feel uncomfortable.

'What's going on?' she asked Susan. 'Why do they all keep asking my opinion?'

'Oh, Carla, I'm sorry.' Susan was so helpless with laughter that she struggled to get the words out. 'When you were in the restroom, they asked me who you were, so I told them you were a talent scout from London.'

'You didn't!'

'I did.'

'We'll get shot if they find out the truth. Let's get out of here.'

Carla raced outside, and when Susan caught up with her, she was holding her sides, tears of laughter running down her cheeks.

'Oh, come on, you've got to admit it was funny. They were all good, but they were taking themselves far too seriously.'

Once they were at a safe distance, Carla stopped and joined in with Susan's laughter.

'What are you trying to do to me? I don't want to be talking to the police twice in one day.'

'I know, I'm sorry. I just couldn't resist it,' Susan replied, still giggling. 'Let's go back to the hotel for a nightcap.'

A taxi dropped them off at the hotel entrance. Susan grabbed hold of Carla and they climbed the steps arm in arm, looking like they'd been friends for life.

* * *

Next morning, a valet brought the Corvette round to the front of the hotel.

'I took the liberty of giving her a clean and polish, Ms Bright. A car like this needs as much attention as a good woman.'

Carla shook her head, pursing her lips in mock disapproval before generously tipping him.

'It's time to say goodbye,' she said to Susan, sadly.

'I guess so. Keep in touch, won't you?'

'Of course I will.'

They hugged each other tight, and Susan turned away. Halfway up the steps, she looked over her shoulder. 'Call him!' she cried.

Then she turned back, ran up the remaining steps, pushed against the revolving door and was gone.

CHAPTER 27
Santa Monica, California

T he final stretch of Route 66 proved to be terrifying, boring and depressingly urban in equal measure. The Mother Road was lost in the annals of time, swallowed up by I-40, I-15 and other motorways. Carla ventured onto yet another freeway in error and struggled to find her way out of the tangle of tarmac spaghetti to get back on track. She was conscious she mustn't flip off any crazy LA drivers in case they pulled a gun on her. Her blood pressure was through the roof and her heart was beating like a metronome on speed. If one more idiotic driver cut across all six lanes from the central reservation to the exit in front of her, she was sure she'd have a heart attack. Oh, and the noise of it all, and the fumes – suddenly, an open-top car didn't seem so smart after all. Thank goodness she hadn't started her journey this side of the country, otherwise she'd have been on the next flight home with her tail between her legs.

Eventually, she pulled into the car park next to Santa Monica Pier, switched off the engine, closed her eyes and took several deep breaths. Calm once more, she opened her eyes...

and couldn't believe what she saw. In the next parking lot was a man in skis, complete with goggles and a woolly hat, flying forty feet in the air. On second glance, Carla saw that he was attached to a winch on a crane. It was almost ninety degrees Fahrenheit and here was a skier, in the air, at the beach, being filmed. Yup, she was in La La Land all right.

Carla strode to the pier and soon found the sign she was looking for: 'Santa Monica, 66, End of the Trail.'

'Excuse me, sir. Would you take a picture of me, please?' she asked a young passer-by.

'Sure.'

He shot several photos of Carla standing by the sign, capturing her beaming face and clear pride in her achievement.

'Did you drive all the way from Chicago?'

'I did indeed.'

'That's sick,' he said, leaving a puzzled Carla staring after him as he walked away.

She spent the rest of the afternoon meandering around Venice and people-watching. There was plenty to see, especially the body builders displaying their well-oiled physiques on the gym equipment at Muscle Beach. Goodness, it was enough to get anyone hot under the collar.

* * *

Back at the car, Carla looked for the scrap of paper with Martha's phone number on it.

'You have reached the phone of Martha Brady. I can't take your call right now, please leave a message.'

'Um, hi. My name's Carla Bright, Olivia's friend. She said I was to call you when I got to Santa Monica. And I am.' As she spoke, she rolled her eyes at the inanity of her last comment.

She sat on the beach wondering what to do next. It all felt

rather anti-climactic, and her mind started drifting to Tom, and how she wished she was enjoying the sunshine and the LA madness with him. She was eventually distracted from her maudlin thoughts by a statuesque model in a handkerchief-sized bikini. A photographer yelled instructions at her while she attempted to sexily lick an ice cream, but it was melting faster than she could eat it. The cream was running down her arm while a Pomeranian dog circled her legs, tangling his lead around her ankles.

Carla shook her head.

Definitely as mad as a box of frogs – all of them.

Just then her phone rang. She didn't recognise the number so answered it tentatively.

'Oh, hi, ma'am,' said a cheery voice. 'My name is Annie. I'm Ms Brady's PA. She's real sorry she can't be here to meet you but she's in Montana, on location.'

'On location?'

'Yes, ma'am. She's directing her new movie there.'

Directing? Wow, Olivia hadn't mentioned that her cousin was a bigshot film director in LA, though she should have got the clues. If she lived in Malibu, it was odds-on she would be part of Hollywood's royalty.

'Oh, how lovely for her.'

'I don't think she'd put it like that. She hates being away from home. Anyway, she won't be back for some time, so she wants you to have the run of her house for as long as you want.'

'Really? That's so kind of her. Thank you, I'd love that.'

Carla's initial reluctance to accept hospitality from strangers had gone west – figuratively and literally. She wasn't about to turn down the opportunity of staying in a film celebrity's house.

'Great, where are you?'

'Santa Monica beach.'

'Oh good, that's close by. Meet me at the house in fifteen minutes.'

Carla noted the address and directions, jumped into the Corvette and drove north along the Pacific Coast Highway. With a mounting sense of excitement, she arrived at her destination and turned into the driveway, where Annie was waiting for her. The house was big, but it wasn't in the same league as the Beverley Hills properties she'd seen on TV and had been expecting to find.

'Hello, Ms Bright. Why, that's a beautiful car you have.'

'Indeed, she is. She's looked after me all the way from Oklahoma. She's called Carla, the same as me, and she belongs to Martha's cousin's husband. They've been so kind to me. It obviously runs in the family, as Nancy's sister took me in and now Martha's doing the same.'

'She's never done anything like this before. I was surprised, I can tell you. You must be a special lady for Ms Brady to open her home to you. She is such a private person, so she rarely has anyone to visit what she refers to as her sanctuary.'

'Then I feel very honoured, and I promise I will take care of the place while I'm here.'

'Stay as long as you like. I have to run, so I'll just leave you the key to get in. The alarm is switched off. You can park the car in the garage and there are provisions in the kitchen. Help yourself to anything you want, and if you need anything else, just give me a call.'

Annie left in her little car and Carla watched as the electric gates closed behind her. She was surprised to see the garden was small and easy-care. Most of it was block-paving, edged with borders filled with colourful, sweet-smelling hibiscus. The beautiful red flowers stood out against the white stuccoed walls. She couldn't wait to find out what was behind the heavy oak doors in this fortress of a house.

She let herself in and was immediately struck by the calm atmosphere: no wonder Martha called this her sanctuary. She gazed around in wonder at the high-ceilinged, white-walled entrance hall. A spectacular spiral staircase at its centre was lit by a modern, crystal chandelier, which dangled majestically from the roof. To her left was a small, functional study and to her right a large yoga studio, which was fully kitted out with equipment, mats and even singing bowls and gongs. She admired a giant mural of the Himalayas and the state-of-the-art entertainment system fixed to the opposite wall. A small statue of Laughing Buddha crouched in the corner. She inhaled the aroma of lavender and felt the tension from the manic drive around Los Angeles disappear from her body.

Walking into the room at the back of the house, she gasped. It was a giant space that covered the whole width of the house. To the left, a sitting area was tastefully decorated and furnished exclusively in white, and to her right was a vast, gleaming kitchen with red cupboard doors, black granite tops, a pristine Aga and a triple-sized refrigerator. An enormous island dominated the centre of the room and brand-new copper pans hung from a rack overhead. Impressive as all this was, the *pièce de résistance* was the view. The whole of the back wall comprised floor-to-ceiling glass, creating the illusion of a giant painting of the ocean.

This wonderful house had its own access to a private beach and an uninterrupted view of the sea. Had there been anyone to talk to, Carla would have been lost for words. She had never been in such a beautiful house before. She could never have dreamt of such a place, and yet, bizarrely, she knew she belonged here. She couldn't quite put her finger on what it was about this house, but she knew it would protect and comfort her. She opened the side door and stepped onto the decking, took off her shoes, skipped down the steps onto the sand and ran into the cool water. The waves lapped gently over her feet as she gazed out to sea, becoming aware of a strange sensation that she realised was contentment. It didn't make sense when there was still so much to be resolved in her life. For now, though, she would just enjoy the moment.

CHAPTER 28
Malibu Beach

S everal days passed without Carla ever leaving the property. She relaxed on the deck, swam in the sea and consumed the plentiful supplies in the fridge. Best of all, she slept for hours in the comfortable and comforting bed upstairs, snuggled under a feather duvet, and woke every morning to the ocean view, which was visible through the curtain-free patio door.

In the studio, Carla tried to follow a YouTube meditation session and found it unsatisfactory. To get in the right frame of mind for meditation, she felt she needed someone with her in the room, not some random person on a TV screen. She was fascinated by the bronze and crystal singing bowls on the floor next to the Himalayan wall. They were so beautiful to look at and she wondered what they would sound like in full flow. On the cork board in the kitchen, she'd noticed a business card advertising the personal services of a yoga instructor, healer and sound bath expert. Carla wondered whether she dare invite a stranger into another stranger's home to spend time doing unfamiliar things with her. Why not? After everything else she'd done lately, she was past worrying about making a fool of herself. Carla dialled the number.

'Hello, LA Shanti Sound and Yoga, Loki speaking. How may I help you?'

'Hi, my name's Carla Bright. I'm staying at Martha Brady's house in Malibu, and I found your business card —'

'Oh, Martha didn't mention anything about a house sitter when she told me she was going to Montana.'

'I'm not exactly house sitting. Martha is kindly letting me stay for a while. I was wondering if you were available to come and perform a sound bath for me?'

'It must be your lucky day! I'm usually fully booked for months ahead, but I've just had a cancellation for tomorrow at 5pm, if that suits you. We'll need three hours together, otherwise you won't get the full benefit. We'll sit and talk first so I can get to know you and understand your needs. Does that work for you?'

'That would be lovely, thank you.'

'You're welcome. See you tomorrow, then.'

* * *

The following morning, Carla opened the door to an impossibly beautiful woman – a real, live 'California Girl'. In fact, she was probably the most beautiful woman Carla had ever seen, although Susan came a pretty close second. Not only was she tall with a perfect body, she exuded an air of peace and tranquillity.

'Come on in,' said Carla, ushering her into the sitting room. 'Would you like to sit here or go outside?'

'Let's start outside, so we can enjoy the sound of the ocean.'

Loki repositioned two chairs on the deck and sat opposite Carla, her never-ending legs stretching out in front of her. The late-afternoon sunshine made her appear even more gorgeous. It occurred to Carla that Loki's usual customers would be celebrities and film stars. Old Carla would have been intimidated by this incredible woman, but New Carla relaxed, conscious of how far she'd come.

'So, tell me about yourself.'

Encouraged by Loki's calm voice, Carla spent the next ten minutes imparting information about her life. Loki leaned forward and looked at her closely. Her penetrating blue eyes seeming to peer right into her soul.

'OK, so you've given me your resume. How about you tell me what's actually going on with you?'

Carla couldn't hide her astonishment.

'Come on, you're like an open book, spill!'

So, she did.

When Carla had finished talking, Loki was silent for a moment, before saying, 'Thank you for sharing everything with me. It's certainly been an exciting time for you, and despite all the trauma you seem pretty grounded and in a good place. You've already worked out for yourself most of what you need to address, and I can help you to jump the final hurdle.

'We'll start with some Reiki to release the physical tension in your body, then we'll move on to a guided meditation to clear your mind, and we'll finish off with a sound bath. How does that sound?'

'What's Reiki?'

'That's a great question. Reiki is an energy healing technique, which can relieve pain and tension and reduce stress. I will use a gentle touch to deliver energy to your body and improve its flow to support healing. You will probably feel heat, tingling and maybe a pulsing sensation, and you may even fall asleep.'

Old Carla would have been sceptical, but New Carla had learnt to accept so many things, however odd they might seem, and this was no exception.

'It sounds amazing.'

'It is. It's fortuitous that tonight is a full moon, which is a time for letting go of things that no longer serve you – it will make our meditation session an even stronger experience than usual. Are you ready for this?'

'I am, I really am.'

'So, let's get to it. Go and change into something loose and comfortable and I'll get the studio ready.'

When Carla came downstairs again, she was wearing harem trousers and a loose, multi-coloured top she'd bought on impulse in Chicago. At the time, she hadn't a clue where she would get to wear them, but she was drawn to buy them anyway.

Loki had created a welcoming space, with a treatment table on one side of the room and two yoga mats spread out on the floor. The sound bath equipment was in position ready for the feast of harmony to come, and Carla decided the distinctive aroma of lavender was a good omen. She settled herself on the treatment table and Loki covered her with a light blanket.

'Close your eyes and relax,' she instructed.

Carla did as she was told, and she soon felt the power of Loki's touch. Heat transferred onto her body and her skin went goosepimply. Becoming more relaxed by the minute, she soon drifted off to sleep.

Aware that Loki was gently shaking her, Carla opened her eyes. Loki touched her lips with her index finger and gestured for her to get off the table. She motioned for her to lie down on the mat, covered her body with another, fluffier blanket, and placed a little purple cushion over her eyes. Then Carla heard Loki settle herself on her own mat.

'I want you to take three deep breaths, paying attention to the movement and direction of your breathing. If you find your mind beginning to wander, bring it back to your breathing. We are going to practise Yoga Nidra together. The English translation is yogic sleep, but you need to remain awake, just at the edge of consciousness.

'Before we start, I want you to think of a *sankalpa*, which is an intention expressed in just a few words to bring about a positive change in your life. When I tell you to, repeat it in your mind, not to me. Say it as though it has already happened.'

Carla thought for a moment and settled on, *I am happy, healthy and fulfilled*.

Loki began the practice. Her silky-smooth voice was hypnotic, and Carla's already relaxed body melted further into the mat. Then, as Loki guided her through the different parts of her body, any remaining tension she'd been holding on to was miraculously released. She drank in the instructor's voice until she was able to let go of all external thoughts. All the while, she hovered on the edge of sleep without succumbing to it, completely at peace.

Loki padded across the room and began to play the bronze Tibetan and crystal singing bowls, softly at first before gradually raising the volume. The beautiful sounds penetrated Carla's body and took her to another level of awareness, the vibrations making her tingle all over. Right at the moment she really felt herself drifting off to sleep, Loki moved onto the gongs, just the small ones at first. The sound was enough to bring Carla back into the room. Loki then shifted to the larger gong, which she began to stroke with her wand. She started slowly and gently before gradually increasing the speed and ferocity, the reverberations getting stronger and stronger until they reached an almighty crescendo, bouncing off the walls and crashing around inside Carla's ribs. Her whole body reacted to the sound and to the incredible power of the vibrations. Carla had never felt anything like it, and she didn't want it to end. When it did, she felt relaxed and at peace with the world, almost as if she was floating on air.

As Loki rose to leave, Carla remembered the important issue of money. Crikey, she hadn't even asked Loki how much all this was going to cost and, thinking about the usual super-rich clients she saw, she wondered how much the experience would set her back. No matter. Whatever it was, it was worth it for how she felt.

'Thank you so much for such a wonderful experience. I feel amazing.'

'I'm so glad to hear that,' said Loki with a beatific smile.

'How much do I owe you?'

'Nothing at all. It's been my pleasure. Martha has done so much for me over the years, and this is my chance to pay it forward.'

Carla was stunned by Loki's generosity. 'That's really kind of you, thank you so much.'

'You are so welcome. The only thing I ask is that you continue to meditate and keep repeating your *sankalpa*; I guarantee that whatever it is, it will happen.'

And with that, Loki was gone.

Totally elated and utterly exhausted by the experience, Carla tumbled into bed, falling into a deep, restorative sleep.

* * *

From her bed, Carla savoured the spectacle of the beautiful morning sky, the clear blue sea and the powdery white sand. The open doors let in the sound and smell of the ocean. She could get used to this. She *had* got used to this. After yesterday, she was fully restored, her mind and body at one with each other. She eased herself out of bed and moseyed onto the balcony. She stretched her body to its limit and breathed in deeply, inhaling the cool sea air. She watched, fascinated, as a flock of grey pelicans flew in line with the shore, so close to the water they were almost touching the surface. She felt like she could stand here forever, but she knew this couldn't go on indefinitely: it was time to think about her future.

She had come so far and done things that only a few weeks ago she would not have believed possible. She'd learnt so much and been overwhelmed by the kindness of strangers. It had been an incredible adventure, one that could have gone disastrously wrong or been a serious disappointment. But since meeting Nancy and Merle, she'd had a strange feeling of being protected, as though she had a guardian angel looking over her, keeping her safe. All the people she had encountered along the route seemed to have appeared out of nowhere, just when she'd needed them. They had supported her physically and emotionally, guiding her along the way. They may have been strangers, yet she often got the feeling she knew them. Every one of them had been selfless, helping her while demanding nothing in return. Carla thought of them all with fondness: Robyn, Nancy, Merle, Curtis, Olivia, Susan, Ryan, Chris, Martha, Loki and Randy – yes, even Randy – and she was grateful to them all. They were all such different people and yet somehow the same.

It hadn't all been one-way traffic. In her own way, she'd given something back and paid favours forward, too. It hadn't just been a tourist jaunt, though there was no denying her enjoyment at visiting so many attractions and historical landmarks. She had been brought to tears by the wondrous landscape of the Grand Canyon and from learning about the trials and tribulations of the Okies. Nothing had moved her more than holding her tiny little namesake in her arms. Carla was proud of the part she had played in the baby's safe delivery, and in return, the child had reminded Carla that her life was of value. Then there was Pandora's Grandpop and all the people who had been so excited when she drove by. It had been wonderful to bring a smile to so many faces, and she felt it was serendipity that had brought about these opportunities.

Absentmindedly, she picked up the photo frame from the bedroom dresser, admiring the diamante-encrusted edging. It held a photo of a young woman, taken, Carla guessed, several years ago. Was this Martha? She studied the photo closely. The woman was attractive, though not in an obvious way, and she had a kind face. There was something about her that seemed familiar, and after a while Carla realised what it was.

Her eyes.

Martha's beautiful, startling blue eyes. That was the connection. Everyone who had helped her had had blue eyes… the same blue eyes. That was why they'd all seemed familiar to her: she'd been looking at the same eyes ever since meeting Robyn at the concert in Chicago. Even baby Carla had them. Awareness gave way to confusion as Carla realised how crazy all this sounded. It was ridiculous, yet she couldn't shake off the feeling it had been one person all along. Maybe she did have a guardian angel after all. And maybe that angel had taken over the bodies of all these people to help Carla find her way. The thought sent shivers down her spine and a pang to her heart. When she left home, she'd had no idea what adventures and powerful experiences awaited her. She felt immense gratitude for having the courage to embark on this voyage of self-discovery, and now she was finally ready to move on with her life.

* * *

Carla awoke with a start, feeling confused and disorientated. She looked around the room and her eyes focused on the dresser. The picture frame wasn't there. She realised she'd been dreaming, and yet it was such a powerful, vivid dream, enough for it to seem real. She couldn't quite shake off the feeling there might be some truth in it. Did it matter either way? Whether some divine intervention had taken place, or whether she'd just been lucky to meet some very special people who happened to share the same optical characteristics wasn't important. In their own ways, they had all saved her and encouraged her to find herself again. She thought of Susan. Her ethereal quality had made such an impression on her, and even though they weren't together now, she could really feel her presence.

'Call him,' she heard her saying.

Carla realised it was time. She knew she couldn't avoid the conversation any longer. The rest and reflection at the end of her journey had given her the mental and physical strength she needed. She had been lost, too fragile to think about the future, but now she had found herself, and she felt strong enough to handle whatever Tom had to say, assuming he would agree to talk to her at all.

Her mind clear, she realised she was no longer afraid to speak to him. Did she still love him? Yes. Could she find it in her heart to forgive him? Probably, but she would not do so unconditionally. Things would have to change. She was not prepared to go back to being Old Carla, who had been taken for granted by her family for far too long. If Tom fell short of her expectations, she was prepared to start a new life on her own. She knew she wanted him, though. The question was, did he want her? What if he was happier with his new life? She knew speculating was pointless. She needed to know what had happened to cause him to leave, and the only way she was going to find out was to call him.

She showered, dressed, drank two cups of coffee, dithered, brushed her hair, dithered, sat on the sofa, dithered, stood up and stepped outside. She sat on the beach and stared out to sea. Unable to put it off any longer, she took a deep breath and dialled her husband's number.

* * *

'Hello,' said a bleary voice.

Carla realised she had completely forgotten about the eight-hour time difference and woken him up.

'Hello, Tom, it's me.'

'Carla?' His voice was now alert. 'Where are you? I've been so worried about you.'

'You have?'

'Yes, of course I have, we all have. Where are you?'

'I'm in California.'

'California? Well, I didn't see that coming.'

'We need to talk.'

'Yes, we do, but I don't want to do it over the phone. Tell me where you're staying, and I'll get the next plane out. Are you OK?'

'I'm fine. I'll text you the address. Let me know when you land at LAX. You'll need to get a taxi from the airport.'

As neither of them knew what else to say, they rang off. Carla felt glad Tom was coming to see her. If their marriage was over, it needed to end face-to-face. However, she wasn't sure she wanted Tom to come to Martha's house. She was afraid it might spoil the magic, the aura of the place. She felt calm and secure here. Then again, surely Tom would be moved by this beautiful house, too. If nothing else, it might ease the tension between them and help them behave like civilised adults.

She mulled over their brief conversation, trying to work out what he wanted to say to her and gauge his mood. He'd given little away, and though she wished she'd pushed him, she knew he was right: this conversation was far too important to be conducted remotely.

Was he going to tell her he was staying with Jane, or was he going to admit that leaving was a big mistake and beg for her forgiveness? If it was the former, there was nothing she could do about it. But as Susan had said, at least she would know.

Unable to infer anything from the tone in his voice, she decided there was little point in going over the different scenarios in her head. All she could do now was wait.

CHAPTER 29
The Pacific Ocean

C arla had butterflies in her stomach as she went to answer the door.

How the hell was all this going to play out?

Catching sight of herself in the hallway mirror, she paused briefly to inspect her reflection. Her short-sleeved, floral-print dress accentuated her trim figure, while her elegant diamanté sandals showed off her shapely legs. She was pleased to see that despite the weeks of exposure to wind, sun and dirt, her hairstyle was holding up. She wore only a touch of mascara and a hint of lipstick: it was all she needed. Since arriving at Martha's, Carla had raided her fridge of its healthy contents while avoiding her vast wine collection. The lifestyle had been good for her, and she had a clear and glowing complexion as well as a taut tummy. The knowledge that she was looking good helped to settle her nerves.

Let's get this over and done with, she thought, pulling open the big oak double doors.

Tom appeared to have shed a few pounds, too, but his eyes

had a haunted look. As soon as he set them on Carla, his jaw dropped and his eyes widened in surprise.

'Wow!'

Carla blushed, and it took her a moment to gather herself. 'Come in, come in,' she eventually said, conscious that her voice was too loud.

Awkwardly, he stepped over the threshold, and his eyes widened once more. 'What a place! How did you get it?'

'It's a long story. Come through to the beach and I'll get you a drink.'

He followed her along the cavernous hallway, through the kitchen and outside onto the deck. Tom stared, flabbergasted, at the spectacular view of the beach and the Pacific Ocean. The orange sun had begun its descent towards the horizon, its rays forming a shimmering pathway on the water.

'Beautiful, isn't it?' Carla whispered.

He nodded, clearly speechless. She motioned for him to sit down on one of the luxurious patio seats.

'Beer?'

'Yes, please.'

She went back inside, leaving him alone with the view and his thoughts.

Standing in the kitchen, she realised she was shaking.

Breathe, Carla, breathe.

She took a few minutes to calm herself, then returned to the deck with a bottle of beer, an empty frosted tumbler and a large glass of cold Californian white wine, all balanced precariously on a silver tray. She placed the bottle and tumbler on the table in front of Tom and sat on the chair next to him, side on, facing out to sea. She wasn't ready to look him in the eye.

A few moments of awkward silence ensued as they each

wondered where to begin. Then Tom asked, 'So, tell me now, how did you end up in this incredible house?'

Carla collected her thoughts before replying, 'In the grand scheme of things, this house is irrelevant. It belongs to a very kind person I haven't even met. She's letting me stay here for a while.'

Her voice was stilted, and she was convinced Tom must be able to hear the pounding of her heart. 'I'll tell you about it another time.'

She looked at him surreptitiously, wondering if there *was* going to be another time. His face gave nothing away.

Let's just get to the point, Carla decided.

'You owe me an explanation, Tom,' she said, 'but before I hear it, I want you to know what happened to me after you left.'

He winced.

'And then you will understand why I ended up here.'

'OK, I'm listening,' he said quietly.

'After you'd gone, I fell apart. I can't remember anything about the following few days, and when I finally dragged myself out of bed and began to pull myself together, I realised no one had noticed my absence: not you, not Mum and Dad, not James or Emili, and not Sally. I was broken and no one cared. I could have been dead, and none of you would have known.'

Tom looked stricken. He started to speak, but Carla held up her hand. 'Please, Tom, there will be plenty of time for you to have your say when I'm finished.'

He nodded, sat back and gave her his full attention.

'One by one, I received phone calls from everyone except you. Initially, my heart lifted, but no one asked me how I was or what I'd been doing. They all wanted me to do something for them, and none of them even had the courtesy of engaging in small talk first. For once in my life, I didn't agree to their demands and cut them all short, yet they neither noticed nor cared that my behaviour was strange, and not one of them called me back. They were so wrapped up in their own lives it never occurred to them that my unusual behaviour was a cry for help. I felt so alone, so unwanted. My whole life playing happy families was a lie… a sham. I couldn't understand how you could walk out on me like that, and when I discovered you had someone else —'

'But that's —'

Carla turned and glared at Tom. He snapped his jaw shut.

'I just couldn't comprehend how I'd got it so wrong. I hit a low point, and I had no idea what to do or where to go. There was no one in this world I could turn to. Then I had a light-bulb moment. I dug out the plans I'd made for us to do Route 66 together. As you well know, I'd already done all the legwork for it – I just had to wait until you retired so I could book the flights. Well, you weren't going to be there to do it with me, so I thought, what the heck, I'm going to do it anyway, and when I'm done, I'll think about what to do with the rest of my life.

'So, here I am. Over two and a half thousand miles and one hell of an adventure later, I'm looking at the beautiful sun setting over the ocean and wondering what I'm going to do next.

'I called you because I realised I couldn't move forward without finding out what happened to us first. Only then can I begin to make a new life for myself.'

Carla had run out of steam and fell silent. Tom slumped back in his chair looking dejected, apparently lost for words. A chasm of silence opened between them and only the sound of the waves and the gulls calling out punctured the deathly stillness.

Carla gazed at the ocean. The gigantic sun was now low in the blood-red sky and reflected in the shimmering sea. The glitter in the water caught the fins of a pod of dolphins as they swam by and surfed the waves. The romantic beauty of this picture seemed incongruous with the tension between them.

'Carla, I am so sorry. I didn't mean for all of this to happen. I've been so stupid and, as usual, trying to do the right thing has ended up with me totally messing everything up.'

He reached into his pocket, pulled out a crumpled letter and handed it to her.

'What's this?'

'I wrote this letter to you on the day I left. I know I acted rashly, but even so, I couldn't understand why you weren't there when I came home. When I tried to call you, your phone was switched off, and then I found it in a drawer with your wedding ring. That's when I got scared. You never go anywhere without your phone, and leaving your ring seemed like an over-reaction.'

Carla bristled.

'I should have known you wouldn't understand. I was so stupid. Why on earth I didn't talk to you first, I'll never know. It never occurred to me that you might leave the house you love so much. I panicked. I phoned everyone I could think of to try and find out where you were, but no one knew. I had no idea how to find you and no way of knowing if you were alright. I was frantic. This is so unlike you. You've always been reliable, so dependable.'

'How dare you—' It was her turn to interrupt.

'Please, Carla, let me finish,' Tom implored. 'I couldn't understand what was going on. I was paralysed with fear wondering what might have happened to you, and I got into quite a state. I soon discovered Scotch wasn't the answer to my troubles. I can't tell you how relieved I was when James phoned me with news of your postcard. It gave me hope.

'Thank God you hadn't walk through the door at that moment – you'd have surely turned tail and run for the hills if you had! Both me and the house looked a right state, but I cleaned myself up and then made a start on the kitchen. I was wiping the table down rather too enthusiastically when I knocked a mug over and sent it flying. It smashed to smithereens on the floor, and it was when I was kneeling to clear it up that I saw my letter to you. Before I went, I left it on the table, propped up against the wall, but somehow it had fallen down the back of it, out of sight. I picked it up and realised what had happened. You must have thought I'd lost my mind, walking out without a by your leave. Then it got worse. I found a card from Jane in the bin. No wonder you cleared off. I feel ashamed for being such a coward and causing you so much pain.'

He paused and glanced at her. She turned towards him and saw a lost boy.

'Please read the letter. It explains everything,' he pleaded.

She stared at him, wondering how on earth he thought a letter was going to solve anything. Anger and resentment were rising. He'd put her through so much, and now he'd travelled all this way to give her a letter. It looked like he wasn't planning to shack up with 'the lovely Jane' for good, which was something, she supposed. But how could he have walked out, and then been shocked to find the house empty when he deigned to return from his tryst with that woman?

The sheer arrogance of the man.

She gripped the letter, ready to rip it up and throw it back at him. Who did he think he was?

And yet… and yet his body language was giving off a

different vibe – one of a man who was anxious, beaten. If nothing else, she owed it to herself to find out what was in the letter that made Tom believe it would explain everything. She sighed, inhaled deeply, then slowly opened the envelope and looked down at the familiar handwriting.

Dear Carla,

I know I'm going to look like a coward for writing you a letter instead of talking to you, but if I talk to you, I'm not sure you will listen... really listen to me. I feel I've got to do this, without any suggestions, changes or, dare I say, interference from you. If I ran it by you first, we'd either end up arguing or I would let you talk me out of it, which could backfire on us both. I need some time alone to sort out what I want to do with the rest of my life, and I feel you also need some time away from me to think about what you really want.

I know you've wanted me to retire for a long time now so we can experience the world, find ourselves again and get away from the humdrum of daily living, but is that what you really want? You are so tied up with taking care of your parents, looking out for the children and Mariah, and even dropping everything for that dreadful friend of yours, that you don't have much time left over for me. Don't get me wrong, I have been perfectly happy with the situation, as I've got my work to occupy me, and you know I've always loved my job.

I need to have a long, hard think to make sure I won't regret it if I do retire. My work has always defined me, and I worry that without it, I might feel useless or like a nobody. I'm frightened I will lose my identity and my social life. On top of that, even if I do feel ready to start a new adventure together, I'm not sure whether deep down, you do. What if I end up hanging around the house while you're off on your latest mercy mission? I'm not blaming you. I know when I was building the business, I had little spare time for you and the children, and it's probably my fault that your life now centres around them and not me. I worry that instead of following your interests after you finished work, you allowed everyone to take advantage of your good nature, and you deserve so much more.

I'm really excited about the prospect of making new memories, but for now, I need to get away for both our sakes. I need to think about how I can make changes to my life without feeling less of a person, and I need you to think about whether your hopes and dreams for us are achievable, and if you will be able to overrule your kind heart and withdraw from being at the beck and call of everyone else.

I'm going to stay at cousin Jane's holiday cottage in the Lake District. She's going to be there for a couple of days, and it will be good to catch up with her. Then she goes off on one of her hush hush jobs, leaving me to the peace and quiet of her cottage, where there'll be no phone signal, internet or TV to distract me. It'll just be me, my thoughts, a fishing rod and, hopefully, a few fish to keep me company. I'll be back in two weeks' time.

Whatever we do, I need you to know that I love you as much as I did when we first met, and I will love you until my dying day.

Forever yours,
Tom x

Carla bowed her head, tears in her eyes. She turned to Tom and said, 'Oh, what a mess! You weren't being a coward; you were spot on with how I'd react if you'd tried talking to me. You know me so well. If only you'd left the letter in a safer place, we could have avoided all this heartache. I was so messed up that it didn't occur to me that it could be your cousin who'd sent the card. I didn't even know she had a holiday cottage, and I don't understand this hush hush job. I thought she was a civil servant?'

'She is. The civil service is a broad umbrella. She's not allowed to talk about what she does. As for the cottage, she's only just bought it. She phoned me to tell me about it, and that's when I told her I was looking for a place for some time out. I was going to tell you about it, but then I lost my head and came up with this stupid grand gesture.'

'Well, maybe it was for the best. If this hadn't happened, I probably wouldn't have realised I was being taken for granted and would have struggled to let go. Then if we had gone away together, I would have felt guilty for letting everyone down, and that would have been the worst of both worlds. But discovering I'm not as important to the people around me as I believed myself to be was a terrible wake-up call, and I'm struggling to come to terms with it.'

'Don't be too hard on them, Carla. James was mortified when he realised how selfish he'd been. He's had a lot of problems of his own, both at work and with Melissa's mother. He was so wrapped up in his own problems that he failed to notice your distress. He feels terrible about it now, and he just wants to say sorry and give you a big hug. As for our daughter, well, Emili is Emili. She's young and in love, and yes, she's selfish, but we have to take our share of the blame for that, don't we?'

Carla nodded. 'And did Kev get to her place OK?'

'Of course he did. Emili was just making a drama out of nothing. Kev got her message and was perfectly happy to make the journey to her flat by train. He hadn't realised how much he would miss her and, after his four-month stint in New Zealand, they are both determined to spend every possible waking and sleeping moment together, to the exclusion of everyone else. They haven't got time for you, me or anyone. I think she'll change eventually, she just needs time to grow up and become a fully functioning adult. Regarding your parents, I've never understood their attitude towards you, but they are not going to change now, are they? You don't owe them any more than you want to give. As for that good-for-nothing woman, Sally, you really need to choose your friends more carefully.'

Carla smiled wryly. 'Yes, you're right, of course you are. And did you come to any conclusions while you were messing about on the river, and I was at home behaving like a mad woman?'

'Yes, I did. I realised that as much as I love you and want to be with you, I would never be happy to completely retire. Mark's been my manager for fifteen years, and in that time, he's put as much into the company as I have. He coped exceptionally well while I was away, and since I've been back from the Lake District, I've been as much use as a chocolate teapot, so he's more than proved his worth. I thought I'd offer him a partnership on the understanding he does most of the running of the business. I figured if I could persuade you to cut down your commitments, without walking away completely, we could go on our travels for weeks at a time while continuing to do the things we already do in between. Obviously, all those plans went out of the window. But now you know them, what do you think? Can you forgive me and give it a try?'

Carla eased herself from her chair and into Tom's lap. She put her arms around his neck and kissed him. 'Tom, there's nothing to forgive. You did what you did with the best of intentions, and I misread the situation. Between us, we've made a right dog's dinner out of everything. One thing's for sure, though, we'll never take each other for granted again.'

'No, and I won't be making any more grand gestures!'

Carla snuggled into him, and he held her tight as they watched the sun disappear below the horizon.

'So, where do you want to go for our first trip?' Tom asked.

'Anywhere but Route 66.'

CHAPTER 30

Home Again

B efore Carla even had the chance to unpack her suitcases, the front door opened and James rushed in, took her into his arms and gave her a big hug.

'I'm sorry I was so selfish, Mum. Can you ever forgive me?'

'Don't be silly, darling, there's nothing to forgive. Your dad told me you were having a tough time of it. Come into the kitchen, I'll make us a coffee and you can tell me all about it. Now, start from the beginning and tell me everything.'

'OK, well, I was absolutely frazzled when you called. My boss had summoned me to an urgent meeting. After you said you couldn't look after Mariah, I was so busy trying to find someone else to step in that I didn't stop to think about how weird you were acting. In the end, I took Mariah to the office and my PA took care of her while I was in the meeting. Not that Pat minded, she adores her. The meeting dragged on for ages and, thinking she was doing me a favour, Pat took Mariah to McDonald's, but you know what Melissa and Andrea are like about fast food. And of course, Mariah was so pleased with her treat that the first thing she did when we got home was to tell her mum she'd been to Maccy D's. And if that wasn't bad enough, Andrea was present, and she kicked off big time, complaining that I'd left a stranger in charge of her grandchild, one who didn't know how to feed her right. I didn't want to make a fuss in front of Mariah, so I patiently explained what had happened. Then Andrea started on about you.'

Carla's eyebrows rose. 'And what did she say exactly?'

'She said, "Well, you'd think your mother would show more interest in the child."

'I was as mad as hell, I can tell you, especially as Melissa just stood there saying nothing. Then I told her that wasn't fair, and that you must have been busy doing something that you couldn't stop at such short notice. I wasn't about to tell her that I was mad at you too. Anyway, she kept demanding to know what you were doing, and, in the end, I shouted at her that I didn't know. That left Mariah in tears and Melissa giving me daggers, so I left them to it and drank myself to oblivion in my study.

'Andrea broke me, Mum, with her constant barrage of criticism. And with Mariah crying, Melissa failing to support me and you hanging up on me, I felt like all the women in my life had turned against me. I wasn't sure how much more I could take.'

Carla leant over and touched his arm. 'I'm sorry, James. I didn't mean to make trouble for you.'

'Don't apologise, Mum. It's all my fault. Melissa and I shouldn't have allowed Andrea to sideline you the way we did.'

'So, what happened?'

'The next day, Melissa refused to speak to me, and if it hadn't been for Mariah climbing onto my knee and telling me she loved me, I swear I'd have packed a suitcase and headed off. Instead, I played the dutiful husband and father and took myself off for another tedious day at work.

'I'm embarrassed to say I didn't notice your lack of contact after that. It was only when Dad called asking me if I knew where you were that I realised we hadn't spoken for several days. When Dad told me what he'd done I was mortified. I'd been so mad at your attitude that it hadn't even occurred to me there might be something wrong with you. What must you have thought of me?'

'To tell you the truth, love, I wasn't really thinking at all. I was so confused, I just had to get away. I should have told you where I was going instead of worrying you like that.'

'At first, I thought you'd intended to punish us by going off like that, but I know you haven't got a vindictive bone in your body, so I realised you wouldn't have upset us on purpose. You proved that by sending the postcard. Unfortunately, it was delayed, which only prolonged the agony. Once I got it, I stopped worrying about you, and, best of all, it changed everything. Thank goodness you sent it.'

Carla looked at him, an expression of sheer confusion on her face.

'I was on my own on the morning it arrived, and it cheered me up no end. When I got home from work, I was still so happy that even the sight of Andrea's car in the driveway didn't upset me. I felt like a huge weight had been lifted from my shoulders.

'Melissa saw how happy I was and asked if I'd received some good news. I read out your postcard and that was it, that bloody woman was off again. She said in this really snarky voice, "Well, I don't know why you're so cheerful, James. I think your mother has been totally irresponsible with all the worry she's caused. Who does she think she is?"

'Just then, something snapped. I kept calm as I spoke, but

my voice was as cold as ice. I said, "I really don't care what you think, Andrea, it's none of your business. I am sick to death of you coming round here interfering in our lives. Maybe if you hadn't done everything possible to exclude my mum, she would still be here now. The only time she gets a look-in with Mariah is when it suits you, so butt out from now on, will you?"

'She wasn't having any of it and spat, "How dare you talk to me like that?"

'There was no stopping me now, and I said back to her, "This is my house, and I will speak to whomever I wish, and however I like, when I'm in it. You have made mine and Melissa's life a misery, and I won't stand for it anymore. No wonder Harry left you. Now, please leave and don't come back until you are ready to apologise. Remember that Mariah is our child, and we will decide what is best for her, not you."

'I thought her head would explode when Melissa didn't support her. Thank God she backed me by repeating my demand for her to leave.'

'And did she?'

'Yes, she did. She even apologised later, and she's been meek and mild ever since!'

'Good for you. I'm so glad you stood up to her, and that some good came out of all the worry I caused. Come and give your mother another hug.'

* * *

The front door slammed so hard that Carla was surprised the glass didn't fall out. She and James rushed into the hallway just in time to see Emili disappearing up the stairs, a suitcase in each hand.

'I'll go after her and find out what's wrong,' James said.

He ran up the stairs to Emili's old bedroom, banged on the door and demanded to be let in. Carla could hear muffled voices and the occasional wail from Emili. It seemed Carla's absence hadn't bothered her daughter much and, as always, the only thing that concerned Emili was Emili. James came back fifteen minutes later, shaking his head.

'Kev's dumped her, and apparently it's all your fault!'

'How can it be my fault? I haven't been here.'

'Don't shoot the messenger! It seems that Dad phoned Emili when he was looking for you, but all she could do was moan about you not picking Kev up from the airport and how rude you'd been to her. She wasn't at all bothered that you were missing, and Kev was disgusted by her attitude. I think the scales fell from his eyes. Anyway, she managed to distract him – I think we can both guess how – and for a while, things were OK between them. Then, when he heard you'd arrived home, he suggested a visit, but Emili petulantly said she wouldn't see you unless you contacted her first to apologise for being so horrible. That was the final straw for Kev. He told her some home truths and said it was over. And here she is.'

'Oh dear. Let's hope she acknowledges the error of her ways once she calms down. Your dad and I *are* to blame in a way; we've let her get away with murder all these years.'

'Stop blaming yourself for everything, Mum. She's a fully grown adult and it's time she took some responsibility. Whatever you do, don't go up to her. She needs to come to you and say sorry, OK?'

'OK. Bless you, what would I do without you?'

* * *

Carla was woken from her afternoon nap by the shrill sound of her phone. Still getting over her jetlag, she squinted at the screen.

Sally.

Oh no, here we go again.

Tempted as she was not to answer, Carla couldn't help herself. She strained to hear Sally's timorous voice.

'Can we meet for a drink?'

Her manners got the better of her.

'OK. I'll meet you in The Bell in half an hour.'

Reluctantly, Carla had decided to face up to Sally and end the friendship; she was unable to bear any more tales of woe, and now was as good a time as any.

When she arrived at the pub, Sally was sitting in a quiet corner with two large glasses of white wine.

Well, that's a first, she's normally late.

Leaping from her chair, Sally enveloped Carla in a massive hug. 'I've missed you *sooo* much,' she said. 'Now, sit down and drink this.'

She pushed a glass of wine across the table and immediately jumped in before Carla had the chance to open her mouth.

Gabbling at breakneck speed, she said, 'I admit it, I've been a crap friend to you. What can I say except sorry, sorry, sorry. I've been so selfish, and so wrapped up in my own problems that I never stopped to think about you. You've been such a good friend to me, and I've been a shitty one back. Did Tom tell you how he called me after you left and shouted at me for being such a terrible friend?'

Carla shook her head.

'I deserved it too. When he put the phone down on me, I realised I hadn't let you get a word in edgeways when you called last, and I felt awful about it. I was so wound up about living in my poky little flat, working in a rotten job to keep the wolf from the door and wishing I was younger, slimmer and prettier that I had no thoughts left for you.

'The truth is, I was jealous of you and your perfect life, perfect kids, perfect house and perfect husband. I felt inadequate and inferior.'

'Jealous of me?' Carla was shocked to the core. 'Oh, Sally, I'm sorry I made you feel like that.'

'You didn't. It was all my own doing. I'm ashamed to say that I was even a tiny bit pleased when I found out you and Tom were having problems. I hate to admit it, but it gave me the confidence to stand up to Mike. I told him he had to start treating me properly or we were finished, and I meant it.'

'I'm glad for you Sally; you deserve more.'

'I know I do, and I promise to be a better friend in future.'

* * *

It was time for Carla to visit her parents and face the music; she couldn't put it off any longer. She walked up to their bungalow, pulled her shoulders back and braced herself, before slipping her key in the lock and silently turning it, delaying the moment her father would notice her presence for as long as possible.

Hearing voices coming from the living room, she stealthily moved to the doorway, gasping involuntarily at the sight of her dazed and pale-faced mother lying on the floor and her father easing himself down beside her. They did not notice her there, and, resisting the temptation to intervene, she stepped back a little to observe what was happening. She was reminded of that time all those years ago when she and Judith had eavesdropped on her parents' private conversation.

'Princess, what's happened?'

Frank cradled his wife's head in his lap.

'I was trying to get my knitting out of the top cupboard when I lost my balance.'

'What have I told you about climbing on chairs?' Frank chided in a gentle voice. 'We're getting too old to be doing things like this, and anyway, your knitting is in the bottom cupboard. I reminded you yesterday.'

'I'm sorry, Frank, I don't know what I was thinking.'

'Never mind, my darling, let's check you out. Can you move your fingers and toes?'

Janet raised her arms and wiggled her fingers.

'I can feel my toes in my slippers, and look, I can move my legs, too. I'm alright, Frank, I'm just a bit shaken, that's all. Help me get on the sofa, will you?'

'I don't think you should move. We ought to call an ambulance and get you properly checked out.'

'Don't be daft, Frank, I'm fine. I'll probably have a few bruises tomorrow and more aches and pains than usual, but all I need now is a lovely cup of tea, so stop fretting.'

'Well, if you're sure.' He helped her up, settled her on the sofa and looked deep into her eyes, concern etched on his craggy face.

'Honestly, Frank, I'm fine.'

'Alright, I believe you. But don't go doing anything silly like that again. I don't know how I'd manage if something happened to you.'

'Hey, now, stop that. Nothing's going to happen to me, we're a team, remember? I'm sorry I was silly. I'll be careful in future, I promise.'

'I'll hold you to that.'

Frank took Janet's head in his hands and kissed her lightly on the forehead. Carla quickly backtracked to the front door, opening and shutting it with a bang to announce her entrance.

Looking at her impassively, Frank said, 'Go and sit with your mother, will you. I'm going to make some tea and cut her a slice of her favourite Victoria sponge. She's had a bit of a shock.'

Carla sat next to her mother and tried to start a conversation, but the stranger beside her made little sense, and before Frank could return, she'd fallen asleep. Carla was shocked at her deterioration.

'What's going on with Mum?' she asked.

Frank hesitated.

He's probably conflicted, thought Carla, *wondering whether to use this opportunity to have a go at me or to open up about his concerns.*

Luckily, it was the latter.

'It's been going on for a long time, but I've hidden it from everyone. She's been doing some odd things and becoming more and more forgetful. At first, I put it down to old age, and I couldn't bring myself to even think about the d-word, let alone do anything about it. I'm so afraid the doctors will take her away from me, and I can't bear the thought of being separated from her.' He caught a sob in his throat. 'But she's just had a fall and I know I've got to do something.'

Carla wanted to take Frank's hand in hers, but she couldn't risk the rejection. Instead, she said, 'I'm sorry, Dad, she doesn't deserve this. I'll help you get the assistance you need for her.'

She didn't think this was the time to tell him that she wouldn't be the one to take care of her. She would visit, but she couldn't allow herself to be dragged down by her parents any longer. And she would not feel guilty. For the first time in her life, she was going to put herself first.

PART THREE
Cruising California

CHAPTER 31
The Anniversary

'Happy anniversary!' chorused the partygoers, clinking glasses and sipping their champagne.

As Tom and Carla smiled warmly at each other, their obvious affection was evident to everyone in the room.

Glass in hand, Tom rose to his feet. 'Thank you for coming this evening to celebrate the thirty-third anniversary of Carla and me pledging to spend the rest of our lives together. I don't know where the time has gone. It means so much to us to have all our special people here to celebrate, and for me to tell you how I love my beautiful wife as much today as I did on the day I met her.' He took Carla's hand. 'Thank you, my darling, for being there for me, and for all you've done for our wonderful family. To Carla.'

Everyone raised their glasses in unison and repeated the toast.

Carla, beaming now, cast her eyes around the table, scanning the happy faces of James, Melissa and Mariah, Emili and her new boyfriend, and Sally and Mike. To her surprise, her mum, dad and Andrea were smiling too. Tom had arranged this dinner party at the fancy Whitehaven Hotel without her knowledge. She was amazed at how he'd been able to assemble everyone in the same room, and she reflected how far things had come since The Day That Tom Left, nine months ago.

Tom and Carla had returned home determined to sort out their daily lives and prepare for the first of their trips together. In her wildest dreams, after everything that had happened, Carla couldn't have imagined them all sitting and breaking bread with each other. How glad she was that the dramas of the previous year were now over.

She caught James's eye, and they exchanged a knowing look. She was overjoyed by the resurrection of their close bond. And what a lot they had to look forward to. Melissa was heavily pregnant with their second child, a boy, and was positively blooming. Old Carla would never have considered going on holiday around the time of Melissa's due date, but New Carla was aware that the smooth running of everyone else's lives was not her responsibility. In any case, Melissa and her mother had reconciled their differences, and Andrea – mostly – appeared to have learnt her lesson. She desperately wanted to be fully involved in the new baby's life, and as such was learning to curb her controlling ways. She was on her best behaviour this evening and hadn't uttered a single barbed comment, snide remark or insult. Carla was hopeful there would be no further friction in her son's household.

Carla saw that Mariah was getting fidgety and called her over. 'And how is my little princess?'

'I'm OK, Grandma. Did I keep the screecret good?'

'Yes, you kept the screecret good, Mariah. I am so happy to see you, and that is such a pretty dress you are wearing.'

The little girl smiled shyly and did a twirl.

'Daddy said my brother is in Mummy's tummy, and he's coming out to play soon.'

'Are you excited?'

'No. I wish they'd send him back and get me a little girl to play with.'

Oh dear, sibling rivalry before the child is even born!

Carla grinned and hugged her granddaughter.

'I'm going to miss you, little one.'

'I'll miss you too, Grandma. Will you bring me back a present?'

'Of course I will, darling.'

Her granddaughter skipped back to her seat and climbed onto the chair in between her mother and Emili.

Emili was looking more beautiful by the day, and her new partner, Adam, was completely besotted with her. It hadn't taken her long to get over Kevin and move onto the next poor sap. Carla knew that nothing she could say would encourage her daughter to be less self-centred; she could only hope that life would eventually teach her humility and thoughtfulness towards others. Right now, she probably wouldn't even notice Tom and Carla's absence.

Her own parents' presence had surprised her: it was probably the first party they'd attended since her wedding. They were still in their own little bubble, engaging only with each other and oblivious to everyone around them. Carla had come to terms with the abnormal relationship she had with her parents and realised they were distant with everyone, not just her. Armed with this knowledge, she had found it in herself to be more forgiving and patient with them. Since her return to the UK, her father had been mostly pleasant when she visited. He could still be short with her at times, but she rose above it and was able to maintain contact with him without dreading each encounter. As for her mother, Carla doubted whether she would remember who she was for much longer. She couldn't feel sad about that; such was the distance between them, the impact on both their lives would be minimal. Her father had accepted that his wife was in permanent decline, and this had motivated him to act quickly. Using his exceptional organisational skills, he'd sold the bungalow and they'd moved into a luxury retirement village, which had all the facilities they needed. He would take care of her for as long as possible, and professional help was available for when he could no longer manage on his own.

But the biggest surprise of all for Carla had been Sally and Mike. Sally was looking particularly radiant, and a diamond ring sparkled on her left hand. Better late than never, Mike had realised how much Sally meant to him. Sally had also kept her promise to be a better friend.

Tom was deep in conversation with Mike, regaling him with his oft-repeated tale of how he'd sat next to the A-list actress, Katie Mason, on the plane to Los Angeles. He was telling Mike how she looked just as beautiful in real life and was a great conversationalist. He boasted how she'd even given him a lift to Malibu in her limo. Mike was enthralled. Carla grinned to herself: she knew the full story. What Tom omitted was how he'd embarrassed himself by first failing to recognise her and then admitting to having never watched any of her movies. Neither did he mention that he'd spent most of the flight discussing his marital problems with the poor woman.

Carla surveyed the scene. All in all, it was a satisfactory outcome – almost. Above the hubbub of conversation, Mike piped up, 'When are you off to San Francisco, Tom?'

Carla rolled her eyes and Tom looked sheepish. She'd been trying to get him to commit to the trip for the last three months, but he kept putting her off. Instead of cutting back his hours and Mark taking over the bulk of the work, the pair had signed up for a big building project, which had not been without its problems.

'Soon, Mike, soon.'

'Next Saturday!' said Carla firmly. 'I booked the flights this morning. That gives Tom a week to get organised.'

Tom caught the determined look in Carla's eyes and kept his mouth shut. Nothing should be allowed to spoil this wonderful evening.

* * *

While Carla was packed and ready to go, Tom had yet to bring his own suitcase down from the loft. He'd worked late every day that week to make sure everything would run smoothly in his absence, and he'd promised to be home early to prepare for the holiday. He broke his promise, and by the time he got home, Carla was pacing the floor, banging saucepans on the hob and handling the crockery in a manner likely to end in tears if she didn't calm down.

'I'm sorry I'm late, love. I've been on the phone all afternoon trying to avert a crisis.'

Carla was not in the mood to listen to his excuses. 'Well, you're home now. Dinner will be ready in half an hour. Go and pack your things. The taxi is coming at 6am, so there'll be no time to do it in the morning.'

'About that —'

'What?'

'I've just had the day from hell. The plumbing subbies have screwed up and the property owner is threatening legal action. He's summoned me to a meeting on Monday. Hopefully, I can smooth things over with him. I'm sorry, love, but we can't go tomorrow – I promise we can on Tuesday, though.'

His pleading eyes and hangdog expression pulled at Carla's heartstrings, and she wavered.

'I warned you not to get in over your head. You were supposed to be winding down, not up.'

'I know, I should have listened to you, and I'm sorry. Mark and I have learnt our lesson, though, and when this project is over, we'll go back to doing small builds only. Tuesday, then?'

'No, Tom. I'm not waiting any longer. Nancy and Merle are flying to San Francisco tomorrow, and they'll only be there a few days. I'll go on my own and you can come and join us on Tuesday. Now, before I say anything I might regret, I'm going to cook dinner. I suggest you stay out of my way until it's ready.'

CHAPTER 32

San Francisco

Carla, Nancy and Merle were relaxing forty-six storeys up in the Cityscape Bar & Lounge. After the excitement of their reunion and a bit of sightseeing, a few celebratory drinks and dinner were in order.

'What an amazing view,' said Nancy. She had a childlike quality about her, and her eyes sparkled with excitement. 'We can see the whole of San Francisco from here. Look, there's the Golden Gate Bridge, the Coit Tower and the Transamerica Pyramid.'

'It's beautiful, isn't it?' said Carla. 'I've always wanted to come to San Francisco, and it's every bit as good as I'd hoped.'

Even Merle was impressed.

'Hey, Merle, I've just had a thought,' said Carla. 'When I was in Oklahoma, you told me you couldn't drive Carla anymore because of your poor eyesight, yet you don't seem to be having trouble seeing what's out there. Were you having me on?'

'No, he's had his cataracts fixed,' explained Nancy. 'He's like a new man.'

'Yup, I wish I'd done it years ago. So, what shall we do tomorrow?'

Merle had lost weight since Carla last saw him, and he looked healthier than she remembered. Despite their advancing years and declining mobility, Carla knew that he and Nancy wanted to explore.

'We could get the hop-on, hop-off bus around the city,' suggested Carla. 'That way, we'll get to see all the sights – Fisherman's Wharf, Chinatown, the Embarcadero, Golden Gate Park, and the Bridge, of course. How does that sound?'

'That's a great idea,' said Nancy.

Merle nodded, the relief evident on his face. Carla leaned forward and patted his belly. 'You've shed a bit of timber since I last saw you,' she commented.

'Yes, I have. Nancy's stopped baking her delicious pot pies and is making me eat that darned rabbit food.'

'Well, you look good on it.'

Merle didn't seem convinced.

'We must stop at the Ghirardelli chocolate shop tomorrow,' said Nancy. 'Matthew's given us instructions to bring him back a big bag of chocolate squares. He says it's the best chocolate in the US of A.'

'Chocolate is always a good plan to me,' said Carla.

'Do I get to eat any of it?' asked Merle.

'If you're a good boy, I guess you can have a few squares,' said Nancy, giving her husband an affectionate hug.

* * *

Their busy bus tour was a successful one; they absorbed the feel and vibe of the city while taking in most of the sights, though Nancy was disappointed they didn't get to cross the Golden Gate Bridge due to the aftermath of an accident.

'I know it can't be helped, but I was looking forward to the bridge more than anything else,' she said. 'Still, if that's the worst thing that happens to me today, I can't complain, can I? What's on the agenda for tomorrow, Carla?'

'We'll take a boat across to Alcatraz, if that's OK with you two?'

'We need to be back for two o'clock,' said Merle. 'I've got a delivery coming.'

Next morning, Merle ducked out of the trip. 'I'm beat after yesterday,' he said. 'This ole man needs a bit of extra rest after all that rushing around. You go without me, and I'll take a nap while you're gone. Anyways, I guess you two ladies would welcome the chance to talk trash without me.'

Nancy looked affronted. 'How dare you say such a thing, Mr Taylor? Seriously, though, you alright?'

'Quit fussing, woman, and git going.'

'Alright, if you're sure.'

'I'm sure.'

He kissed her on her forehead, turned away and lumbered over to the hotel's elevator.

'Is he really OK?' asked Carla, once he was out of earshot.

'Sure. Neither of us is getting any younger and it's been a while since we've had such an active day. And what with the flight and all, he's just wore out. He'll be better company later for taking a rest.'

* * *

The tourist boat cruised through the choppy, uninviting waters of the bay and sailed towards the infamous island. The clouds had gathered, the wind was picking up and rain threatened. The inclement weather magnified the former high-security prison's gloomy atmosphere, a sombre reminder, should they need one, of its isolation from the mainland. They gazed at the Golden Gate Bridge in the distance and were lulled by the movement of the boat.

'Anyways, what's going on with you and Tom?' said Nancy. 'I thought you'd sorted out your differences?'

Nancy looked at Carla intently, her expression deepening the worry lines around her mouth and temples.

'There's no need to be so solemn, Nancy. Everything's fine.'

'Come on, he's not here. There must be a problem of some sort.'

'No, there really isn't. Tom has got himself embroiled in a project that has gone wrong, and he's having to sort it out. He'll be here tomorrow, and then we'll start our journey. I'm just sorry he won't get to meet you and Merle.'

'Me too. We would love to have met him. I guess it wasn't meant to be.'

'I'll make sure we come and see you in Oklahoma on our next trip.'

As the boat was now docking, Nancy's response was lost in the kerfuffle of people scrambling into a disorderly queue to disembark.

They toured the dark, depressing buildings before venturing into the grim exercise yard, from where they could see the Golden Gate Bridge in the distance. Carla imagined the prisoners seeing the same view and, when the wind was in the wrong direction, hearing the sounds of freedom wafting from the San Francisco shoreline. Headphones clamped to their heads, they learned about the prison's history, which confirmed the visual proof of how awful life was for the men incarcerated on this bleak island. One of the speakers told Carla that ghosts haunted the island. As she entered one of the tiny cells, she shivered as a waft of cold air rushed through it.

A ghost?

You've got an overactive imagination! she scolded herself. *It's just the wind!*

Even so, the thought of sleeping in this cold, miserable cell made her shudder.

* * *

That afternoon, the three of them sat in Carla's hotel room surveying the street below.

'What are we waiting for?' Carla asked.

'You'll see,' said Nancy with a grin. A lorry pulled up to the kerb across the street. The driver got out of his cab, lowered the ramp at the back and, a few minutes later, out rolled a sleek, red Corvette.

'Carla!' The human Carla clapped her hands in delight. 'How wonderful.'

At his friend's reaction, Merle seemed to grow a foot taller. 'I had her shipped up from Martha's,' he explained. 'We didn't get around to bringing her home, and we thought you and Tom would enjoy driving her through California.'

'Oh, thank you both. I can't wait to get behind the wheel again, and I know Tom will love her too. He was so jealous when I told him all about my adventures on Route 66 in this incredible car. He'll be glad of the opportunity to take her for a spin.'

'You can have her tomorrow,' said Merle. 'Tonight, Nancy, my queen, I am going to make your dream come true. You and I are going for a little drive across the Golden Gate Bridge to Sausalito, where we are going to have dinner and watch the sunset.'

'I didn't know you were such a romantic,' said Carla in surprise.

'Oh, he has his moments,' said Nancy with a wink.

* * *

Carla enjoyed a solitary walk along the quayside before stumbling across a restaurant serving delicious seafood. It was so nice to spend time with Nancy and Merle again, and she took great pleasure from watching the starry-eyed couple enjoy a rare holiday away from the farm.

She planned to spend a few days showing Tom around the city before heading south with him in the Corvette.

As if on cue, her phone rang.

'Hello, darling. You've missed a lovely couple of days here. Never mind, I know my way around now, so I'll take you to all the best places when you get here tomorrow... Tom, are you there?'

'Yes, I'm here. I'm sorry, I really can't tell you how sorry I am. I can't be there tomorrow. I've pacified Mr Peaks for now, but there's one or two things I'll need to sort out before I can get away with a clear conscience. I'll make it up to you, I promise.'

'You keep making promises you can't deliver, Tom. Frankly, it's not me you're hurting. I'm used to travelling alone, remember? It's you who's missing out, not me. Nancy and Merle fly home tomorrow night, so I'm not hanging around here waiting for you to arrive. I'll start the drive down the PCH to Los Angeles on my own.'

'PCH?'

'The Pacific Coast Highway. It's another name for Highway 1. It hugs the coast all the way to Los Angeles, and it's supposed to be one of the finest in the world. And best of all, I'll be doing it in the Corvette. Like I said, it's your loss not mine.'

'I know, I've screwed up... again. What else can I say other than sorry?'

'Oh well, it's your loss. Martha is letting me use her place for a few days, and now you're going to miss out on that luxury too. I don't want any more excuses. I'm warning you; you've got one week and then I expect you to be here, otherwise I'm going on without you. Is that clear?'

'As crystal.'

* * *

'Morning, lovebirds.' Carla sat down at the breakfast table, overjoyed to see Nancy and Merle gazing at each other like smitten teenagers. 'How was your evening?'

'It was wonderful, just like old times,' said Nancy. 'Merle looked so cute driving Carla, and it was great to get another chance to enjoy her. I just loved looking up at that big, red bridge, and crossing it was exhilarating. We had a romantic dinner in Sausalito, with soft music and flowers on the table, and I swear it was the most beautiful sunset I've ever seen in my life. You could drive Tom there tomorrow night.'

'I'm afraid that won't be happening, he's not coming,' said Carla, the words sounding sharper than she intended.

'Oh, I'm sorry, honey, what happened?'

Carla told them about the phone call.

'Tom can't help himself. He's a workaholic, and he always has been. He's frightened to face a future without the business, but he just won't admit it to himself. He talks as though he and Mark got themselves embroiled in this big project by accident. It's his own fault; he wouldn't listen when I tried to talk him out of it. I think he's terrified he'll be less of a man if he takes a back seat. You of all people must understand that, Nancy.'

She nodded and Merle shifted uncomfortably in his chair.

Nancy said, 'Coming here made me realise we've missed out on so many things because we couldn't let go of the farm, and now we're too old to do much. Surely you can't be happy he's scuppered the plans you both agreed to in Los Angeles last year?'

'I'm fine with it, honestly, though I'm not letting on to Tom. I'll let him go on thinking he's in the doghouse.'

'Even so, you must miss him.'

'Of course I do, though you know what, I learnt so much about myself when I drove Route 66. I didn't realise it at the time, but I'd let so much of myself go into hibernation, and the trip allowed me to find the real me again. I'm going to enjoy my Californian adventure, with or without Tom. He doesn't define me.'

'Aren't you worried that Tom will end up having the same regrets we have?'

'No, not really. If I leave him to his own devices, I'm hoping he'll work it out for himself. I can't tell him – that man doesn't like being told what to do. What bloke does? If he doesn't work it out, then it'll be his loss. All I know is that *I've* got the travel bug now, and nothing and nobody is going to stand in my way.'

'Good for you.'

'Anyway, he made a promise to be in LA next week, and I'm pretty sure even he realises it would be a mistake to break this one.'

Nancy looked intently at Merle. He nodded. Carla was amazed to note their apparent telepathy. It was clear an important exchange had taken place, even though no words had been spoken.

'I don't have to go home today. What would you say to me coming with you to Malibu for a few days?' said Nancy. 'I could always fly home from Los Angeles.'

'That would be wonderful. Can you manage on your own, Merle?'

'What is it with you and details, girl?' he grumbled. 'I'm perfectly capable of getting on a plane on my own. Matthew can pick me up from the airport in Oklahoma City. And I'll git to eat what I like without Nancy fussing.'

'If you're both sure, I'd love to have your company, Nancy.'

'Of course we're sure, it'll be quite an adventure.'

'Not too much of an adventure, I hope,' said Merle, gruffly.

'It's a shame Martha won't be in Malibu, but I can give Olivia a call and see if she can visit; I haven't seen her in a while.'

'What a great idea,' said Carla.

Nancy went off to phone her sister, while Merle handed over the keys to the Corvette.

'Now, you look after both my ladies, won't you?'

'Of course I will. Are you sure you're OK with this?'

'You'll be doing me a favour. I feel real bad for not bringing Nancy to California when I had the chance. That woman has never made a fuss about anything, and she deserves more. I can tell she's excited to do this trip, and she loves spending time with you. You've been a breath of fresh air for us both.'

'Aw, thanks, Merle. You've both made such a difference to me, too. Anyway, how come Carla's got a California license plate now? What happened to the Oklahoma plate?'

'When you told us you were coming back with Tom, Nancy and I decided to leave her at Martha's. It was always our plan to let you have her for your next adventure, and it's a bonus Nancy gets to share it with you. State laws say we must register her in California if we keep her here, so her home is at Martha's. It's no big deal.'

'Thank you so much for your kindness. I'll never forget how good the two of you have been to me.'

Merle blushed with pleasure. Seconds later, Nancy came back into the room, grinning from ear to ear.

'She's coming! It's going to be wonderful to see her again, and I'm so excited about our road trip too.' She hesitated and linked arms with Merle. 'Are you sure you'll be OK on your own, honey?'

'Quit fussing, woman. Anyone would think we'd never spent a night apart.'

'We haven't! This will be the first time since we married.'

'Well, it's time we did. Now go and pack your suitcase.'

CHAPTER 33
Pacific Coast Highway

They were bowling along the Big Sur section of the PCH, sunshine on their faces and no sign of the dreaded fog. With the fresh sea wind in her hair, Carla was in her element. The road afforded them glorious, postcard views of the Pacific Ocean below. This dramatic stretch of coastline rose from sea level up to a thousand feet, from where sheer cliffs dropped into the ocean. Hills and forests lined the opposite side of the road, adding yet more drama to the vista. Carla could understand why so many people judged Big Sur to be the most beautiful coastline in the world, but in her not-so-humble opinion, the detour they'd made earlier on the 17-Mile Drive was even more spectacular. Was it the rugged coastline, the harbour seals, sea otters and Monterey cypresses that had made her feel that way, or had the fancy lunch they'd enjoyed at Pebble Beach Golf Links clouded her judgement?

Feeling elated, Carla looked across at Nancy and saw tears streaming down her face. She quickly pulled into a layby and switched off the engine.

'What's the matter?'

'Nothing. I'm just so happy, is all. I can't help crying; I'd never seen the ocean before this vacation, let alone dreamed I'd get the opportunity to do a road trip in Merle's favourite car.'

'Really, you'd never seen the sea?' said Carla in disbelief.

'Most of the folks at home have barely left the county, let alone Oklahoma, so they sure as heck haven't seen the sea.'

'Wow! Do you wish Merle was driving instead of me?'

'No, I don't. He can't drive far these days, and I would have spent the whole journey worrying about him. With you at the wheel, I can just relax and enjoy the view.'

'How does Merle feel about it?'

'He's real happy for me. He feels bad we didn't get round to it when we were young enough, and he thinks he's let me down, so this trip has made him feel better about all that. I just hope Tom doesn't make the same mistake we did.'

'Me too, Nancy, me too.'

* * *

They completed their four-day journey along Highway 1 without incident by taking it easy and stopping off several times along the way. Carla didn't want to tire Nancy out, so she had factored in plenty of time for them to see all the coast had to offer. She couldn't resist a pilgrimage to Cannery Row. Originally named Ocean View Avenue, the waterfront street in Monterey was once lined with sardine canning factories and was the setting for John Steinbeck's Great Depression novel, *Cannery Row*. To honour one of the greatest American authors of all time, the street's name was subsequently changed. Of course, Steinbeck's most famous novel of all, *The Grapes of Wrath*, was the one that had made such an impact on Carla as she travelled Route 66, and this is why she'd put the street on her 'must do' list for this trip. They took a walking tour around the now gentrified area, which was teeming with hotels, restaurants, spas, boutiques and galleries. Carla wondered what the late author would have made of it all.

To thank Nancy for her kindness, Carla paid for all their hotels and meals. She wanted to give her friend a trip of a lifetime, and for her to experience things she'd never experienced before. She booked them an overnight stay and dinner at a stylish hotel in the kitsch town of Carmel-by-the-Sea, where, it seemed to her, anything went in terms of architecture: from Hansel and Gretel houses to glass-fronted modernist mansions. The houses all had one thing in common: they were all eye-wateringly expensive. The exclusivity of the town was highlighted by its lack of traffic lights and street lamps. Who needs them in such a civilised society?

Nancy looked uncomfortable in the hotel's posh restaurant.

'Are you OK?' Carla asked.

'Sort of. I'm just a little worried about disgracing myself. What am I supposed to do with all these knives and forks?'

'Don't worry about it. Start on the outside and work your way in. No one cares whether you know dining-room etiquette, and anyway, after we've drunk our way through this delicious Korbel California Champagne, you won't either.'

'True. I don't know whether to order the sanddab or steak.'

'Have you eaten sanddab before?'

'No.'

'Then you need to live a little, take a chance. What's the worst that can happen? If you don't like the fish, you can still order a steak.'

'You're right, of course, but being in a place like this sure does make me realise how small my world is.'

'And is that world a happy one?'

'Oh, yes.'

'Then you've made all the right choices in life. Look around you. How many women in this room do you think have had a long and happy relationship with the same man?'

'I don't know.'

'I'd guess it's about ten per cent. Most of these people are probably on their second or third marriage, and I'm sure a lot of them will be looking for an excuse to get out of their current one. Being rich doesn't guarantee happiness, though I'd rather be rich and unhappy than poor and unhappy. Better still, I like being the way we are, neither rich nor poor, and happy most of the time. The last thing I want is to make you feel insecure in any way. I want this to be a memorable trip for both of us. Just because these people have lots of money, don't think they are better than us. They're not.'

'I won't, and you're right, this champagne is helping me to relax and enjoy the evening.'

'If you think these people are rich, we need to visit Hearst Castle. Have you heard of it?'

'Vaguely. Is that where the newspaper magnate William Randolph Hearst lived?'

'The very same. Now, he *was* rich. We'll go there tomorrow, and you just won't believe the opulence and excesses of his mansion and gardens. They even have zebras on the estate!'

'How do you know all this?'

'My trusty travel guidebook tells me where to go and where not to bother with.' Changing the subject, Carla added, 'How are you coping being without Merle for the first time in your married life?'

'Do you know, it's been fine. I was really worried about leaving him, and last night, in bed, it felt strange being alone, but he would have hated being in this hotel, and that would have spoiled it for me, too. We're so intertwined that we

276

haven't given each other the chance to do our own thing, so I'm really glad to have had this opportunity.'

'Well, we've got Tom to thank for that. Let's make a toast. To Tom!'

'To Tom! I wonder if we'll see Clint Eastwood tonight. Did you know he used to be the mayor of Carmel, and he still lives here?'

'Yes, I did. Is this a good time to admit that's why I chose a hotel in this town? He was my favourite actor when I was a teenager.'

Nancy laughed and said, 'Next you'll be telling me the reason you made a reservation in Santa Barbara is because Tom Cruise lives there.'

'Not me. Only Clint and David Cassidy ever made it onto my bedroom wall.'

What Carla didn't admit was that ever since they'd arrived, she'd been keeping an eye out just in case Clint happened to be out and about. It was a long shot, and she wasn't surprised when she failed in her quest, especially as she didn't even know if he still lived in Carmel!

CHAPTER 34
Los Angeles

Martha's place was Carla's new spiritual home. She loved its atmosphere and was looking forward to spending some time there with her friends. As soon as Olivia arrived, she took her out to the deck and opened a bottle of Californian white wine.

'You've come a long way since I last saw you, Carla,' commented Olivia.

'Yes, I certainly have.'

'And yet you're still on your own?'

'Indeed, I am, but it's different this time. I'm not fretting about Tom or worrying about the family. I'm totally relaxed and enjoying every minute of this holiday.'

'Aren't you mad at him?'

'No, he can't help being a workaholic. It's his loss he's not here, and if he were, then I wouldn't have spent these special days with Nancy. She's been more of a mother to me in the short time I've known her than my own mum ever was. It's a win-win for me. And, for that matter, with Tom in the picture, you wouldn't have been here, either!'

'True.'

Hearing a commotion, they turned to see Nancy stumbling through the door, her arms flailing. She was frantically waving something at them, and in her excitement, she tripped over the step. Only Carla's lightening reactions saved her from a tumble and an inevitable visit to the ER.

'Steady on, Nancy, where's the fire?' said Carla.

'These are from Martha,' said Nancy breathlessly. 'Tomorrow night is the premiere of her new movie *Angel at Moon River* at the Chinese Theatre, and she's sent us tickets!'

The three of them squealed and jumped around like schoolgirls, hugging each other with glee. When they'd calmed down, Nancy poured herself a glass of wine and proposed a toast to Martha.

'To Martha!' they chimed in unison. Carla couldn't believe her luck. Whenever she spent time with a member – or two – of this marvellous family, something magical happened. The irony of the film's title wasn't lost on her, either: another angel was making her day.

'If Martha has to be in LA tomorrow, I wonder why she isn't here now?' said Olivia.

'She's in New York tonight and flying in tomorrow,' explained Nancy. 'She's straight off to Hawaii after the screening, so she won't have time to see us. It's a shame, as I'd like to see her one last time.'

'What do you mean?' asked Olivia.

'Oh nothing. It's just that I can't see me travelling away from the farm again.'

'Hush now,' said Olivia. 'There's plenty of life left in you yet.'

'You're right, as always, big sis. I was being silly. Let's get something to eat, I'm starving.'

'Me too.'

'Me three,' Carla giggled, glad to see the mood lighten again.

* * *

The following morning, Annie, Martha's PA, trotted into the house, her arms loaded with garments.

'Hi, Nancy. Ms Brady sent me to give these ballgowns to you and Olivia. She said Carla was to wear something from her personal wardrobe: it's a formal dress code. She also managed to get you passes for the after party, and with a bit of luck, she'll catch up with you then. I've arranged for a hairdresser to come here at midday, a make-up artist is arriving at two, and a limousine will pick you up at four. Is there anything else I can get for you?'

'No, I think you've got it covered,' said Nancy. 'Thank you so much for arranging everything. We are so excited, and we're really looking forward to the premiere.'

Annie bid the three women farewell, leaving them in peace to prepare for the evening ahead.

Several hours later, they were ready for their big night out. Carla was wearing a crimson, Louis Vuitton evening gown. Her hair shone, and her subtle make-up accentuated her glowing skin. Olivia insisted she looked beautiful, and she graciously accepted the compliment. Nancy's dress, a purple velvet creation by Armani, had her clapping her hands with glee. Along with her fashionable new hairstyle, it had the impact of making her look both taller and younger.

'Is that really me in the mirror?'

Carla nodded and smiled at her.

Olivia was wearing a glorious, multi-coloured Prada gown that suited her perfectly. Her normally flowing hair was piled up on her head in a classic style. Carla thought she looked magnificent. They all stood together admiring their reflection in the hallway mirror.

'We scrub up better than the Weird Sisters, don't we?' commented Carla.

'Who are they?' asked Nancy.

'The three witches in *Macbeth*. Nancy was always more interested in the farm than school,' said Olivia with a chuckle.

'We should give ourselves a name,' said Carla.

'Well, we're certainly not the Three Little Pigs or the Three Blind Mice,' joked Nancy.

'I was thinking more along the lines of the Three Amigas or the Fabulous Three,' said Carla.

'Lame,' retorted Nancy.

'Now then, ladies, when you've finished your little game, you might notice there's a big fat limo outside,' said Olivia. 'It's waiting to take the three Cinderellas to the ball, so let's go, shall we?'

'What about the Three Wise Women?' Nancy whispered on the way out.

'Hardly,' said Carla, giggling. 'I think that champagne we just drank has gone to our heads.'

'Well, it's a good job one of us is a grown up,' Olivia snorted while chivvying them into the car.

'Aw, lighten up, Livvy. You can't have forgotten what it's like to live in the boondocks. This is the most exciting thing that's ever happened to me in my life!'

'I've got it. Instead of Charlie's Angels, how about Martha's Angels?' said Carla.

'Oh, do shut up the pair of you.'

Carla and Nancy exchanged glances and sniggered.

The limo proceeded slowly along the bustling Hollywood Boulevard before coming to a stop outside the Chinese Theatre.

A small crowd had gathered behind the makeshift barriers to wait for their favourite movie stars to arrive. When the chauffeur opened the door for the three women, an anticipatory hubbub of noise rose from the crowd, who were eager to see who would emerge. Sighs of disappointment filled the air when the Three Nobodies clambered out. Expecting to enter the theatre via a side door, they were surprised to be ushered onto the red carpet, where they were stopped for a photoshoot despite the fact no one seemed interested in who they were.

If Tom could see me now, Carla thought.

She knew she was at her best, while Nancy oozed elegance, and Olivia's bold, stylish new look had her exuding confidence. Carla thought how much they all deserved this moment in the limelight.

They sat at the back of the theatre, nudging each other as a host of celebrities filed past to take their seats, adorned in beautiful evening dresses or tuxedos. Even Olivia was giggling now. They spotted Martha breezing into the auditorium with the inevitable lackeys following in her wake. Carla gasped in shock. Martha in the flesh was identical to the woman Carla had manifested in her vivid dream all those months ago in Malibu. *Spooky!*

Martha acknowledged them with a wave and a little smile before taking her seat at the front of the theatre.

'She looks tense,' said Nancy.

'Well, so would you,' replied Olivia. 'It's a big moment for her; the critics' opinion will make or break this movie.'

Before Nancy could question her further, the lights went down. There was a hush, and the music began. They all settled down to what they hoped would be an entertaining movie, and they weren't disappointed. The audience was spellbound by the stunning locations and innovative cinematography as the intricate tale of star-crossed lovers, watched over by the heroine's guardian angel, unfolded.

When the movie ended, everyone in the audience rose to their feet, cheering rapturously and applauding. All three women were crying and, for once, were lost for words. They dried their eyes and hugged each other, proud to have witnessed such a phenomenal event.

* * *

Carla woke up with the hangover from hell. She put on some sunglasses to hide the dark circles under her eyes and went outside, where she found the two sisters sipping coffee. Nancy was shivering and Olivia's face had a green hue.

'My head hurts,' groaned Nancy.

'I feel sick,' moaned Olivia, 'but it sure was a great night, as far as I can remember.'

'Yes, it was, one of the best of my life. I ain't gonna forget it in a hurry,' said Nancy.

'Me neither,' Olivia replied. 'I kept pinching myself, thinking I'd wake up any minute.'

'Me too,' said Carla. 'It's a shame we didn't get to talk to Martha, though.'

'She's hot property now, everyone wants a piece of her,' said Nancy, proudly.

'Clint Eastwood told me the chance of anyone else winning an Oscar for best director has gone down the pan,' confided Carla. 'He said Martha's movie was one of the greatest he's seen in a long time.'

'Woo hoo, get you, girl, with your name-dropping,' said Olivia. 'I saw you chatting to him in the corner like you were best buddies.'

'I did rather monopolise him, didn't I? I'd never have dared to speak to him if it wasn't for the free-flowing champagne. It all seems so surreal now; I can remember watching *Play Misty for Me* when I was a teenager. I've seen most of his films since then, including all his spaghetti Westerns.'

'And she had posters of him on her bedroom wall back in the day,' said Nancy.

'He's so old,' wailed Olivia.

'In case you hadn't noticed, we're not exactly spring chickens ourselves,' said Carla.

'Yes, but he's at least thirty years older than you!'

'Well, I don't care. He was charming, and if I bored him, he didn't let on, so he's still my hero.'

They laughed at the incongruity of it all, which lead to another bout of head-holding grimaces.

'I don't know what you two are planning for the day, but I'm not moving any further than the sun lounger,' said Carla.

'Me neither,' said Olivia.

'I'm just going to call Merle and then I'll join you.'

They lazed on the beach all morning, nursing headaches that showed no signs of receding. Olivia was scrolling on her laptop when she shrieked, 'Oh my God, look at this, Carla.'

'What?'

'You've been papped! You're headline news in *Celebrity Gossip*. There's a picture of you and Clint Eastwood looking very cosy together. It's captioned, "Who is the mystery woman with Clint?" What do you make of that?'

'Jezebel,' quipped Nancy, and they all roared with laughter.

* * *

It was the end of their stay, and Nancy and Olivia were waiting for a taxi to take them to the airport for their flights home. Meanwhile, Tom would be arriving at LAX in a couple of hours' time, and Carla had agreed to pick him up in the Corvette. He'd managed to get away at last, and she couldn't wait to see him.

'Don't be too hard on Tom, will you?' said Nancy.

'I won't. After all, it all turned out for the best, didn't it? The three of us got to spend this precious time together, and I got to meet Clint Eastwood!'

'True, and you'll never know how much this week has meant to me. I got to see the Pacific Ocean in Carla the Corvette, and the days we've spent together will stay in my heart forever.' She was fighting back tears. 'You are the daughter that Merle and me never had.'

'You and Merle mean the world to me, too, you know that, don't you?'

Nancy nodded. She gave Carla a sealed envelope. 'I want you to keep this safe and don't open it until you get back to Los Angeles at the end of your trip. Can I trust you to do that?'

'Of course,' said Carla, mystified.

The taxi had arrived. The three misty-eyed women hugged each other and said their goodbyes. Carla waved them off, then prepared to shut up the house in readiness for the drive to the airport and Tom's arrival.

CHAPTER 35

Huntingdon Beach

Carla scanned the crowd coming through the arrivals gate. There he was.

'Tom,' she called out. He sprinted over, dropped his bag on the floor and threw his arms around her. They hugged each other tight, oblivious to the obstruction they were causing.

'It's so good to see you, Carla, I've missed you so much.'

'I've missed you, too.'

'I'm sorry for everything.'

'It's OK. Let's forget about it and focus on having a good time.'

'Sounds good to me.'

She saw the worry lines around his eyes disappear and felt the release of the tension in his body. She could tell he was relieved to be let off the hook so easily.

'Can I drive the Corvette?'

'As soon as we leave LA. I've just got used to the crazy traffic around here, and I don't think this is the place for you to drive her for the first time. You can take over as soon as we start heading south. Before we do that, I've booked a motel in

Surf City, also known as Huntingdon Beach, for three nights. It's not too far away from here, so let's go.'

They dumped their bags at the motel and headed straight for the beach, where they watched surfers tackling the waves while listening to a collective of drummers, which they found strangely soothing. Afterwards, they ate dinner at a restaurant next to the pier before sitting around a firepit back on the beach, drinking Sex under the Pier cocktails made from peach Bacardi, cranberry juice and lime, and listening to reggae music. As the sun disappeared behind the silhouetted pier, a solitary paddle boarder glided by.

'This is the life! I could get used to this,' Tom said contentedly. Carla looked at him askance but kept quiet.

* * *

'What's on the agenda for tomorrow?' asked Tom as they got ready for bed back at their motel.

By way of explanation, Carla handed him two tickets.

'NHRA drag racing tickets for Pomona! You little beauty. I can't believe you did this for me. All those times I failed to get you to come with me in England, and now you're taking me to the daddy of drag-racing tracks. Thank you!'

He took her in his arms and twirled her around.

'VIP seats and premier parking no less,' Carla replied smugly. 'I might not know what's going on, but at least I'll be comfortable.'

However, the next day, they discovered the VIP tickets were more about providing them with an endless supply of food and drink options rather than comfortable seating. Their start-line seats were no more than bleachers, which would have been fine had they not been sharing them with some extremely large Americans. Carla felt like a slice of processed cheese in a McDonald's burger.

Just as the event was about to begin, a woman pushed past to get to her seat, announcing at the top of her voice, 'I've come all the way from New York to see John Force race!'

Carla noticed people turning around to look at her.

So, the stereotypical New Yorker does exist! she thought.

Tom decided to up the stakes. 'Well, *I've* come all the way from England to see John Force race.'

A ripple of laughter was accompanied by some friendly back slaps. The only person who wasn't amused was the New Yorker, who made a hasty retreat, never to be seen again.

'Who's John Force?' Carla whispered.

'Only the greatest drag racer that ever lived, that's who,' replied Tom. 'He drives a Funny Car.'

'Oh,' Carla replied, still none the wiser. But Tom's comment had broken the ice with the crowd, and before they knew it, they had a new set of people to add to Carla's growing list of kindly American friends.

Carla had been acting purely altruistically when she bought the tickets for her and Tom, and she hadn't actually expected to enjoy the racing, but the sheer power of the incredible machines, the noise of the 10,000-horsepower engines, the smell of nitrous and the unbelievable speeds – in excess of 300mph – as the cars sped along the 1000-foot track in less than four seconds, blew her away. She was immediately hooked. When the monsters launched off the start-line, the noise and vibrations from the powerful engines channelled into her chest, creating an incredible feeling of excitement. She was reminded of Julia Roberts's infamous line in *Pretty Woman* when Richard Gere's character asked if she'd enjoyed the opera and she replied that it was so good she'd nearly peed her pants.

In the commotion, it was a while before Carla noticed the helicopter flying past with what appeared to be a giant bucket dangling underneath it.

'What's that?' she asked Jerry, the man sitting next to her.

'It's for putting the fires out.' Seeing her look of surprise, he added, 'Didn't you hear about the wildfires?' She shook her head. 'They just started this morning. We've had a dry spell and they're spreading real fast.'

'Are we OK here?'

'Yes, but a couple of the freeways are already closed, and the traffic is backing up on the others.' He asked where she was staying, and when Carla told him, he added, 'You won't be able to take the direct route back, and if you go round, it'll be about ninety miles in crawling traffic. I suggest you head west on I-10 and check into the first available motel.'

Carla didn't like what she had heard.

'Tom, I think we should leave right away,' she said.

'OK,' Tom replied, clearly disappointed to be missing out on the final race.

* * *

It was dark by the time they hit I-10. The interstate was chock-a-block with traffic moving at a snail's pace while spewing smog into the atmosphere. Behind them in the distance, flames flickered in the sky. Ahead of them stretched mile upon mile of red taillights. Twice they pulled off the freeway to find a place to stay, and both times they were unsuccessful.

'I'm getting really worried,' said Carla, coughing. The smoke coming down from the hills was getting into her lungs.

'Me too, but we've got no choice; we've got to stick it out.'

An uneasy silence followed.

'Shall I check the traffic news?' said Tom, trying and failing to hide his anxiety from his wife.

'It's worth a try. Maybe we'll get some advice on making a detour.'

He switched the radio on – nothing. No radio, no lights and no engine: the car had broken down.

'What do we do now?' said Tom in a panic.

'Look, there's an exit ramp a hundred yards up the road. Thank God we're so close to it. We can push the car from here.'

They manoeuvred the Corvette onto the hard shoulder, pushed it to the exit ramp and came to a stop on a traffic island. They were huffing and puffing from the exertion, but Carla was eerily calm. 'I spotted a Motel 6 sign from the freeway,' she said. 'I reckon it's just around the corner. You stay with the car, and I'll run round and see if they've got a room for the night.'

Luckily, they had. A few minutes later, Carla was back at the Corvette. 'I'll jump in, and you push the car down the hill. Hopefully, she'll get enough momentum to get round the bend and up the slope to the motel's entrance.'

They were just about to start this manoeuvre when a policeman glided by in his black and white LAPD car, completely ignoring their predicament.

'Well, thanks a lot,' grumbled Tom.

They managed to get the car safely around the bend and parked up without causing any damage to themselves, the car or anything else. Carla heaved a big sigh of relief.

'Do you think the gates around these premises are to keep the guests in or the intruders out?' said Tom. 'It looks like a prison.'

Carla shrugged, preferring not to think about it.

'I really don't care, Tom. I'm just glad they left the light on for us, just like Motel 6's slogan says.'

'Where are we anyway?'

'Baldwin Park, apparently.'

The suburb didn't appear in any of Carla's guidebooks, so she kept her fingers crossed that everything would be fine, and it was. In their innocence, and in true British style, oblivious to the potential dangers of being mugged, or worse, they walked to a Walmart and bought toothbrushes, toothpaste, a change of clothes for the morning and a snack. Back at the motel, they collapsed straight into bed and were asleep within seconds.

* * *

Fortunately, the car issue was an easy fix. At the motel, they sought the assistance of a Mexican man who spoke little English but was keen to help. Despite the language barrier, he managed to communicate that the radio had blown the main fuse, which was easily replaced, and they were soon on their way.

'We're not touching that radio ever again,' said Carla.

'All's well that ends well. It looks like that guardian angel of yours has come up trumps once more.'

'Don't make fun of me, Tom. The more this sort of thing keeps happening, the more I think there might be something in it.'

'I'm sorry, love, I won't tease you again, and maybe you're right.'

'Well, maybe I am.'

Back at Huntingdon Beach, they spent an idyllic day relaxing on the beach, content in each other's company. Carla forgot her frustrations with Tom and was happy to see he'd put his work problems behind him at last. A romantic dinner and copious amounts of wine sealed their renewed sense of intimacy.

'It's been a great day, hasn't it, Carla?'

'It certainly has.'

She raised her glass and clinked it with Tom's.

'Here's to us and the rest of our Californian adventure.'

'To us!'

* * *

Something woke Carla up. It wasn't Tom, even though he was snoring loud enough to wake the dead. She was used to that cacophony of noise. She lay there, ears pricked. The room was shaking, not much, but it was definitely moving. She could hear glasses gently rattling in the bathroom.

'Tom, wake up. There's an earthquake. What are we supposed to do?'

'Huh? What are you on about?'

He yawned, struggling to come round.

'There's an earthquake.'

The movement had stopped. Tom got out of bed and peered out of the window.

'There's nobody out there and I can't hear anyone moving around the motel. You must have dreamt it. Go back to sleep.'

He got back into bed and immediately fell back into a deep slumber.

I know I didn't imagine it, thought Carla.

Then it happened again.

Well, if no one else is going to worry about it then neither shall I, she thought before promptly falling asleep.

In the breakfast room next morning, Carla said loudly, 'Did anyone else feel the earthquake last night?' Everyone in the room looked at her as if she was mad, shook their heads and carried on eating.

'Will you be quiet, you're embarrassing yourself,' Tom hissed.

Carla silently seethed.

* * *

They were packed and ready to leave the motel when Tom's phone rang.

'It's Mark, I'll have to take this.'

He went outside to answer the call. Five minutes later, he returned, his face ashen.

'What is it?'

'Mark's broken his leg. I must go home and take care of the business, I'm sorry.'

Carla stiffened. She turned away from Tom, her heart thumping in her chest. She looked out of the window, but the view blurred. Her body started to shake, and she wrestled to control it. She dug her long fingernails into the palm of her hand, fighting back the tears that threatened to spill over her lower eyelids. She bit her lip so hard it pierced the skin, leaving her with the salty, metallic taste of blood in her mouth. She was shrinking back into Old Carla, and when she caught sight of her reflection in the window it made her recoil. Staring back at her was a face she barely recognised. Pinched and lined, it was as if she had aged ten years in two minutes. Her shoulders sagged, her head drooped, and her backbone shrunk. She was beaten.

'Do whatever you need to do, so long as you're not expecting me to come home with you.'

'I wouldn't dream of it. It's taken me thirty years to realise you're a free spirit, and there's no way I'd try to clip your wings now,' Tom said lightly.

He came up behind her to put his hand on her shoulder. She shrugged him off and twirled round to face him. 'Don't patronise me, Tom.'

The words came out louder and harsher than she'd intended them to. Tom stepped back, shocked.

Carla glared at him, hard-faced and thin-lipped.

'I'm not patronising you,' he insisted.

'Yes, you are. Do you think I want to do this on my own? I'm not a bloody free spirit, I'm doing it alone because you don't want to be with me. You'd rather be at work.'

'That's not true!'

'Isn't it? Then why did you commit to this sodding project?'

'I told you it was a mistake.'

'No, it wasn't. You asked my advice and I counselled against it, but you did it anyway. Jesus, Tom, you're only interested in my opinion if it backs up your own. If I say anything different, you ignore me and carry on in your own sweet way. I've been kidding myself, and everyone else, by telling them that you're a workaholic and can't help yourself. How do you think I feel knowing your work is more important to you than me? What have I got written on my forehead?'

She wrenched up her fringe and gripped it tightly to the top of her head. Tom frowned, looking confused.

'It says "fool". All these years, I thought you were the one person I could rely on. I thought you loved me unconditionally. Turns out, it was conditional after all, conditional on me massaging your ego and agreeing with you.

'That's not it at all.'

'So, what is it, then?' She spat out the words. Tom opened his mouth to speak, but before he could say anything, Carla continued with her rant, words falling out of her mouth, all thought and reason gone. 'You just don't get it, do you? Until I met you, I was alone. For the first time in my life, I felt important to someone, and yet here I am, alone again, with only Judith for company.'

'Who's Judith?'

'My imaginary friend. The person who made my childhood bearable, the person in the mirror, the person I talk to when I'm on my own. At least I can depend on her when all else fails.'

She paused to catch her breath. Her body was shaking, and her eyes were alight with fury.

Tom was stunned, speechless.

'You have no idea what it's like to be unloved and lonely; you had Barney and Brenda. It was only when I became part of your family that I understood why I didn't feel right when I was a child. I thought you'd fixed me, but I've been kidding myself for all these years. My life will *never* be normal.'

When Tom tried to reach out, she pushed him away.

'Have you forgotten that it was you who let the genie out of the bottle when you went AWOL? You said you'd sorted your head out, and I was happy with the compromise of you working part time. But there is no compromise, is there? It turns out it was nothing to do with work, otherwise you'd be staying with me now. You just don't want to be with me. Did you stop just once to think about my feelings? No, of course you didn't, because it's all about you.'

Carla had run out of steam. She turned away from Tom and stared out of the window.

'Just go,' she said quietly.

'I can't leave you like this. We need to talk, to sort things out.'

'Please just get out of here, I can't talk anymore.'

Carla had never been so angry in front of Tom, and nor had she ever spoken to him so harshly. She felt totally drained.

'I'll call you when I get home.'

'Don't. I'll contact you when I'm ready.'

She stood, immobile, still gazing out of the window while seeing nothing.

'OK, I'll go. I do love you, Carla, you must believe that.'

He picked up his suitcase and quietly slipped out.

CHAPTER 36
Ortega Highway

'Hi, Susan.'

'Hello, Carla! I wasn't expecting to hear from you so soon. Are you OK?'

'Yes, I'm fine. I was wondering whether you could get off work tomorrow?'

'I wish I could, but I've got a couple of busy days ahead. We had an earthquake last night and the lobby sustained minor damage.'

Vindicated!

'Never mind, it was just a thought. Tom's gone back to England, so I'm reorganising my plans.'

'Really? What happened?'

'Oh, just some business issue he needs to sort out.'

'I have an idea. The owners have been putting off doing some important maintenance work for a while, so they've decided to close the hotel and fix the place up while checking for quake damage. After tomorrow, we've all been given time off, so I could come with you on your road trip.'

'Fantastic! I'd love you to join me; we'll have so much fun together. Is there much damage?'

'No, it's mostly cosmetic. We've been lucky.'

'That's good. I'll come and pick you up on Thursday and we'll take it from there.'

'Great, see you then.'

* * *

It was Susan's idea to have dinner at Ye Olde English Grille in Palm Springs; she thought Carla might be missing English food. Despite her scepticism, Carla had to admit the décor did make it look like a pub, and her turkey roast dinner was tasty. She wasn't so sure about the waitress, a friendly lady who probably should have retired years ago. She was wearing a smart suit and a pair of pink fluffy slippers.

'I'm not sure if she thinks slippers are de rigueur in English restaurants or if she's got sore feet!' laughed Carla.

'Do you mean they're not?' said Susan. 'Another illusion shattered. So, what's the plan?'

'I haven't made one. I want to drive down the coast all the way to the Mexican border, otherwise, I really don't mind what we do. I'm happy to put myself in your hands.'

'OK, here's what we'll do. Tomorrow we'll do a bit of sightseeing in Palm Springs. Then we'll drive cross-country via the Ortega Highway and spend the night in Dana Point, on the coast. How does that sound?'

'Bring it on.'

* * *

Susan and Carla jumped on the revolving Palm Springs Aerial Tramway and rode from the Sonoran Desert up to the San Jacinto Wilderness Park.

'Blimey, Susan, if you'd told me it was going to be cold up here, I'd have brought my gloves.'

'What do you expect? We're nearly eleven thousand feet above sea level. Stop whining, woman, and look at the view.'

'You're right, it is impressive, but it doesn't seem real. Golf courses look out of place in the middle of the desert, and there's so many of them.'

'It takes a hundred million gallons of water a day to keep them like that. What can I say? It's a wealthy town and the residents like their golf. Can you see that row of palm trees over there?'

'I see them.'

'Do you remember the big earthquake in 1989 that destroyed parts of San Francisco?'

'How could I forget.'

'My uncle told me he was up here, standing right where you are now. The San Andreas Fault runs through the valley, and according to him, the ground opened up and all those palm trees were left bobbing up and down. I don't know if it's true or not, but it sure is a good story.'

'Wow, my rattling hotel room tale seems boring now.'

'Come on, let's go back down and hit the road.'

'Would you like to drive the Corvette?'

'Would I? Hand me the keys, girl, before you change your mind.'

With Susan handling the car like a pro, Carla was able to sit back, relax and enjoy the scenery to the full instead of keeping her eyes peeled on the road. Susan wasn't exaggerating – Highway 74 was a stupendous road to drive. They passed Lake Elsinore in the valley and saw it again from the viewpoint at the summit, where the parking area resembled a Sunday afternoon at a classic car show.

'This is a great place to take a photo,' said Carla. 'The view takes your breath away. Frankly, I'm running out of superlatives to describe the beautiful sights in your country.'

'It is rather wonderful.'

'I've loved the twists and turns of the road through the mountains and the gorgeous smell of the pine trees. We wouldn't get that in an air-conditioned saloon, would we?'

'True. I'll need to concentrate super-hard on the downhill section. This highway is one of the deadliest in the US. There's a good reason why the roads have nicknames such as Blood Alley, Dead Man's Curve and Ricochet.'

Carla paled.

'It's nothing to worry about if you keep to the speed limit, which of course I will be doing, but I'll need to lookout for any dopes on the road.'

'I trust you implicitly. Let's go.'

Carla enjoyed the winding descent of the highway, as she took in all the sights and breathed in the scents. Today, she'd seen desert, mountains, lakes, pine trees and palms. Sand and sea would soon be in sight. Only in California! She glanced across at Susan and noticed her hands were gripping the steering wheel as she anxiously looked in the rear-view mirror.

'What's up?'

'There's a car tailgating me. He's been on my ass for a while now. There's nowhere for him to safely overtake, and I guess he's in a hurry, so he keeps pressuring me to speed up. I'm not going to risk it on this road, so I'll pull over and let him pass as soon as I get the chance.'

The driver of the late-model Mustang was becoming more and more impatient. He pushed closer, then dropped back, repeating the manoeuvre over and over again, each time getting closer to the Corvette's bumper. When he realised Susan was not going to be intimidated, he repeatedly honked his horn. She ignored him and continued at the same pace, staying within the speed limit of fifty-five miles per hour and slowing down for the bends. The man's patience ran out. Even though a blind bend was just ahead, he suddenly pulled out onto the other side of the road and roared forward to overtake them. Just then, a speeding motorbike came hurtling round the bend. The rider was leaning heavily into the curve, his wheels clinging to the road at the centre line. He was right on course for a head-on crash with the Mustang. Carla screamed as the Mustang's driver cut in on the Corvette. Instead of wiping out the bike, a collision with Susan and Carla now seemed certain. But somehow, Susan deftly steered the car to avoid both vehicles, whilst maintaining full control of the Corvette. The Mustang disappeared into the distance while Carla shook uncontrollably. She looked at Susan and saw that she was completely calm.

'What the heck, Susan?' she shouted. 'How can you act so normal?'

Susan shrugged and, cool as a cucumber, said, 'Didn't I tell you I used to drive a race car?'

'No, you didn't. Thank God you knew what you were doing. If I'd been driving, we'd have gone over that edge and into the canyon. It would have been curtains for us and the scrapyard for Carla. You're my real, live guardian angel. Now, get me to Dana Point; I need a drink.'

CHAPTER 37
Dana Point

C arla and Susan sipped cocktails at a bar overlooking the beach. The more they drank, the more they relaxed, and soon their terrifying experience seemed nothing more than a bad dream.

'Wow, look at that sunset, Susan. I've seen so many since I've been here, but this one is exceptional.'

'That's because of the wildfires. I don't understand the science of it, but when the air quality is poor, the sun and the sky appear redder than usual.'

'Who knew? Look, there's a pod of dolphins surfing the waves over there. Aren't they amazing?'

'Yes, they are. I'm so glad I met you, Carla. Morgan and I used to come to the coast all the time, and we always loved the sunsets and the wildlife. I haven't done this since he passed. I'd put all those precious memories to the back of my mind, and you've reminded me of the little things I've been missing. I need to move on; I'm nearly ready.'

'I'm glad to hear it. You deserve some happiness, and if you find it, your love for Morgan won't be diminished. You know he would want you to be happy, don't you?'

Susan nodded and smiled, her eyes moist.

'So tomorrow, we'll take a detour inland to see your parents?'

'If you don't mind.'

'Of course not. I'd love to meet them.'

'I also want to go to church, and you're more than welcome to come along. If you don't want to, you can do your own thing and we'll meet up afterwards.'

'Well, I've heard that gospel services are pretty full on, and I'd love to compare it with my limited experience of attending the Church of England.'

More to the point, though she didn't say it, Carla wanted to see what lay behind Susan's fervent and unshakeable faith. In some ways, she envied her friend's certainty and ability to take comfort from the unknown, even in adversity.

'You'll need to dress sharp; we all dress up for worship. It's a serious business in the house,' Susan told her with a twinkle in her eye.

'Will your parents be there?'

'I hope so, my father is the pastor!'

* * *

The two women approached the entrance to the church. Dressed in a canary-yellow dress and a matching fascinator, Susan exuded self-assurance. An electrifying aura surrounded her. Impossible to describe, it seemed to have an impact on everyone in her wake. Carla followed behind, but even her eye-catching scarlet dress and heels couldn't detract from Susan's larger-than-life presence. She didn't envy her, though, she was simply proud to be her friend. They joined the line of elegantly dressed worshippers waiting to be greeted by the pastor and his wife.

'Susan! What are you doing here?' Her father's caramel-brown eyes widened in delight.

'Well, that's no way to greet your favourite daughter. I couldn't miss this special day, could I, Papa?'

She hugged him and then her mother, who was equally pleased to see her. When they finally drew apart, she introduced Carla.

'I'm honoured to meet you,' said Susan's father, shaking her hand vigorously. 'Susan has told me all about you. I'm Edwin, and this is my wife, Cassie.'

Cassie gave her the warmest of hugs.

'I'm delighted to meet you both,' said Carla.

'Welcome to our church. Please, come inside.'

They were ushered into the building and directed to the front row seating. Cassie whispered something in Susan's ear and then left.

'Will you be alright here on your own?' Susan asked Carla. 'I've only been here for five minutes and already my mother has allocated me a role in the service.'

'I'll be fine. Go and do what you need to do.'

From the comfort of her seat, Carla gazed around in wonder. The modern, round building was the complete antithesis of her magnificent, old, not to mention chilly, parish church back home. The seating was laid out in a semi-circle, facing a large stage. The walls were brightly decorated in a mosaic-style pattern and there were none of the relics to the dead that Carla was so familiar with. Were it not for the stained-glass windows lining the top of the walls and the enormous, neon-lit cross positioned above the centre of the stage, she would have believed herself to be in a theatre. Beautiful arrangements of flowers adorned the stage, their sweet smell permeating the air.

The seats quickly filled with an assortment of immaculately dressed people of all ages and sizes.

Crikey, the congregation in my church isn't even this smart at a wedding! Carla thought.

The women were clad in beautiful dresses representing all the colours of the rainbow, and many of the older ladies wore lavish hats. The men were not to be outdone, sporting smart suits, crisp white shirts and colourful ties. The hubbub of noise rose as the people around her chatted amiably. It was so different to the quiet formality that Carla was used to, and she enjoyed absorbing the room's happy vibes.

The stage soon filled: a group of guitarists to the left, keyboard players and percussionists to the right. Centre stage, a choir assembled, resplendent in maroon and yellow robes. It was an arresting sight. A robed man approached the oversized perspex lectern positioned under the cross and held his hands aloft. A hush descended.

'Welcome to the house on this very special day, as we come together to celebrate twenty-five years of service and sacrifice from our brother, Pastor Edwin Cole.'

For the next ten minutes, the man regaled the congregation with stories about the pastor, before calling him onto the stage amid thunderous applause.

'Thank you for your kind words, Elder Brown, and for all the love I feel around me. I have tried to serve you all to the best of my ability. But I couldn't have done it without the first lady of the church, my wife, Cassie, so come up here, my darling, and share in the love of all these good people.'

Susan's mother seemed faintly embarrassed as she walked towards her giant of a husband, but the look she gave him was one of pleasure and satisfaction. She was clearly glad of the recognition and looked even more petite as he wrapped his big arms around her in a loving hug. They waited for the applause to subside so the service could begin.

The pastor's voice was in turn booming and whispery, never losing the attention of the congregation. He danced around the stage as he preached, leaping into the seating area and bounding around the hall, grasping outstretched hands and mopping sweat from his brow with a linen handkerchief, all the while bellowing his message without missing a beat. He spoke with such passion and eloquence that it was clear his enthusiasm hadn't dimmed throughout his years of service.

Carla glanced at the congregation behind her and marvelled at the impact Edwin was having. She was amazed by the informality of it all and loved the audience participation. Some people sat silently with their heads bowed in contemplation, while others were on their feet and swaying with their hands in the air. At seemingly random intervals, people called out 'Hallelujah' and 'Praise the Lord', or else they cheered and applauded. One woman appeared to be in a hypnotic state. Carla smiled at the incongruity of it compared to a traditional English church service, where no one stood up unless told to do so and the congregation remained silent except for hymns and prayers. She loved the spontaneity and inclusion.

Afterwards, Carla would remember little of the words of the sermon, but the tone affected her greatly. Putting aside her ambivalent attitude towards religion and the church, she was moved by Susan's father's passion and became caught up in the joyfulness of the occasion and how it lifted her spirits. When the music started, she was dazzled by the sophisticated sound system and the incredibly talented musicians and choir. It was like watching a musical at the theatre, with a hefty dose of

Jesus thrown in. The high-octane energy was infectious. The congregation wasn't hampered by hymn books: a big TV screen on the wall displayed the words, karaoke style. Many of the worshippers sang along. Some danced, while others sat quietly, tears sliding silently down their faces. One woman even had her own tambourine.

Clearly, anything went in this church.

It wasn't until the service was nearly over that Carla spotted Susan in the body of the choir. She was camouflaged in her uniform and nestled amongst the other singers. She stepped forward to the front and picked up a microphone.

Edwin introduced her. 'Most of you will know my precious daughter, Susan,' he said. 'It's been a while since she visited us in the Lord's house, and I am honoured to have her here today to lead us in our final hymn, *Here I Am To Worship.*'

Carla was entranced, and it was only when the woman on her left nudged her and passed her a tissue that she realised tears were trickling down her face. She had never been so moved by a song or heard such an incredible voice. The words her friend sang were beautiful, just like Susan herself.

* * *

After the service, they went to Susan's parents' house for lunch. Susan's father sat at the head of the table, facing her mother, while Carla, Susan, Susan's brother, Samuel, and her grandma filled the remaining seats. The table groaned with food – fried chicken, sweet potato pie, creamed corn, black-eyed beans, collard greens, cornbread, and dishes that Carla didn't even recognise. Plates were loaded high before they began to tuck in. Carla bit into a piece of fried chicken and marvelled out loud at how delicious it was.

'Have you heard of soul food, honey?' asked Susan's

grandma. Carla shook her head. 'Well, this is it – it's good for the soul but maybe not the heart.'

'Well, it's the best fried chicken I've ever tasted,' said Carla. Then she tried a mouthful of one of the mystery dishes. 'Mmmm, this is good too, what is it?'

'Chitlins.'

'What's that?'

'Pigs' intestines.'

A look of horror crossed Carla's face, which she quickly rectified, aware of the five pairs of eyes staring at her.

'I'm really sorry, that was very rude of me. I'll be honest, if you'd told me what they were before, there's no way I would have tried them. I know it's irrational, but the idea of eating a pig's intestines seems wrong, though I have to admit, the dish is delicious.'

'Well, honey, you wouldn't have been so choosy if you'd been an African slave on a plantation in the Deep South. They had to survive on any scraps the slave masters didn't want to eat, so they did whatever they could with whatever was available to make their food more palatable. Over time, their methods developed into the delicious dishes we have today, and we get the benefit of recipes that were born out of the struggle for survival. This particular one has passed through my family from generation to generation.'

'I had no idea,' said Carla, chastened and mindful that she still knew so little about this complex country.

After lunch, they sat back in their chairs, holding their stomachs in satisfaction for the wonderful feast they had shared, content at being together on such a special day.

* * *

As it was getting late, Carla and Susan accepted her parents' invitation to stay overnight in their rather beige guest room. Carla got straight into her single bed to continue reading her guidebook, while Susan sat gazing out of the window. Carla noticed that she was uncharacteristically quiet.

'Are you alright?' she asked.

'I guess so. I'm just feeling a little nostalgic for my teenage years. This used to be my room, and I hate what my parents have done to it. I used to have a poster of Madonna on the wall, and the bookshelf was filled with teenage romances and my schoolbooks. I also had a fluorescent pink quilt, which I can't claim to miss. I saved for months to get a cassette player, which I had over there in the corner. I was so proud of it and, of course, I had all sorts of knick-knacks that no self-respecting teenager could live without. Obviously, I couldn't expect Mama and Papa to keep it as a shrine, but my heart aches at the severance of another part of my connection with Morgan. This room was full of happy memories of him. He used to sneak in here all the time, unbeknown to my parents. I feel like he's slipping away from me.'

She paused. 'Anyway, enough of that, let's talk about something else. It's been a great day, hasn't it?'

'It certainly has, and your voice is incredible. How come you didn't sing at the karaoke?'

'I have no interest in singing other than at church.'

'I'm sure you could be a big star if you chose to be. You could be the next Whitney Houston.'

'And look how that turned out!'

'True. I'm just glad I had the opportunity to hear you sing. Thank you so much for letting me be part of today, it's been amazing.'

'I'm glad you think so. My family loved meeting you and sharing what they do.'

'Can I ask you a personal question?'

'Shoot.'

'How come you've got those incredible blue eyes when everyone else in your family has brown ones?'

'I don't know for sure. My grandparents originally came from Trinidad. Neither of my grandmas know anything about their ancestry on the side of their fathers. It's a possibility they have Scottish blood in them, and the blue eyes manifested in me, generations later. I'm the only one with blue eyes amongst all the family we know, so it could be that a genetic mutation has popped up in me.'

'Well, however you got them, your eyes are stunning, and I find myself wanting to stare at you all the time, just like one would gaze at a rare, beautiful painting.'

'I'm sort of used to it, Carla. A lot of people stare at me because I look different. At least people leave me alone now, but I had to develop a thick skin to deal with all the insults I used to get.'

'Insults, whatever for?'

'You name it, I've had them. When I was a child, the adults used to whisper around me and go silent if they thought I was listening – even some of my aunties. I didn't know why until I got older, and kids would tell me my daddy wasn't my daddy and my mommy was a whore. I didn't even know what a whore was!'

'How did you cope?'

'Well, let's just say my big brother got into a lot of fights on my behalf. When I was older, the girls in high school would call me out for wearing blue contact lenses, which alienated me even more. I felt like an outsider.

'Then I met Morgan. He was the first person to make me feel special. He told me every day I was beautiful, and I believed him. He gave me strength and self-belief, and before long, the insults were nothing more than white noise. I guess once people realised they couldn't get to me anymore, they left me alone. I know people still point and stare, but I refuse to let that upset me, and I rarely notice it now.'

'It must have been tough for you growing up, but things have changed, and I see how people look at you now. It's not just because you look different, it's because you're beautiful. Of course, there will still be some people who disrespect you, and there's nothing you can do to change that, but I'll wager they stay in the shadows these days, as they wouldn't want to risk you standing up to them. You see, you project an image of confidence and self-assurance, so no one is going to mess with you. For the rest of us, your aura adds to your obvious physical beauty, and I can tell you, the only looks I've seen you receive are ones of admiration.'

'Really? I had no idea. Like I said, I've been wearing a thick shell to protect me all these years.'

'Just know that when you are ready to start dating again, there'll be no shortage of suitors!'

'I'll bear that in mind,' Susan said, laughing. 'Now, can we get some sleep?'

CHAPTER 38
Carlsbad

'Shall we relax today for a change?' said Carla.

'Sounds good to me. What did you have in mind?'

'There's a really nice apartment hotel in Carlsbad. It's got suites with views over the ocean, an outside swimming pool and a hot tub, sun loungers and a private beach area. Do you fancy it, or would you rather spend the day shopping? Apparently, the city has exceptional retail therapy. Or we could go to Legoland?'

'Are you kidding me?' Susan replied, giving Carla a withering look. 'Unless you want this friendship to end, you need to make that reservation right now. And as soon as we hit those sun loungers, you're getting the first round!'

* * *

Carla and Susan sipped champagne as the sun sank inexorably towards the ocean. Their suite was perfectly situated with direct access to the beach.

'How do you keep snaffling these amazing rooms at such good rates?' asked Susan.

'Stick with me, kid, I'm a master at this. I use my best English accent and ask for a discount. Who can fail to fall for my obvious charm? I'm sure my discount voucher book helps too!'

'Well, thanks to you we have an incredible view at a bargain-basement price. Cheers!'

'Cheers! I'm loving this champagne.'

'Only the best Korbel for us.'

With nothing else to add, they silently watched the waves rushing to the shoreline, enjoying the last of the evening sun's warmth.

'I think I've seen more beautiful Californian sunsets this year than I've had hot dinners,' mused Carla.

But Susan didn't appear to want to listen. 'OK, girl, time to spill the beans.'

'About what?'

'Oh, come on, Carla. I wasn't born yesterday. There's something in your eyes telling me that however good a time we're having – and it is pretty special, I grant you – something is bothering you.'

'I'm fine. Can't we just enjoy the evening?'

'No, because your problems will still be there after the sun goes down, so why not share them while there's still light?'

'Honestly, I'm fine.'

'OK, then, if you aren't going to tell me, I'll tell you what I think is bothering you.'

Carla arched her eyebrows, shifted uncomfortably in her lounger and stared out to sea.

'While incredible, your Route 66 adventure was tinged with anxiety because you thought Tom was having an affair and your family didn't care about you, so you couldn't fully relax into the experience. Am I right so far?'

Carla nodded.

'That was the easy bit. I'm guessing you were having a ball this time around because you felt secure in Tom's love for you, and you've enjoyed experiences beyond your wildest dreams. True?'

'True.'

'You were fine about him not being here because you now trust him, and you understood his need to work. His absence allowed you to do things you would never have done had he been with you, and you blossomed, discovering things about yourself you hadn't realised were lurking beneath the surface. You've realised that you are still a strong woman, and a fearless one at that. This revelation came as quite a shock to you. How am I doing so far?'

'Jesus, Susan, I've only known you five minutes and it seems you know me better than I know myself. You're wasted in hotel management.'

'But – and this is a big but – you know you can't carry on this fantasy life forever. Nancy's gone home and I'll be returning to work, and then you'll be on your own again. Maybe you'll meet other people along the way to share your adventures and maybe you won't. At some point, you'll have to face up to the fact this new life of yours is only a distraction and you need more to make you complete. You were vaguely hanging on to Tom seeing sense and joining you on further travels, but he's blown you out three times now and you don't think he will. So, what are you going to do? Are you going to go home and slip back into the life you had before? Or are you going to issue Tom with an ultimatum? If he says no, what are you going to do? Kick him to the kerb? And if he says yes, then problem solved. Is that what's going on in your head?'

'I love your expression, kicking him to the kerb. I take it that means splitting up? You're almost right with everything you say, but it's a bit more complicated than that.'

'So, tell me!'

And she did.

'Wow, even I didn't see that coming. I knew you were feisty, but... I'm so sorry. When you told me about your parents before now, you didn't mention how bad your childhood was.'

'That's the point, I didn't think it was until I met Tom. Without him, I would have sailed through life as a single, career-driven woman, blissfully unaware that my life wasn't normal. He changed my perspective and made me feel like I belong, but now I've been cut adrift. I'm so used to Tom working, so I really was OK with it until he was summoned home. And when he called me a free spirit, I don't know what happened to me. I just lost it. I realised he doesn't understand me at all.'

'Have you ever talked to him about your childhood, I mean really talked?'

'No, not really. I wanted to leave the past behind me, and I didn't want to dwell on it. I'd found happiness, so why should it be tarnished by old memories? Anyway, I'm not one for oversharing. The past should be left where it belongs.'

'Not if you end up with the misunderstandings that you and Tom keep having. You said he's been living a lie, but it's you that's living the lie. All these years, you've acted like you've got your shit together when you haven't. Your parents' neglect is a considerable part of who you are, and Tom has the right to know about it. In any case, you haven't left the past where you say it belongs, otherwise you wouldn't be insecure about Tom's feelings for you.

'Last time, you let him think you were upset with him

because you thought he was having an affair. You never told him it was about much more than that. Even if I bought into the "my childhood doesn't bother me" and "I wanted to leave it in the past" crap, it was a big deal after he left you, and when he came to Santa Monica, you should have told him everything, but you didn't. So, when the misunderstanding about the affair was cleared up, he thought everything was fine between you. How was he supposed to know it wasn't?'

'You're right, of course. In my defence, though, I thought it was fine too.'

'Well, clearly it wasn't, and I can't believe you've never mentioned Judith before; it sounds like she's been another big part of your life.'

'She was, *is*. But it all sounds ridiculous saying it out loud. She went away when I grew up and only came back when Tom left me, when I saw her in the bathroom mirror. She kept me company from time to time on Route 66 but disappeared again after Tom and I got back together. She only seems to visit me in times of trouble. God, I sound stark raving mad, don't I?'

'No, you don't, it sounds like an effective way of dealing with trauma to me. But it's not really fair for you to expect Tom to understand you when you've kept so many important secrets from him, is it?'

Carla cast her eyes down and inspected her hands, mulling over Susan's words.

'Tom told you he loved you when he left. He wouldn't have said that if it wasn't true. I'm not saying this is all your fault, of course it isn't. It sounds like he's been pretty dense not to recognise that you need him, and he was certainly stupid not to listen to you about the business. I'm sure he knows that now. You told him not to call you and I'm guessing he is respecting your wishes, but I'm sure he's just as devastated as you are.

Let me ask you another question. What was your original motivation behind your Route 66 plans?'

'To drive across America, of course.'

'Really? I don't believe you. It was a means to an end, wasn't it? It wasn't about the trip, which of course was a great idea. It was so you and Tom could focus on each other without anything or anyone standing in the way, wasn't it?'

Carla took her time before replying. 'I hadn't articulated it, but you're absolutely right. It should be our time now, but Tom doesn't see it.'

'How is Tom supposed to know if you don't tell him? Think about it, Carla. You've been self-sufficient all your life, giving the impression you are in control and don't need anyone else to make you whole. You've had a great time here without Tom. He probably thought you didn't need him, and that suited him because it gave him the freedom to work as much as he wanted to without having to worry about you. All I'm saying is that at some point, you and Tom need to have a proper conversation.'

They watched as the last of the sun disappeared below the horizon and was swallowed up by the sea. The red sky left in its wake invited optimism for a clear night and another morning of brilliant sunshine.

'Enough of this doom and gloom,' Carla said. 'I'm starving. I spotted a restaurant advertising the best ribs in town and two-for-one margaritas. Come on, let's go.'

CHAPTER 39

Baja California, Mexico

The following day, Carla and Susan jumped on the trolleybus for the forty-five-minute journey from Chula Vista to San Ysidro at the Mexican border. The majority of the passengers were Mexican, many of them on their daily commute home: working in San Diego, living in Tijuana. They chatted loudly in Spanish, their words often accompanied by laughter.

From the terminus where they disembarked, they could see the giant ugly fence in no man's land, which separated the two countries. It dominated the landscape. In the distance, a massive Mexican flag fluttered in the wind, drawing attention to the high-density housing nestling in the hills.

'We need to walk across that bridge to get to Baja California,' said Susan, pointing ahead.

'I'm not sure about this, Susan. I've read that Tijuana is a dangerous place.'

Susan burst out laughing. 'I can't believe you just said that considering some of the places you've been to, and now you've got me staying in Chula Vista instead of a nice hotel in downtown San Diego because you wanted to be authentic. Of course, there's some risk, there is wherever we go, but it's broad daylight. We'll be fine. I want you to try some genuine Mexican food in a real Mexican town. Come on, it'll be fun.'

They followed a sea of people across the border, which, according to Carla's guidebook, was one of the busiest in the world. Immediately, Carla felt the atmosphere change. This really was a different country: hustle and bustle, tooting car horns, colourful window displays, and multi-coloured flags draped from rooftops. And of course, the aromas of delicious street food. They spent a pleasant day strolling around the town, drinking in the vibrancy and absorbing the sights and smells around them.

'You were right, as always,' admitted Carla, 'we really did need to visit this amazing town. If you'd only told me about the Birria tacos and how good the margaritas are here, I'd have been over in a flash.'

Susan grinned at her tipsy friend. 'Well, I had to keep something as a surprise for you. Much as I'd like to hang around, I guess we'd better head back to San Diego.'

* * *

Susan breezed across the US border flashing her American passport. Meanwhile, Carla was called forward. As soon as she looked at the customs official, she knew this wasn't going to be the easy passage she'd had in Chicago and San Francisco. He glared at her with malevolent eyes.

'Passport.'

She silently handed it over to him.

'Purpose of visit; vacation or business?'

'Vacation.'

'Why haven't you got any luggage?'

'Because it's in San Diego. I just went to Tijuana for the day.'

He looked at her doubtfully. 'On your own?'

'No, with my friend, she's American. She went through ahead of me.'

'Where are you staying?'

'The Travelodge in Chula Vista.'

He looked at her incredulously, his eyes surveying her closely. 'You expect me to believe that?'

'Yes, because it's the truth.'

And on it went. She glanced over her shoulder, feeling bad for the people stuck in the line behind her. They remained impassive and showed no sign of irritation. Clearly, these delays were common.

'You came into San Francisco, you say?'

Carla's patience was running thin. 'Yes, I've told you that already. If you look at my passport, you'll see the stamp,' she said, barely able to keep the sarcasm out of her voice.

Careful, Carla, you don't want to be stuck in Tijuana, especially now it's getting dark.

The official gave her a dismissive look and flicked through her passport, his cursory inspection failing to find proof of her legal entry into the USA a few weeks earlier.

Check your damned computer, she wanted to scream, but she daren't.

'Give it to me, I'll show you.' She almost snatched the passport from his hand, before turning the pages until she found it. 'Look, here is the stamp from San Francisco Airport. Now, can you please let me through or get your superior to come over?'

She knew she was in dangerous territory, but she could no longer stand by and allow this surly man to intimidate her. Her heart was pounding nineteen to the dozen. Had she gone too far? The first rule of travelling was not to upset border officials, but he was already upset with her for no good reason, so she couldn't make it any worse, could she? He glared at her, took the passport and pretended to scrutinise the stamp. Finally, he added his own stamp and handed it back to her.

'Have a nice day,' she mumbled under her breath, scuttling away before he had the chance to change his mind.

Susan was waiting for her outside.

'What kept you? I was starting to get worried.'

'You and me both, I thought I was going to get stuck in Mexico. Give some men a bit of power and it goes to their heads. Come on, let's go get a drink. I need one.'

* * *

At a busy bar, they found a table and ordered two beers. A more relaxed Carla recounted her tale to an amused Susan.

'Stop laughing, it wasn't funny. Why is it that every time I go anywhere with you, I get into trouble?'

Susan shrugged.

'Excuse me, ladies, is it OK if I sit here?' asked a man, gesturing to an empty seat at their table.

'Sure,' said Susan.

'No!' said Carla at the exact same time. The man looked from one woman to the other, decided he liked Susan's answer better and sat down.

'Can I get you ladies a drink?'

'No thank you, we're sorted,' said Susan.

The man called over the waitress. 'Get me a beer,' he said.

She raised an eyebrow. 'Of course, *sir*.'

There was something about the way she'd said sir that put Carla on high alert. She'd already taken an instinctive dislike to the man, and now she was convinced he was a creep. He was talking to Susan, and she was responding politely. Carla said nothing. She was trying to work out if Susan liked the guy. If she did, it wasn't Carla's place to interfere. It was hard to tell, as her friend's body language was completely neutral. Carla didn't want to cramp her style, especially as she'd had so little fun since Morgan died, so she drank her beer and remained silent.

'I'm John, by the way.'

'Susan.'

'And what's your friend's name?'

Susan belatedly realised that Carla hadn't been engaging in the conversation. She looked at her friend's impassive face and hesitated. John looked at Carla, his affable veneer slipping, and then back at Susan.

'Your little friend doesn't have much to say for herself, does she? I think she's being a little rude, don't you?' His voice had an edge to it. He stared at Carla. 'What's your beef?'

Susan looked at Carla in alarm. Carla leaned in closer and said in a quiet but firm voice, 'Well, John, it's like this. I've travelled six thousand miles to see my friend, not you. She's a very polite person who is always nice to people. Me, not so much. So maybe you could just pick that drink up and take it back to the bar where you came from.'

'I think I'll stay exactly where I am, missy,' he replied, menacingly.

Carla leaned in closer still, almost reeling from the smell of stale beer and cigarettes on the man's breath. 'You are the second arsehole I've had the misfortune of speaking to today. The first I couldn't do much about. You, I can. So, if you don't want me to call security, you'd better get out of your seat and fuck off.'

With a face like thunder, he jerked his chair back and stormed out of the bar.

The waitress rushed over. 'Are you OK, ma'am? Was he bothering you?'

'Yes, he was. It's OK, though, he's decided he needs to go home. Do you have a lot of trouble with him?'

'Not so as we can really do much about it.'

'You might want to bring him to the attention of your bouncers if he comes back. He was in too much of a hurry to get out of here when I threatened to call security. That's not the behaviour of a trustworthy man.'

Susan looked astonished. 'How did you know he was a creep? I didn't get any vibes until it was too late.'

'He just had something about him, and I didn't like the way he spoke to the waitress. I think you've been out of the dating game for so long that your antennae are switched off.'

'I know. I didn't like the man almost from the start, but I'm so used to being pleasant to obnoxious guests at the hotel that it's second nature to be polite to everyone. I think you need to be more careful, though, even if you do have a guardian angel watching over you. You really flipped him off, and it could have turned nasty.'

'I'm sorry I worried you. Maybe I did come on a bit strong, but I've spent too much of my working life putting up with arseholes and I'm done with all that. In any case, it was a calculated risk. You obviously didn't notice those burly bouncers hovering near our table. They're trained to sense trouble, so I wasn't being totally reckless.'

'Well, just be careful, won't you?'

'Of course I will. Now, drink up. We'd better order a taxi to take us back to the hotel in case John is hanging around outside. I'm not going to make the same mistake I made at your hotel.'

CHAPTER 40
Palm Springs

Sadly, their time together was up since Susan had to return to work in preparation for the hotel's reopening. But rather than parting ways fully, she offered Carla the same master suite she'd stayed in previously.

Carla wasn't one to look a gift horse in the mouth, but as much as she enjoyed the luxurious surroundings, her thoughts inevitably turned to Tom and the quandary they were in. She mulled over all the things Susan had said to her in Carlsbad, hating to admit that she'd been right about everything. She and Tom had never been big on deep, meaningful conversations, and now she could see how this had led to misunderstandings. She should apologise and bare her soul to him. And yet, there was a niggling doubt at the back of her mind. They wouldn't be in this mess if he'd listened to her when she'd asked him not to take on the new work project. Was her opinion that unimportant to him? Her husband had dismissed her views without a second thought, and he had reneged on his promise to be with her. It was all so confusing. In the past year, she'd reinvented herself, or, more precisely, she'd found the feisty, independent Carla of her youth, and now here she was full of self-doubt once again.

* * *

Carla's phone pinged with a message from James.

'Can we Skype?'

Carla's mobile didn't even have a camera, let alone the facility to see someone on the other side of the Atlantic. Should she just call him back? Surely it had to be news about the baby. No, he wanted to Skype, so she would find a way to do so. She stepped into the elevator and pressed the button for the lobby, shuddering at the memory of last year's narrow escape. She found Susan in her office.

'Hey, Carla, what's up?'

'I've had a message from James; he wants to Skype.' Mournfully, she showed her phone to Susan.

Susan laughed, shaking her head in disbelief. 'I told you to get yourself a decent cellphone. You're such a dinosaur.'

'I know.'

'Have you got James's Skype address?' Carla nodded. 'Come on, I'll set you up on the PC in here. Send James a text and tell him you'll be online in a few minutes.' Susan bashed the keyboard until she got to the required screen. 'There you go. I'll leave you to it.'

Carla sat at the desk and there they were on the monitor – James, Melissa and their newborn.

'Meet your new grandson, David James Bright,' said James.

'Oh, he's beautiful, and so, so tiny.'

Melissa grimaced. 'He doesn't look small to me.'

The little baby was swaddled in a blue blanket with just his tiny pink face poking out as he slept in his proud mother's arms. There was no disguising James's elation at the arrival of his son. Even so, he looked more exhausted than Melissa.

'When was he born?'

'Just over an hour ago.'

'That's wonderful. Thank you for doing this for me, I don't deserve it after running away and leaving you all to it.'

'Don't be daft,' said James. 'We didn't want you to miss out on seeing him.'

'Tell me all about him. How much does he weigh?'

'Seven pounds and two ounces, and he's fit and healthy too.'

'That's great news. I didn't think he was due for another week?'

'It seems he was in a hurry to get into the world.'

'How are you feeling, Melissa? Was it a difficult birth?'

'Is there such a thing as an easy one? I'm tired, obviously, but that's hardly a surprise, and I'm in better shape than I was with Mariah. Thank goodness I didn't have to go through another marathon labour like I did with her.'

'I know we've had a few hiccups along the way, but I want you to know I am so proud of you both, and my heart is bursting with joy. I'm so glad you resolved your differences; you were made for each other, don't ever forget that. And you've given me two beautiful grandchildren.'

Tears streamed down Carla's face.

'Are you OK, Mum?' asked James. 'I've never seen you cry before.'

'I'm fine, son. I've turned into a right old blubberer lately.' She wiped her eyes and placed her hands on her heart. 'I feel like you're in this room with me, not six thousand miles away.'

'It's even better than that,' beamed James. 'We're still in the delivery suite, so if you had been at home, you'd still be waiting to see us. The midwife is going to check Melissa and the baby over before we move onto the ward. Then Andrea will be able to see David. Must go.'

'Take care, all of you.'

The significance of the call wasn't lost on Carla. It was James and her daughter-in-law's way of saying that she was no longer going to play second fiddle to Andrea. She guessed they would tell Melissa's mum about the introduction, as a gentle reminder for her to continue watching her step. How clever of them! What a simple way of redrawing their domestic boundaries without the necessity for awkward conversations.

Susan came back into the office. 'And?'

'I have a beautiful baby grandson called David James Bright,' said Carla, looking every inch the proud grandmother.

'Congratulations, I'm so pleased for you. Tonight, we are going to celebrate in style.'

And they did.

* * *

Carla was homesick. Her time in America had certainly been eventful, and she'd never forget the fun she'd had with Susan, Nancy, Merle and Olivia. But with Susan back at work, she was on her own again. Her appetite for solo travelling was waning. As Susan had said, she couldn't go on like this forever. Despite everything, she missed Tom. She longed to see the rest of her family and to hold her new grandson. It was time to go home, face the music and, hopefully, resolve things with Tom. She would tell Susan of her plans first thing in the morning and then book the next flight home.

Decision made, she ran a warm bubble bath before curling up on the sofa in a fluffy white robe. A feeling of déjà vu washed over her. So much had happened since she'd last relaxed on this sofa, and however things ended, she wouldn't regret anything that had happened in between.

She was just dozing off when a thought struck her. *Nancy's letter!* She had given it to her with strict instructions not to open it until she was heading home. Now was the time. Better to do it here in the comfort of her beautiful suite than in a packed airport.

Carla hunted through her suitcases and found it in a side pocket. She slit the envelope open and removed the letter; haltingly, she read it and then wept.

* * *

There was a knock at the door. The only person who knew Carla was staying in the suite was Susan. She must have squeezed in a break.

I'll invite her in for drinks and tell her I'm going home, she decided.

She opened the door before stumbling back in surprise.

'Tom, what are you doing here?'

'Well, that's a fine welcome to give someone who's just crossed the Atlantic and left no stone unturned to find you.' He spoke cautiously, a hopeful glint in his eyes.

'Sorry, I didn't mean it like that. It's just so unexpected, that's all. You took me by surprise.'

She ushered him into the suite.

'Wow! How do you keep blagging these fancy digs?' asked Tom.

'It's my natural charm and personality, of course. How did you know I was here?'

'I called Susan.'

'Ah, so that explains her sudden work commitments and lack of availability to spend time with me.'

'If you'd rather I left...?'

'Of course not. Sit down, I'll get you a drink.'

He nodded. Carla poured Tom a beer and a glass of Chablis for herself. She sat on the sofa next to him and raised her glass, feeling a little awkward.

'So, how come you're here? Surely Mark hasn't recovered already?'

'No, he's still in plaster and he's stuck at home feeling sorry for himself, but I couldn't bear to be on my own at home any longer. I am so sorry for being such an idiot. Honestly, when Mark phoned, I was devastated. I didn't want to leave you; I was enjoying our time together. The mess I was in was of my own making, so I felt I had no choice but to fly back. I knew you'd been having a good time without me, so I thought it wouldn't bother you too much if I left. I was stupid, I know that now. I shouldn't have made assumptions, and I should have asked how you felt. The truth is, it was convenient for me to believe you didn't need me here, but the last few days without you have been torture. I couldn't bear to think of you in the state I left you in.'

'Oh, Tom, I'm sorry too. I shouldn't have lost my rag like that. I should have told you how I felt and been honest about my insecurities when we were in Malibu. I've been so used to keeping these things to myself, I just didn't know how to open up. And I didn't realise how much I needed to tell someone.'

'Apart from Judith?'

Carla smiled wryly. 'Apart from Judith. Anyway, thinking I was fixed, she left me after we got back from Malibu. Too soon as it turned out. After all these years, I can't suddenly tell you all my thoughts and feelings, but I can try harder.

'Saying all that, I can't take all the blame for this, can I? I made my feelings pretty clear about you expanding the business and yet you ignored me and ploughed on regardless.

That was the time when you should have dug deeper to find out why I was so against you taking on the project.'

'I know, and I'm ashamed of myself. I've had a lot of time to think things over and I've realised that I've never tried to reach below the surface and look into your soul. I've never tried to understand you, and I should have acknowledged the damage your parents inflicted on you. I hated the way they treated you, yet I never bothered to find out how you felt about them. Just because you've never opened up doesn't mean I shouldn't have seen your pain. You've shown me so much understanding over the years and I haven't done the same for you. Bless you and your kind heart; none of this is your fault, it's mine, and I truly am sorry.'

'But how could you be expected to understand when I didn't even realise I had a problem myself? Meeting you was a revelation, and you gave me the love I didn't know I'd been missing. It was only when it all went wrong last year that my buried emotions resurfaced, and even then, I didn't really understand them.'

'If I'd listened to you in the first place none of this would have happened. I've been so selfish. My only pathetic excuse is that I'm a spoilt only child with parents who thought the sun shone out of my backside, so I'm used to getting my own way.

'The truth is, I was genuinely frightened of retiring. I know we had the discussion in Malibu, and that it made sense for me to go part time, but when it came to it, I lost my nerve and couldn't relinquish control. I should have discussed my fears with you, I know, but I could see that you were having an amazing time out here, and it honestly didn't occur to me that it would be a problem for you. I thought your objections were out of concern for me taking on more than I could handle – which, as it happens, turned out to be true. I have no idea why I went in the opposite direction and took on more work. An old man trying to prove he's still got it, I suppose. It seems we're both rubbish at talking about the big stuff.'

'Yes, it does. What a pair of idiots we are; we deserve each other! Come here.'

He slid across the sofa and kissed her lightly on the lips.

'That's from our new grandson.'

'Have you seen him?'

'Of course. He's going to be a bruiser when he grows up.'

'Don't be ridiculous. You can't possibly know what a seven-pound baby is going to look like when he's older. Anyway, I think he's beautiful.'

Their second embrace was more passionate. They were both now confident that the iciness between them was melting; it really was time to kiss and make up. They cuddled on the sofa, enjoying the warmth of each other's bodies. There was still more to discuss, but they both sensed a need to let what they had shared so far sink in, and for a few minutes, the only sounds disturbing the silence came from the ticking of the grandfather clock and the faint noise of the traffic outside.

Tom stroked Carla's hand. 'I felt so bad leaving you on your own. I was jealous too. You're having experiences that we should be sharing and... well, I still haven't driven the Corvette.'

Carla thumped him hard and let out a little giggle, then her face clouded over.

'You can drive her as much as you want.'

Tears filled her eyes.

'Hey, what's the matter?'

She didn't answer. Instead, she moved over to the bureau, picked up Nancy's letter and wordlessly passed it to him.

Tom began to read it out loud...

Dear Carla,

I hope I didn't sound too cloak and dagger when I gave you this letter, but I want you and Tom to enjoy your trip without any distractions. I hope you have a wonderful time and create many happy memories with him.

Tom looked guiltily at Carla. 'I feel terrible. Not only did I ruin your plans but I also disappointed your friends.'

'I won't deny that they were sad they didn't get to meet you in San Francisco. They were really looking forward to getting to know the man they'd heard so much about.'

'Well, I'm here now, so we'll just have to put that right, won't we?'

Carla stood up and walked over to the window. Tom carried on reading.

Even though we haven't known you for very long, you hold a special place in our hearts. You can know some people for a lifetime and never truly feel a connection, but once in a blue moon, you meet someone just the once and it feels right. This is how we feel about you, and we get the impression you have the same connection with us. Because of you, Merle and I got to realise my dream to cross the Golden Gate Bridge in the Corvette, and what with the dinner and the sunset and all, it was one of the best days of our lives. We'd never have gotten around to doing that without you. Thank you for making two old people very happy.

I will always treasure the memories of driving Highway 1 and the fun we had in the City of Angels. My time with you has been special and you have become very dear to me.'I don't feel so bad now. If I'd been here when I should have been, you and Nancy wouldn't have had the opportunity to create those memories for her.'

'True.'
Tom read on.

You gave our Carla new life, a new purpose, and you made all the years that Merle tinkered with her worthwhile. Through you, we feel we've been on an adventure too. We won't get the opportunity to drive her again, and so we want you to have her. The enclosed 'pink slip' will allow you to register the car in your name. Feel free to keep her stored at Martha's so you can carry on touring with Tom – she's fine with that – or if you'd rather take her home to England, you can do so with our blessing.

'Woo hoo! I can't believe it: our very own beautiful, red Corvette. It's a dream come true. Now I feel doubly guilty for not coming to San Francisco. What incredible people they must be.'

'They are,' Carla whispered. 'Now read the last bit.'

The truth is, Merle is dying. When he had his cataract operation, the doctors ran a whole bunch of other tests and discovered he has cancer. They did all sorts of investigations, but there was nothing they could do for him. He only has six months left to live, a little more if we're lucky. I'm sorry we couldn't tell you before: it was important to us that our last visit with you be a happy one. It isn't true that I've stopped baking pot pies; we just said that to explain away his weight loss, and we didn't want you to suspect anything. As it happens, Merle looks healthier now than he has done in years. It doesn't seem fair, does it?

I know you will want to come to us, but we want to spend the little time we have left on our own, just the two of us. Merle wants you to remember him as he is now, not as the shell of a man he is likely to become in the months ahead. We've got a good support system in place for when we need it, so it isn't necessary for you to worry about us. And don't be sad for us, either, we've had a long and happy life together, and we feel blessed.

I'll be in touch when the time is right, and we can get together when I feel up to it. I know you will treasure Carla. Please take care of yourself and tell that husband of yours to take good care of you, too.

With love,

Your 'Mom', Nancy

Carla broke down. Tom gathered her up in his arms. 'I'm so sorry. I know how much they mean to you.'

They continued to cling to each other until Carla's sobs subsided.

'Is there anything we can do to help them?' asked Tom.

'No. Nancy says they want to be alone. She sounds pretty definite, and I doubt they will change their minds. The best I can do is write and tell her I'll come as soon as she wants me to. She's being strong now, but I think she will need me when Merle dies.'

'We must go to her.'

'*We?* But you'll be too busy.'

'No, I won't. I don't want to be away from you for a second longer, Carla. I'm done with being an idiot. I'm selling my share to Mark's brother and retiring for good.'

Carla smiled at him, not caring about her blotchy face and swollen eyes.

'Oh, Tom, that's the most wonderful news, and it means the world to me. I'm not going to lie, I've had some fabulous experiences without you, and I've met many amazing people. I still want to travel, but I don't want to do it on my own anymore. Before you arrived, I was about to book a flight home. I'm so glad you've said you are ready to be with me. Do you really mean it this time?'

'Most definitely.'

'So, what do you want to do?'

He thought for a moment. 'Despite what her letter says, I'm sure Nancy would like to talk to you. I don't think writing to her is what she needs. You should call her and check if she means what she says. If she does, tell her to call you the minute she needs you and you'll be there.

'Meanwhile, we should go home to see our gorgeous grandchildren and finalise the sale of the business. Then we can come back and start a grand tour of Central California, Oregon and Washington. What do you think?'

'That sounds like a great idea, Tom. But before we do that, and while I'm feeling like the luckiest woman in the world, shall we spend a few days in Las Vegas together before flying home?'

'It's a deal.'

Acknowledgments

I would like to thank a number of people who, unbeknown to them, have played a big part in my quest to write a novel. As a renowned bookworm, I have harboured an ambition for decades to create a story of my own, and finally, here it is.

To Christian Baker for planting the seed. Adele Hartshorn for motivating me to begin. Sue Forsdike – my biggest cheerleader and cherished friend. Karen and Monte Strand for correcting my use of the American language and urging me on. Juliana Durrant and David Wilkins for their observations and encouragement. Kanti Freeman for introducing me to yoga and teaching me that you must look after yourself first to be able to help others. Caroline Alexander for her positivity and for keeping me focused. Hazel, Louise and Natalie, for torturing me in cycle spin and forcing me to distract myself by allowing my imagination to run riot, which is how this story unfolded. My editor, Danielle Wrate, for making great suggestions, tidying everything up and holding my hand at the business end of things. Rachel Middleton for bringing 'Carla' to life on the front cover. Last but not least, my husband, Dave Brown, for sharing a multitude of adventures with me on our travels in the USA.

About the Author

Lesley Anne Brown was born in Luton and, following a brief spell in Australia as one of the 'Ten Pound Poms', she has spent most of her life in the Bedford area.

She attended the Dame Alice Harpur School in Bedford and worked at an international bank in London before joining her husband, Dave, in business. They owned and ran a number of successful convenience stores for more than twenty years before 'retiring' to a less frenetic way of life. Lesley spent four years working part-time for the Bedford Library Link service, which she likens to a chocoholic working in a sweet shop. Her already eclectic taste in books exploded, and she was lucky to come across many amazing authors previously unknown to her. However, her almost life-long addiction to all things Agatha Christie remains unabated.

Between 2007 and 2014, Lesley and Dave travelled extensively in the USA, covering 28 states and 32,000 miles in their 1931, hot-rodded, Ford Model 'A' Phaeton. The car has a passing resemblance to Bonnie and Clyde's car – without the guns. Their incredible experiences and meeting so many special people in such a beautiful country provided much inspiration, and together with Lesley's imagination, the result is this, her first novel.

For photos and author updates, you can follow Lesley's Facebook page: *Lesley Anne Brown – Finding Carla*.